A DIFFERENT WISDOM

Guide to Supervision Series

Published and distributed by Karnac Books

Other titles in the Series

Supervisor Training: Issues and Approaches
Edited by Penny Henderson

Orders

Tel: +44 (0)20 7431 1075; Fax: +44 (0)20 7435 9076

E-mail: shop@karnacbooks.com

www.karnac books.com

A DIFFERENT WISDOM

Reflections on
Supervision Practice

Penny Henderson

KARNAC

First published in 2009 by
Karnac Books Ltd
118 Finchley Road, London NW3 5HT

British Library Cataloguing in Publication Data

A C.I.P. for this book is available from the British Library

ISBN 978 1 85575 614 4

Cover image: "In discussion" by Helen Martino. Photograph by Peter Mennim.

Edited, designed and produced by The Studio Publishing Services Ltd
www.publishingservicesuk.co.uk
e-mail: studio@publishingservicesuk.co.uk

www.karnacbooks.com

CONTENTS

ACKNOWLEDGEMENTS

This book contains some stories to show vividly how the supervision I have received has influenced me, and how much I have learnt from my own supervisees. These experiences have formed the heart of my learning, without which the book could not have been written, and I thank those concerned for permission to share them, and for our interesting exchanges as we debated them.

I want to thank Hazel Johns, who read almost all of the book, was my ally and coach, and gave me sensitive immensely helpful advice and feedback about structure, language, punctuation, and ideas, and affirmed my approach. Her encouragement was crucial to the process of finishing the book.

Particular appreciation also goes to those who have read individual chapters, and those with whom I have discussed the issues and the book more generally, who have shared their thoughts generously: Hazel Johns, Caro Bailey, Anthea Millar, Brigid Proctor, Francesca Inskipp, Charlotte Sills, Rosie Bell, and Sue Weaver: I have learnt so much from being with you all.

Helen Martino, the potter whose woman is on the front cover, generously gave permission for me to use the image of it, as did Peter Mennim, the photographer of the piece. It is called " In discussion". I do appreciate your generosity.

ABOUT THE AUTHOR

Penny Henderson is an accredited Counsellor and Supervisor, and Fellow of BACP. Her career has encompassed many years of Open University work as a tutor and tutor-counsellor, developing adult learning materials, and institutional research. She has been a training officer in Social Services, offering in-service and group work training there, and then a staff counselling service. Her self-employed work, in addition to counselling and supervision, has included consultation to organizations and teams, and development of training materials for group work, exam anxiety, experiential training methods, counselling in Primary Care, and supervision. She is the author of many articles, chapters, and books on these topics.

For over a decade she has also been involved in education for medical students, and latterly in supervision of doctors.

Introduction

I have a favourite fountain in the University of Cambridge Botanical Gardens, which has five spouting upright features from which the water falls into a small pool of water, made turbulent by it. This is edged with a ring of steel, and then there is another larger circle encompassing the whole, which has still water in it, some water plants for oxygenation, sometimes a duck paddling and seeking food hopefully. A low, wide wall encircles the whole, around the top of which children sit, skip, or march. Supervision can be like the outer layer, a separate reflecting space, offering a sense of being contained, holding what might otherwise spill over the edge. A gardener there told me that the ring of steel had to be inserted after initial building, because, like a supervision contract, it stops the turbulent water from disturbing the roots of the oxygenating plants and the reflective space. Positioned on the wall that also buffers what is within, a supervisor of supervision can get an overview of systems and a perspective on details as well as the whole, despite being at a distance from the experience of the turbulence.

Counselling supervision is generally defined as a space offered by one practitioner to another, in which an account of therapeutic work is given and reviewed. It is an educative, co-operative and rigorous process, useful when permeated by encouraging profes-- sional values.

Proctor's definition (1997, p. 192) is widely used:

> A working alliance wherein the counsellor can offer an account or recording of her work, reflect on it, receive feedback, and where appropriate, guidance. The object of this alliance is to enable the counsellor to gain in ethical competence, confidence and creativity, to give the best possible service to her client.

A core aim of supervision is that the supervisee feels enabled to ask for what they want and need, without shame or intimidation. At best, this entails a sense of partnership, so that supervisees also share responsibility through preparation beforehand, reflection afterwards, and playing a part in negotiating and sustaining the working alliance. Supervisees need practice to give a coherent summary account of a session, incident, or relationship. When the supervisee feels stuck or emotionally challenged s/he needs support to take the risk to be honest. A key issue for both supervisor and supervisee is to keep our hearts and minds open as we continue in the work, by dint of "fearless compassion, the courage to both speak the truth and yet do so with respect and compassion for the other" (Hawkins & Shohet, 2006, p. 220).

Effective supervisory work is built on a foundation of agreement about pragmatics. Practitioners are encouraged to get the beginnings and endings in supervision right so that power is equalized as much as is realistically possible, and agreement is negotiated on focus, style, mode, and balance of work. Reviews and opportunities to speak the unspoken can be wrought into the fabric of the sessions in ways that invite the supervisee to take responsibility for their learning and practice. Any structure that can limit the negative impact of supervisee deference is welcome. Both supervisor and supervisee need to be clear that the work of the supervisor is in service of the development of the supervisee, and the best work with and for the client.

Playful seriousness, or possibly "serious playfulness", makes the work go well. Creativity, the use of all the senses, and the inclusion of rigorous reflection combine in differing measure depending on temperament and philosophy of supervision. This play space allows thoughts or feelings to emerge in service of the work.

Carroll (2001a) calls supervision "a way of life, a value system that drives us as much personally as it does professionally" (p. 78).

Sometimes, humour can help, too. When supervisees feel powerless I quote the late Anita Roddick, who wrote on a Body Shop leaflet: "If you think you are too small to be effective you've never been in bed with a mosquito".

I find that metaphors can usefully capture an element of the work. For instance, Waskett (2006) describes supervision as "treasure hunting", looking for the jewels that are in the unaware competence of the client and the counsellor, thus supporting the counsellor to become more aware of her inner resources to be in the work.

A safe and restorative space can sustain and support the emotional resilience of the practitioner in the teeth of challenging work, their personal reactions to it and to upsetting life events. Much supervisory writing highlights the importance of the supervisory relationship for satisfying and effective supervision. Hawkins and Shohet (2006) use Winnicott's metaphor of a supervisor being "like the father 'holding' the nursing mother" to describe, vividly, the containment provided by a supervisor. Often, this is invisible emotional work by a supervisor who responds to the spoken and unspoken needs of the supervisee. This restorative function will be familiar to all readers who have had good supervision, and know the feeling of leaving a supervision session feeling emotionally lighter as well as intellectually or practically clearer. A primary bonus of this restorative function lies in encouragement, to give courage to the worker (Millar, 2007). This necessary containment is not just about emotion. It is also a result of explicit supervisory contracts and unambiguous lines of accountability, protocols for risk assessment, understanding of the legal and moral base for the work, and thought or audit about outcomes (Jenkins, 2006; Jenkins, Keter, & Stone, 2004).

To offer a developmental space that is respectful of differing learning styles, the supervisor takes the stage of personal and professional development of a supervisee or a group of supervisees into account. This will encourage the emergence of a unique "internal supervisor" (see Glossary) in each supervisee. The supervisor may help the supervisee to sustain confidence, to grasp the realities of the context, and to appreciate the different contributions of members of a multi-disciplinary team.

Ethical and effective counselling work is supported by sharing an interest in monitoring this. Supervisors need to explore work and its consequences without attacking the self worth of the practitioner. "Supervision works best when it is respectful, collaborative and pragmatic", writes Waskett (2006). In the early stages of practice, it is a complex process, and a difficult yet necessary balancing act, to encourage supervisees while also helping them to identify the *limits* of their own competence. Specific feedback and both keeping a record of supervisory feedback helps supervisor and supervisee to monitor the competence demonstrated in both roles.

For experienced supervisors, supervision of supervision can be the most collegial, delightfully interesting, developmentally challenging opportunity, as pairs or groups wrestle with complex ethical dilemmas, or the risks of authentic and idiosyncratic relating, while respecting the boundaries of professional practice.

CHAPTER ONE

Building a strong foundation

"What we think we are coming for is not always what we
need"

(Hewson, 1999, p. 77)

Contracts for supervision involve negotiation. Negotiated
contracts create and sustain working agreements to suit
both parties as they begin a relationship, or as they begin a
session, and even as they change tack in the midst of a piece of
work. For each eventuality the aim is to clarify whatever is necessary in connection with expectations, roles, and responsibilities,
preferred methodology and desired outcomes. A new working relationship involves getting to know each other, to begin to build the
trusting base for safety.

If the parties are willing to discuss their prior assumptions and
hopes or fears, this can reduce the arena of undeclared expectations.
Discovering how a supervisee chose me or was allocated to me,
who made a recommendation, or in what other environments we
may have met, sometimes hinted at items for further exploration
about our hopes or fears as we began.

1

As the years go by and practitioners work with a series of supervisors, each may become more and more clear about what they do or do not want, and therefore more confident in negotiating about it. Flexibility is desirable, and, as the need for focus changes in a session, the existence of an explicit agenda and agreement for what the supervisee wants makes this more obvious. A review at the end of a session about what were the most and least helpful exchanges in the session highlights differing perceptions and gives feedback to the supervisor, and performs a really valuable shared monitoring function. A report of supervision research that made this enquiry (West & Clark, 2004) so impressed me that I arranged to include this in my future sessions as supervisor and supervisee.

First steps in creating a contract

Generally a potential supervisee makes the first contact by phone or e-mail, and the pair initiate some enquiries about whether it is possible to meet and work together, on the basis of available times to meet.

I have habitually offered a free first session, to see if we are compatible. Houston (1995) also recommends this, but others believe that, as this is work, they should be paid for the session.

I suggest we both bring a CV. This immediately provides considerable information for each of us, and clarifies that the choice goes both ways. In a recent beginning with a very experienced potential supervisee, as we each looked at the other's patterns of education and experience we could see writ large that I like to read and think and write, and she likes to work intuitively and reflect on experience. We could comment on this being something we would review in six months, if not before, to see how well we were bridging these different styles. It is also a useful reminder with trainees who might have a lot of experience in another role or setting that, although they may be full of novice feelings in this role, there are transferable skills to call on.

Proctor (1997), Hewson (1999), and Inskipp and Proctor (2001) all detail the pragmatics that initial supervisory contracts must address. Agreements need to include:

- form of supervision (frequency, timing, one to one, or group);
- focus and functions: that is, the desired balance between time spent on normative, formative, and restorative tasks (see Glossary for definitions of these terms);
- roles and responsibilities;
- pragmatics about an appropriate venue, payment, and the potentially difficult issues about missed sessions;
- clarity about to whom the supervisor is answerable, and for what;
- clients or other work to be brought, whether there is to be discussion about contextual matters like management of a waiting list, how many clients might normally be presented in the session;
- whether notes, tapes, videos, or transcripts of sessions are expected;
- what sort of preparation each considers useful and necessary for the process.

Where the supervision is paid for by an organization, clarity is essential about feedback to it, and when this may be required, such as in annual appraisals, or in an expectation to contact the organization if fitness to practise issues arise.

Where the supervisees are trainees, requirements for reports, relations with the course or placement, clinical responsibility for clients, and details about frequency of supervisions per number of hours seeing clients all need to be spelled out. Proctor calls this purpose and preference stating (1997, p. 194), distinguishing what must happen from what might.

If there is to be some flexibility on offer, such as the possibility of telephone calls or e-mail contact between sessions if required, there needs to be clarity about when that might suit, why it could be necessary, and what extra fee, if any, is to be incurred.

This long list indicates that the supervisor might need written prompts to remember to cover every element. Often, the process is not completed in one session, but enough must be done for the decision to be mutually made whether or not it seems right to begin. At the same time, a subtle dance of relationship building is progressing in the process of the negotiation, and that element is as important as the pragmatics for creating a safe learning and reflection environment. Houston (1995) always encourages new-comers to go away and reflect after the first session, and then call after a few days to affirm a wish to continue. This makes clear that they are making a positive choice. Planning to review after three or six sessions also allows either party to decline to continue should they so wish.

This summary simplifies a complex process. Even in contracting about session lengths, some theoretical modalities work to a fifty-minute hour as therapists, while others choose to work to a sixty-minute hour. Do both people know how long an hour of super-vision is to be? Not unless it is spelled out. Some training course specify one supervision session to every six counselling hours, but is this those that the counsellor offers, or those that are taken up? How do cancellations and clients who do not attend count here? It might be useful to check the requirements of the organizations involved, as well as between the supervisory pair or group.

I have decided not to supervise someone after the contracting session only on rare occasions. Usually, it was because it became clear that the supervisee's learning style was too different from mine, and I could not discipline myself not to feel judgemental about it, or because I felt the course was unsound, or the supervisee was too unreflective and unaware of their limits to competence. King and Wheeler (1999) discovered that many experienced super-visors take the same route, and choose not to work with someone whose practice or potential they do not feel confident about. In my experiences, I knew I could not sustain my part in creating a safe space unimpeded by my judgemental preoccupations, and so it was better for the supervisee to seek another supervisor. With experi-ence, I became willing to own it in this way, while also telling the person about what my difficulty was in relation to their learning or practice.

Psychological contracts

I have had supervisees who began with me after previously diffi-cult experiences in supervision, and who thus conveyed a wish not to be challenged in any way that would feel like an attack. I had to earn the right to probe or push as trust grew, aiming to be sensitive to what the supervisee could bear before becoming defensive or upset. I had one recently qualified counsellor from a poorly organized course who had managed to get through her whole training without presenting a client in the group supervisions. It took us almost six months, in which she gave me enormous amounts of details about each client so that I could barely comment, before she felt safe enough to tell me this, and say that she was terrified I would be unbearably critical of her work. Once that point was passed, the relationship was on a working footing at last.

Hewson (1999) uses the image of the iceberg to note that the supervisory pair must find out what is below the waterline if they are to stay sensitive to covert agendas. Sensitivity is important to pick up subtle shifts in expectations of each other. Courage is required to enquire about what such shifts might mean. "Parallel process" also occurs (see Glossary) when unconscious elements of the counsellor–client relationship are reproduced or enacted in the supervision or from the supervision back into the client–counsellor relationship. Contracts and regular feedback and reviews in relation to them are useful to disentangle personal agendas in the relationship from enactments of unspoken themes within the therapy.

How long is "too long" for a supervisory relationship?

How long can supervisees usefully stay with the same supervisor? (Henderson, 2003). In its early years, the British Association for Counselling (BAC) debated a two-year norm, at another time a five-year maximum, but neither was included in their original code of ethics for supervisors or put into the subsequent ethical framework. Two to three years is thought appropriate for trainees. For more experienced people, Inskipp and Proctor (2001) suggest "change every three years or so", though they emphasize that there is no ethical requirement to do so. However, informal discussions among supervisors, my current research project studying experienced practitioners, and my own experience, suggest that once supervisees are very experienced, especially when they are working in a specialist area, and particularly when they live in an area sparsely populated by supervisors, 10–15 years is not uncommon. Some supervisors confess that they will have to retire to be released from long-term supervisees who are reluctant to let go. Since the British Association for Counselling and Psychotherapy (BACP) includes some very experienced supervisors and supervisees and requires accredited members all to be in regular supervision, it is worth reflecting on how to stay lively in such supervisory work. A danger is that both rest comfortably on their individual plateaux, and the client or service is also the loser. An annual contract and review provides a vehicle for explicit conversations about what each party is learning from the relationship.

Inskipp and Proctor (2001, pp. 85–86) indicate that it is time for a change when any of these factors apply:

- starting work with a new client group, or in a new context which has different demands and challenges;
- becoming aware of a developing collusion, shared blind spots, merging perspectives, or the supervisor becoming predictable;
- moving locality or one of the pair retiring;
- becoming aware of serious mismatches between supervisee and supervisor;
- being promoted into a role with more managerial responsibilities, so the balance of needs from supervision changes;
- reaching a new stage of professional development—seeking new training or a supervisor who works from another perspective;
- personal development—seeking a different balance of challenge and support, or wish to work with a supervisor of another theoretical orientation, or gender, age, class, sexual orientation, or race;
- wishing to change from a group to one-to-one, or vice versa.

The supervisor has needs, too, and these are relevant to any decisions to change supervisees.

- To deepen expertise in specialist areas: this might lead to a longer span of work with a supervisee, or to seeking new supervisees from a speciality.
- To extend the variety of supervisory work, with supervisees of different genders, ages, or stages of development.
- To meet emotional needs for a new or different relationship.

Supervisors who insist a reluctant supervisee leaves because the supervisor is ready for a change can fear being seen as rejecting. This provides rich material for discussion about handling endings and relationships where each party wants something different.

Metaphors might signal what is happening emotionally in such supervisory relationships.

- Does the collegiality remind us of sibling relationships?
- Does it remain teacher–pupil, to the detriment of both?
- Does it become like a marriage, with predictable ups and downs, but deep intimacy?
- Does the increasing knowledge of each other lead to a relationship more like that of friends?

Certainly friendship can be one aspect of the relationship in long-term supervision, especially between peers. It behoves both to keep a sharp eye on the rigour with which they stick to boundaries for a useful working space.

The hazards of a too long relationship

Indicators to suggest the relationship has gone on for too long include fuzzy boundaries, boredom, predictability, and over-identification. Collusion can arise, avoiding being open about some thoughts or feelings, or assuming both feel the same. A prolonged idealization of the supervisor is not healthy, and there are dangers in feeling special. Page and Wosket (2001) assert that dependency over a long term indicates that the supervisor is failing to point out the degree to which the supervisee has his or her own wisdom. They think that the ethical principle of autonomy requires that when supervision has lasted "a number of years", the supervisor should *actively* encourage supervisees to move on and find another supervisor, and face the discomforts—and opportunities—of letting go. Personal histories of abandonment or vulnerability might create such a strong wish to cling to the known person that other needs for development can be disregarded. It is also debatable whether or not it is more difficult to exercise supervisory authority: the power of familiarity is great, and both parties might slip into familiar interactions that could make it less likely that difficult issues are addressed. Challenge *can* occur effectively within an established relationship. It can also come from meeting a new supervisor who can offer it from a new framework.

Sometimes, supervision persists because of a reluctance to travel further, or a lack of expectation that anyone else would be better, even when the current arrangement is not satisfactory.

The benefits of a long-term supervisory relationship

Mutual challenge and playfulness enable good supervision. The plus side of a long-term relationship comes from trust, familiarity, and building sufficient emotional capital for the relationship to survive uncomfortable conversations. Knowing each other for many years as unique human beings allows better assessment of risk during difficulties arising from life events such as bereavements, accidents, marital changes, and health crises. The supervisor may come to understand how people and systems affect the worker in a specific organization. The supervisor can encourage the supervisee to remember, in moments of gloom, how s/he has developed over the years. There can also be acknowledgement of the existential realities that inhibit or limit development.

Accompanying a supervisee on their journey of professional and personal development is very enriching, and a privilege. When it works well, the supervisor can understand the implications of an issue referred to in shorthand, like the allusions made by old friends, and the multi-layered nature, resonances, and implications of some of the supervisee's reactions.

To ensure a long-term supervisory relationship remains appropriate, the pair should usefully commit themselves positively to regular reviews, at least annually. In these, a learning focus can be named, probably for both of them for this relationship, leading to a shared commitment to monitoring and discussing progress. When the supervisee has a large caseload, it is up to the supervisor to plan these reviews, and ensure that they do happen. It is too easy to let the urgent push out the regular discipline of taking stock.

In addition, regular supervision of supervision might help the supervisor to notice issues they are reluctant to address. If the topic of ending becomes taboo or heavily emotionally charged, it is important to raise it, however uncomfortable, because there may be parallels in the supervisee's practice in relation to ending with clients. If either party is considering ending, it is important to say so. If neither is, and it has been discussed in supervision of supervision, perhaps they should be positively encouraged to continue.

Issues about money

As I was listening soporifically to the radio one day, I heard about a London restaurateur who offers a menu with no prices at all, and asks customers to pay what they think is appropriate once they have had the meal. He relies on the quality of his product, on customer satisfaction after the meal, their sense of fairness, and, to a certain extent, guilt and embarrassment, to ensure his restaurant thrives, and so far it is doing well. It reminded me of Carl Rogers, whom I was told used to ask clients to pay him whatever their hourly earning fee might be, and he, too, trusted that he would thrive with a mix of high earners and poorer clients. He acknowledged that people are not necessarily straightforward in the emotionally laden arena that is payment for services. Some temperamentally overpay, others look for ways to justify withholding, some are oblivious to the extras they are receiving or carefully monitor that they are getting every "mouthful" of their just desserts. I have found it necessary to review my own arrangements to be paid for supervision at various points, and some of my assumptions underlying them, and still find that I "forget" initially to mention payment for missed sessions until it happens, and then feel caught in unprofessional behaviour and dilemmas about how to balance my need for predictable income with my reluctance to be paid for sessions that are missed, because I have not then "earned" it. Sometimes, insight about such "forgetting" is not enough, and it takes repeated coaching to shift such deeply held patterns or values.

Originally, I thought of the supervision payment as a flat fee that would cover all associated "services". I set the fee higher than the hourly rate I charged for counselling, partly to take into account the greater time I routinely spent on preparation, and partly because it seemed a more "grown-up" activity to be engaging in, only available to the more experienced practitioner and thus worthy of a premium. I did assume it was worth more. I was startled, some years later, when a colleague said she charged less for supervision because she enjoyed doing it less, and as a counselling psychologist she thought she did much more preparation for clients. This made me realize again how individually we approach even the most apparently straightforward rationale for decisions.

No market rate

I have found few references about money and supervision. Without good knowledge of what other supervisors charge, except for the fees described in the professional directories, there is little sense of being part of a community of supervisors who all might charge roughly the same, and thus create a local "market rate". Peer group discussions can be very useful to share such details. Interestingly, powerful organizations such as the National Health Service (NHS), which pays for supervision for counsellors who work in a variety of settings, has, in my locality, set their own rate for reimbursement below current norms, and fail to keep pace with inflation, so the supervisee has to "top up" from her own pocket to meet whatever the supervisor charges or the supervisor has to charge less. Voluntary organizations struggle to pay a commercial rate, and usually expect supervisors to offer some reduction in recognition of their battle to sustain funding. Many supervisors offer a reduced rate for trainees. Generally, courses expect supervisors of student placements also to attend college meetings without pay for time or travel costs, even when no one else is paying for their time. Large organizations and salaried employees often do not recognize that the supervisor is offering a commercial service, too, and fees for attending meetings and providing reports are appropriate. Supervisors are entitled to clarity about what services are to be included in invoices and who will pay.

Payment for "extras"

Increasingly, I found that there were extra requirements depending on whom I was supervising. For instance, students on initial training courses, post qualifying training courses, or seeking accreditation, often sought support with written work or listening to tapes, which could be time consuming. I began to realize that I was making decisions "on the hoof", which therefore did not allow supervisees to know in advance what costs they might incur if they requested extras beyond our normal time spent together, and which impaired the ethical basis of "justice" when I accepted payment from one person who offered to pay, but not from another just because they did not offer.

My hardest challenge: short notice cancellations

My initial lack of system was most excruciating to me when people cancelled at short notice. Some assumed they would pay the whole fee, others offered half, a few expected not to pay at all, even if they had given me barely a few hours' notice. I would say, if asked, that they should pay half if they gave me minimal notice in advance, as I could get on with something else. Yet, if I had more than one cancellation in a day, which did happen on rare occasions, and especially close to Christmas, when people seemed more often to get ill or be overwhelmed with the pressures of life, I was left feeling that my calculations for my income were wrong, and so I noticed that I did have feelings and my own needs about this.

I compounded this confusion, as sometimes I wanted to be paid if I was feeling anxious about income, and sometimes not, because I had just been paid well for some other work, and felt calm about it. With some people it was easy to ask for the fee, for others my knowledge of their financial circumstances inhibited me and affected what I did. It took me some years to sort this out. A colleague who commented, "Plumbers don't ask before they hand you their bill", helped me. Eventually, it became important for me to be coherent and predictable and fair to all, including myself, but I can still catch myself being inconsistent with someone who will not pay, or cannot pay, or is simply disorganized about it. Now I can say later, "I made a mistake; this was our agreement." I do not have difficulty saying this once a supervisor has reminded me, yet seldom think of it myself.

This led me to develop an explicit document, outlined below. I consulted some peers for their comments and a view of their practice before giving it to my supervisees.

Supervision

Hourly rate: £40 per hour.

The hourly rate includes, from my point of view, planning and preparation, and reflection afterwards, completion of accreditation or re-accreditation reports, references for courses or jobs, and brief e-mails or phone calls. That is, basically, anything that takes less than a quarter of an hour extra, and is occasional as well as our face-to-face time.

Normal financial arrangements for non-attendance: if you do not attend without prior contact, a full fee is payable.

If there is a cancellation with more than forty-eight hours' notice, no fee is payable, if less than forty-eight hours' notice, a half fee is payable.

Elements attracting an extra fee at the same hourly rate:

- planned telephone calls lasting more than fifteen minutes;
- planned e-mail exchanges in lieu of meetings due to illness/ crises;
- feedback on course essays or audiotapes, or assistance by reading drafts of accreditation documents.

NB For a "monthly" supervision contract I expect that we will meet for a minimum of nine sessions a year, depending on holidays and health, and a norm of 10–11 sessions. If many cancellations occur during a year, it will be important for us to discuss the pattern and its implications, professional as well as financial.

Giving this out to supervisees was straightforward, and greatly improved the situation, but I still found I might forget to do so with a new supervisee and not notice until there was a difficulty, usually arising from a short notice cancellation. Old habits die hard.

Gifts

An extra element which is much more difficult to address in advance with a new supervisee relates to gifts to the supervisor. Some have brought gifts at Christmas, or gifts or flowers to say thank you for help after achieving accreditation or graduation, or as a kindness to me after an illness or operation. Others have brought cards. Many did not do either. This seems more common in female pairs of supervisor–supervisee, but some male supervisors have had a present or flowers, they tell me, though this is rare. I have not yet found a form of words that would clarify with supervisees that gifts are not expected or necessary, and perhaps not appropriate, without sounding pompous. It seems portentous to put such strictures into a contract at the start of a relationship, but if it is not mentioned initially it arises only when gifts are given or discomfort arises, and that is always much more difficult to be congruent about. Spare apples from a tree or flowers from the garden strike me as different from something paid for, though they have taken time and thought in a similar way. So, I give a mixed message of pleasure at it and a feeling that it should not be happening.

Maybe because I am one of the more task-focused people who does not offer presents to my supervisor, I have not felt comfortable receiving them. Or is it that with gifts we move into intimacy and care, and an acknowledgement that, though this is a paid relationship, it is also one characterized by a deep connection when it works well? The complexity of our work is encapsulated by this intimacy within a paid relationship, and people live it differently. As a supervisor, I think it is my job to be clear about boundaries and expectations, and to let go of the illusion that I can control other people's behaviour beyond that.

I think the issues around boundaries and contracts in supervision are under-researched. They replicate the tensions at the core of the supervisory relationship of sustaining a balance between support and challenge. It is a paid, yet intimate, relationship in best circumstances, because the personal and professional development of both the supervisor and the supervisee lie at the heart of it. It is also one that needs to become safe enough that what is more easily unspoken can courageously be put into words in service of the work. When this can happen, it is a precious resource, and people are wise not to let go of it lightly. Yet, letting go and starting afresh is also useful, and may be necessary for further development.

The needs and preferences of both parties are usefully articulated at the start and at reviews. So often I have said "yes" to an enquiry about whether or not I am taking new supervisees, only to have to squeeze myself to stay available to regular supervisees in the maelstrom of other, irregular, work. Supervisors, too, can acknowledge how their personal pathology affects their professional work.

CHAPTER TWO

Beginning as a supervisor

"Practice prepares the mind, but suffering prepares the heart"

(Remen, 2000)

I began supervising when requested by a local voluntary agency, with only a day's training for the role, occasional attendance at conference workshops, and a little reading under my belt. My own supervisors were my models, and yet I made many naïve assumptions. I read early work by Inskipp and Proctor (a tapes and booklet resource now unavailable) and began confidently to negotiate administrative contracts about how we would work together: where, when, how often, and for what fee. We explored whether I was to be the only supervisor, and, if so, what my responsibilities were. We agreed other normative elements such as whether reports would be necessary, which ethical code or framework we each used, and what I would do if I became concerned about the supervisee's practice. I learned to negotiate a more psychological contract by experience that was sometimes difficult for myself or my supervisees, or both of us. Some lessons were about my own style and personality and the way these affected my supervisory style. In particular, there were hard lessons about the skills necessary for creating a safe, boundaried relationship in which I could take authority without slipping into oppressive behaviour.

In the 1980s and 1990s, informal apprenticeship was common as few supervisor training courses were available. Most people began supervising as a career development move once they considered themselves experienced enough, or when some individual or agency asked them. Unaware incompetence is a risk when taking on a new role and responsibilities. Clarity about what skills are transferable from counselling, and what else the supervisor needs to be able to do to supervise effectively is relevant. This is also true for supervisors within medical and social work settings.

Learning to "helicopter", to identify themes, fitted with my prior academic background. In contrast, I had to learn particularly about using intuition and my bodily responses as information that was pertinent to the supervisory process, rather than dismissing this source of information as an irrelevant distraction. I also had to learn to discipline myself about timing of suggestions and "teaching", and to do less of this, since this was a comfortable and familiar mode. Learning to value "not knowing", and to encourage supervisees to do likewise, was a significant step.

Today, more counsellors begin work as a supervisor after some supervisor training. Many obtain experience in a peer group, and then build a practice from there. Some supervisor training courses help applicants to consider how they know they are ready to begin. Some require participants to have begun work with one or two individual supervisees or a group before they begin training.

The necessary knowledge, and grasp of an ethical base

The then BAC codes of ethics were barely formulated when I began, and I did not have them by my chair as I worked, as I came to do in later years. My attitudes to them were that they were a resource *in extremis*, rather than an underpinning for everyday practice. Less routinely, I commented on counsellor competence and context and did not seek liaison with mental health colleagues.

Daines, Gask, and Usherwood (1997, pp. 16–17) indicate issues a supervisor might address in relation to individual clients and the work with them:

- clarify whether the potential client will benefit from counselling;
- clarify whether the counselling needed is within the counsellor's competence;
- point to evidence in clients of medical/psychiatric problems, and clarify their nature and the implications for counselling;
- avoid setting up unrealistic aims in the counselling;
- arrange appropriate liaison with medical or mental health professionals;
- aid resolution of ethical dilemmas.

It is an unwise counsellor or supervisor who works without some conceptual framework about whom they might be able to help within the limits of time and skills available. Counsellor training courses are now much better than in my time in teaching about psychiatric diagnoses and terminologies (Lemma, 1996), whether or not their theoretical modality values these models. It is necessary in many arenas of employment to be able to consult with other professionals using accepted frameworks for psychiatry. Knowing which clients are suitable for the experience level of the supervisee and the time and resources available is also very important.

Working as a novice supervisor

Easy learning: bonding and supporting a trainee

My early supervisees included one who began supervision before she met her first client in a voluntary agency, after only a ten-week agency "introduction to counselling" course. She had had a lot of therapy herself, and this gave her courage to begin. Our early work was pragmatic: how to make a counselling contract; rehearsing what to say at the very start of the first session. We explored the feelings she might find it hard to engage with, and what to put into her notes. As in many voluntary agencies in the 1980s, it was an experience for her of going in at the deep end. The agency did not do prior assessments to ensure the clients were suitable. Dunkley has more recently (Dunkley, 2003) produced a series of helpful short articles to alert trainees to risk assessment, suicide risk assessment (Dunkley, 2006), and placement planning (Dunkley, 2007).

Within two months, my supervisee had worked with a young person who had been raped, a very angry nineteen-year-old gangster who wanted to avoid another spell in prison, a young man who reminded her of her brother, a bulimic art student, and a young man who, it later emerged, was the son of a colleague in the agency. Fortnightly supervision was intense and she often asked "what do I do about this?", or said "I had to dig deep to stay with her about that". As her therapy was continuing, there was relatively little pull to misplacing the therapeutic boundary with me. We would identify issues she could take to therapy, and look in supervision at how her reactions, thoughts, feelings, beliefs, or bodily sensations might be affecting the work with each particular client. The normative issues about fitness to work with such complex needs were constantly in our minds. Yet, she was so willing to explore her own part in the process that I came to trust her approach, value her style, and respect her courage for engaging in some deep connections with clients barely younger than herself. She would talk openly in supervision about how she felt in relation to clients and her own life events, and what she was learning from working with each client, and she was keen to get feedback, challenge, and encouragement from me. I came to respect and admire her, and in our final review named this as "like having a professional daughter". She had difficult relationships with her own mother, yet allowed herself to depend professionally on me. We examined these issues and idealizations, but not in the depth I might do now. The agency became a source of frustration to her, primarily through the attitudes of older counsellors to her and to the young people it served. She stayed at the agency and with me for three years. The match between our styles was good, and we each enjoyed learning as we developed alongside the other.

She was not on an ongoing course, so I did not learn at that stage the necessary skills of writing reports; nor did I test how transferable were my existing competencies in assessing practice. These are major responsibilities when supervising a trainee on a course, and the novice supervisor needs some mentoring about it when first they take it on.

Hard learning: how and when to challenge a colleague

Another supervisee in the same agency was a classic developmental challenge for an inexperienced and untrained supervisor. I was without the support of supervision of my supervision when a difficult relationship developed that had a less satisfactory outcome. Over a period of time, I became concerned about a supervisee, who blamed her clients for leaving therapy prematurely, and had what I eventually called a "combative style" with them. I tried to raise the issue with her. She did not see there was a problem. As we started to talk about it, we wrestled with our increasingly differing perceptions of her approach to her work and to supervision. My concerns grew, and I accepted that I had not given her enough honest feedback as they arose. She would not engage with the feedback when I did so, even though I then offered her the chance to read my notes of our supervision sessions, which recorded issues I had raised month by month. Eventually, I said I must tell the agency of my concerns. She was angry and seemed unable to hear my feedback. Our relationship became unsafe for her, and she would not discuss our impasse. I insisted I would consult the agency with or without her consent. She felt betrayed; I felt incompetent and anxious. The relationship never recovered. Neither of us felt satisfied with our conduct, but I learnt a lot about the importance of contracting for supervision, and about voicing concerns early and being more clear and direct about them.

Through this difficult experience, I learned to identify and share my growing concerns earlier in a relationship. Especially when I feel I have to "walk on eggshells" with a supervisee, I now use this as a signal that I need to take courage to name an issue I am avoiding. When I have an impulse to ask questions about the supervisee's style of relating to clients, I do not avoid or defer them. When I see a pattern of behaviour (like a number of clients leaving without ending), I name it, and invite shared exploration and monitoring.

At some level, I knew at the time that I could and should do all of those things, but lacked courage and confidence in my assessment initially and put it off, and then named it too tentatively. This made it harder later, when my capacity for empathy with her was compromised by my anxieties for the clients. In the end, the agency took on the issue at my insistence and it was resolved professionally. It remains an experience that shifted my under-standing of the courage that is required of a supervisor.

Attending to the supervisees' relationship in the agency

Both these supervisees had combative relationships with the volun-tary organization at some point. The organization was going through a very difficult period of change. As a supervisor, at that stage I had little contact with the organization, and yet my feelings about the changes were turbulent, too. I have since come to value the opportunity for meetings for supervisors working in an agency to offer feedback to the agency through identifying common orga-nizational themes that become apparent to the supervisor group. Examples include considering the individual's choice, as a volun-teer, not to go to available meetings or take up internal training events, and balancing this autonomy with needs for the organiza-tion to convey coherent or changing policies or ideas. When super-visors hear reports of difficulties with the management, or about proposed changes, it can be useful to ensure these have been fed back—with consent—into the system.

Working with supervisees from different theoretical orientations

Many voluntary agencies offer placements or work opportunities to people from a variety of training courses or theoretical modalities. This may create tensions between colleagues. When supervision is in multi-theoretical groups, the supervisor has to respect, under-stand, and explore different ways of working. It is testing for a supervisor, who has to learn how best to make a working alliance with someone who might have utterly different basic assumptions. Herrick (2007) describes her role as both a course supervisor and a placement supervisor, and explores these issues, describing how the supervisory relationship can respond positively to difference, not trying to convert trainees to her model, but being true to it. She has to know enough about the models the trainees on placement are using to be able to challenge statements inaccurate within their model, such as "I'm person-centred, so I am not allowed to ask questions". She relied on the question: "How might you explain or justify that intervention from your own model?"

My first developmental opportunity in this regard revealed my lack of generosity with a new counsellor from a course with a different theoretical modality from my own. The trainee was so excited about the new theory she was learning, of which I was completely ignorant, yet I made no attempt to familiarize myself with it. This meant she had to come more than half way to meet me on my own familiar and safe theoretical territory. She also had much more experience of direct work with young people than I had, yet I do not now recall celebrating this enough. She had chosen me as her supervisor because of a recommendation from a shared friend, and so gave me undue idealization. We met over two years for thirty-four sessions, and did develop our shared language and approach. Certainly, enough trust grew to support explorations of her personal and professional development and her work, but my current assessment of my contribution is that it was less than generous and relatively unaware of her developmental needs.

Supervising a more experienced colleague

A final example of a developmental challenge to a novice supervisor came from working with a colleague who was well respected and a more experienced counsellor than myself. She had approached me because of some shared theoretical base, and my experience in academic settings, and a wish to learn how to do more short-term, focused work, on the basis of a recommendation from her existing supervisor, whom I also knew.

I was flattered to be asked, and uncertain what I could offer. This combination of feelings is a potent predictor of difficulties. I also still thought I was to offer knowledge more than provide a process and a relationship. My feelings switched between feeling superior, comfortable, and knowledgeable, or inferior, less experienced, and uncertain about my contribution and role (Adlerians call this the superiority–inferiority dynamic; see Glossary). Thus, there was potential for abuse of power.

We met for thirty-seven sessions over almost three years, had a working alliance that seemed adequate, and did some careful work on behalf of her clients. Yet, I did not take supervisory authority in a key area of the relationship. The supervisee was struggling with health and relationship issues that meant her counselling role provided most continuity in her life at the time. I thought she was overworking because of a need to keep earnings up and because her self-esteem lay so greatly in her role as a counsellor. Her issue throughout our supervision was reiterated many times: "*Do* I create dependency in my clients?" I noted that the issue kept coming up for her, we explored her assumptions and ways of working, but I did not have the experience to help her wrestle with this key issue effectively, and resolve it to her own satisfaction. Specifically, because my focus was entirely on the client, and her interventions and relationship with her clients, I did not explore how her own history might contribute to the issue. We quickly found ourselves in parallel process about needy clients (and needy supervisees), but I did not have the conceptual base to be able to articulate parallel process either to myself or to her. I just knew in my guts that I was worried about her resilience. She experienced this as me trying to "mother" her, and resisted my restorative enquiries. Our stresses came to a head over her re-accreditation submission. She felt "treated like a trainee when she saw my anxiety shooting up if things were wrongly done in my eyes". I had to say that her case study did not fit with my recall of our discussions, and it *was* important to discuss our differences of perception. She was right, of course. I was much too anxious and rigid with her, and had not the skills or personal development myself to convey concerns without being and sounding critical. I completely overlooked the loss to her of her previous, much-valued supervisor. In the end, I unconsciously created a crisis that she felt as an attack through the re-accreditation report. Our ending eventually leaned on what had been good between us, and what was courageous in each of us. We did explore her "mother transferences" to me, and my anxieties, and my way of being careful about expressing my concerns. We had mutual friends, so also had to discuss whether we might meet at social events. I learnt a lot about misunderstandings, and about surviving what I experienced as damaging attacks, and about courage from her modelling of congruence in conflict situations.

Learning styles

Continuous professional development for counsellors requires "deep learning" (Marton & Saljo, 1976) that is not just about assimilating given material. It is centrally concerned with reflection, bridging between theory and practice, practice and understanding, and the development of hypotheses or formulations about clients and relationships and how a counsellor may best work with them.

Winston Churchill said, "I like to learn, but I do not always like to be taught." Supervisors need a lot of discipline to be aware of differences between their own preferred learning styles, and those of their various supervisees, and differences arising from prior expectations. It is the shared way of matching styles that makes for an effective working alliance.

As Inskipp and Proctor (1995) remind us, one challenge of learning in supervision arises because the individual is the professional tool, so every mistake can come close to his or her sense of identity, and as each develops their own sense of professional identity, previously established ones need to shift. To learn, we need to accept some pain and discomfort.

Emotion and the management of feelings have a major place in learning in supervision. Individual life stories and preferred styles will alter how anxiety is expressed, and what assuages it. Beliefs and assumptions will be exposed and explored, and shame might be attached to discoveries of taken for granted beliefs that are not seen as being accurate, or politically correct.

There is excitement, too, and finding that way of relating with each supervisee that is enjoyable. All supervisees will bring established learning styles and strategies to supervision, and these arise from personality, educational experiences, and learning or assumptions taken from life experiences. Chapter Six reveals some of mine: habits of independence, initial preferences for thinking rather than intuition or sensing, some undue and premature confidence, and too much self-belief. Yet, those who trust themselves and are willing to engage without defensiveness may feel most free to negotiate for what they want and need. Conversely, low self-esteem and prejudices about what one is not good at may limit a supervisee's willingness to try new ideas or practise new skills. If s/he is preoccupied with strong feelings or reactions, concentration might be compromised. Any supervisee who has previously been exposed to serious post traumatic stress is at risk, when feeling attacked, of slipping into panic or rigid patterns of thought.

Claxton (1984) describes four internal drivers that can get in the way of learning, if a supervisee is saying any of the following to himself:

- I must be competent;
- I must be in control;
- I must be consistent;
- I must be comfortable.

Supervision is most useful when the supervisory pair have agreed goals for supervision that include an active learning agenda. Page and Wosket (2001) describe supervisory styles that are authoritative or facilitative, using Heron's six-category model (1975; see Glossary). This reminds us that the way a supervisor communicates and relates with supervisees might either support their differing learning styles or cut across them. Enquiring how a potential supervisee prefers to learn is an important element of the contracting process.

Characteristics of adults as learners

Ideas current in the 1980s strike me as highly applicable to supervision and learning. They may be entirely familiar to readers who work in the higher and further education sector, but not necessarily to others. Knowles (1975) wrote about four useful assumptions about adults as learners, and these ideas also apply to the increasing maturity of counsellors as they become more experienced within their role. These are:

- "As people grow and mature, their self concept moves from one of dependency to one of increasing self directedness." This highlights the importance of making a contract to clarify goals for supervision that support a physical and psychological climate that encourages the supervisee to trust their capacity for practice and reflection.
- "As people mature they become an increasing reservoir of experience, and thus a rich source of learning." This makes group supervision highly desirable, and collegiality within supervision a priority.

- "As people mature, their readiness to learn is the product of the developmental tasks required for the performance of their evolving social (and, in this context, professional) roles."
- "Adults have a problem centred as opposed to a subject centred approach to learning." This makes learning in supervision at all stages of professional development a useful basis for integrating theory and practice.

Clarkson and Gilbert (1991), Inskipp and Proctor (1995), Carroll (1996), Carroll and Gilbert (2002), and many others emphasize that supervision is a place to learn. These authors also have useful things to say to supervisees, to help them become aware of how they prefer to learn. Hawkins and Shohet (2006, p. 17) describe three learning "zones": comfort, learning, and panic. The learning zone is characterized by "beginners' mind", and a relaxed attitude. The comfort zone may be characterized by too much being taken for granted, and individual work not being subjected to reflection.

Honey and Mumford's (1992) framework distinguishes those who learn most easily from coherent, structured, theoretical presentations ("The Theorist"), from other styles that differ in terms of pace and mode. "The Reflector" likes doing projects and case study work, taking time to work out what they think and feel. "The Activist" revels in role-play and thrives on new experiences and active learning. "The Pragmatist" enjoys applying ideas in practice and assessing if and how they work (*ibid.*)

Kolb (1984) developed relevant ideas about learning styles, and about the processes of experiential learning. He proposes a cycle of learning that starts with an experience, as follows:

- beginning with an experience;
- sharing what it was like;
- interpreting: making some sense of what has happened;
- generalizing: looking for patterns, or indicators of what can be generalized;
- applying: thinking about how the insights gained about the process of learning where the content can be applied.

A key point to understand that arises from combining Honey and Kolb's ideas is that people with different styles of learning prefer to begin the process at differing places in the cycle. Their readiness to learn and awareness of the need to do so might also arise because they are moving through stages of development about an issue or skill: from unconscious incompetence, unconscious competence, or self-conscious incompetence towards self-aware competence.

Unconsciously, surely each of us is learning something new each day and with every new relationship. However, the value of supervision is that the reflective space supports us to stop and consciously consider what we have experienced and what sense we are making of it. The supervisory contract forms one base for deciding what to attend to: skills, knowledge, new conceptual frames, or personal issues.

Learning the skills involved in being a supervisee

Carroll and Gilbert (2005) offer descriptions of six skills to help supervisees to reflect on the what, how, and why of learning. Their headings for the skills are:

- Learn to learn
- Learn to give and take feedback
- Learn realistic self evaluation
- Learn to reflect
- Learn emotional awareness
- Learn how to dialogue.

Like Hawkins and Shohet (2006), they use the ideas from neuro-linguistic programming (NLP) about whether the individual learns best from visual, auditory, or kinaesthetic cues (seeing, hearing, or doing).

Realistic self evaluation, or what Inskipp and Proctor (2003) call being "a fair witness" for oneself, involves updating a self concept and reflecting compassionately on efficacy of professional practice. Getting a realistic grip on the internal critic is crucial. However, during training, it is a particularly sensitive issue. Supervisees might be unaware of their strengths, and about how they are perceived. They might be hyper-critical of their work, comparing themselves to examples of best practice rather than with other novices. More rarely, some are unduly sanguine, which might make it more difficult to pinpoint the developmental edge of their current work.

Solution-focused frames of thought (O'Connell & Jones 1997; Waskett, 2006) encourage supervisors to assist in development of more professional self-awareness. The supervisee notices his or her effective practice when the supervisor invites him or her to describe what s/he is doing that is working. Encouragement that is specific and descriptive (Millar, 2007) facilitates self assessment. This creates the platform for identifying what to do differently next time, with minimal threat to the self-esteem of the practitioner. No matter how competent a supervisee may be, s/he will benefit from identifying good practice, and then considering how to use similar insights for a new situation.

Emotional awareness and the management of feelings in supervision is important, because supervision is such an emotional process and the supervisory relationship is potentially so significant to the working confidence of the supervisee. Wilkinson's work on attachment styles in relation to doctors and patients is relevant to supervision (Wilkinson, 2003). The supervisee who is fortunate enough to come with habits of secure attachment from early life will be in a strong position to negotiate for what s/he wants, and to be flexible in response to feedback. The person with insecure attachment styles might choose independence rather than co-operation, or denial of upset feelings rather than naming them and seeking shared reflection of a difficult supervisory exchange, within a context of mutual valuing, respect, and equality.

Prompts for reflection exercises for supervisees

Self-questioning is a very useful process for becoming aware of learning styles, and learning from experiences, and to build the "internal supervisor". I developed these prompts for a workshop. Carroll and Gilbert's (2005) book for supervisees has many more.

How my first supervisor influenced me . . .
Who has influenced my supervision the most, and how?
What was important to me about supervision X years ago?
What is most important to me now?
How has my style of learning changed?

When was supervision a safe space?
What have I learned from a mistake in supervision?
Where is my learning edge at this stage of my career as a supervisee?

Reflections

Supervisee self-awareness, supervisor sensitivity, dialogue, negotiation, and contracting have all been identified as contributing to effective supervision that builds the working alliance by being responsive to the learning style of the supervisee, and yet invites him or her to extend beyond a comfort zone about learning. Some comments about how adults learn are designed to encourage the supervisor to trust that the supervisee can bring jewels of experience to the process. The supervisor also has to be disciplined to work outside her own comfort zone, thoughtfully choosing to work in ways that most help the supervisee to make use of the time, space, and relationship.

The personal examples have been chosen to illustrate developmental challenges for a new supervisor. It is now common to seek supervision of supervision to support early practice, and the chapter on this topic explores this further. Some of my mistakes and shortcomings could have been minimized or averted by attending a good training. I eventually did seek more experienced mentoring.

Now, some knowledge of legal issues and confidence in ethical decision-making would also be considered essential. Chapter Seven, which looks at supervisory styles, also indicates how necessary it is to examine and reflect on attitudes to difference of many sorts.

As Remen, whose words begin this chapter, also said (2000, p. 213), "Curing is the work of experts, but strengthening the life in one another is the work of human beings".

CHAPTER THREE

Relationship climates

"See how the golden groves around me smile,_
That shun the coast of Britain's stormy isle,
Or, when transplanted and preserved with care,
Curse the cold clime and starve in northern air.
Here kindly warmth their mounting juice ferments
To nobler tastes and more exalted scents"

(Addison, 1704)

I am interested in the emotional tone of supervision, what the chemistry might be between people with different emotional styles in order to achieve an enabling supervisory environment. I describe these simply as warmth or coolness, though more complex analyses are available and discussed briefly below. I am curious about how the matches between the supervisor's and supervisee's styles make different supervision relationships work, and use ideas from Myers–Briggs and attachment theory to think about the issues.

A supervisory alliance may be built from, and work within, a comfort zone of shared style, or function as a bridge between different styles. Bonding with someone similar may initially seem easier, but bridging could be more productive in the end. Bridging skills include immediacy, so either can make comments to check out the intentions or meaning of the other, and a curious interest in difference. I make my personal preference for warmth explicit, and I hope that does not wholly distort this discussion, as I am interested in all the variations of relationship, and, in particular, in the opportunities which arise from differences in professional style and theoretical modality, class, race, age, sexuality, and so on. Here, I focus on emotional temperature, but this intertwines with cultural norms and differences and the developmental stage of the supervisee. I am also conscious that differences can, unhelpfully, lead to abuse of power by either party.

Warmth or coolness might refer either to a quality residing in the supervisor or the supervisee, or to the relationship between them. Whether cool or warm, it is possible to create a relationship that communicates understanding and respect, and develop a shared language and ongoing discussion about ideas. An essential element for useful supervision is that the working alliance be characterized by *safety*, that is, the threat to the individual's self esteem is reduced, so that the relationship enables the supervisee to reveal matters about which they feel anxious, uncertain, ashamed, or simply in need of a creative boost from another person's perspective. Of course, the purpose of the supervisory relationship is central. It is a means to an end: to work creatively together for the benefit of the clients, to explore difficulties and failures, as well as progress, learn from them, and feel empowered as a counsellor.

One task for the supervisor is to support the development of the supervisee's internal supervisor. Any supervisor can usefully model this through an ability to "wonder" with the supervisee, to offer curiosity in the context of not knowing, and to tolerate ambiguity.

Intimacy

Professional intimacy includes safety, trust, honesty, risk, openness, respect, psychological contact, and boundaries. This is a powerful mix that may lead to erotic or relationship longings, so the boundaries of professional intimacy have to contain these feelings, yet prevent inappropriate enactment of them.

Intimacy entails separate selves tuning into another's reality, which is an important component of a supervisory style. Through good enough contact with someone else, each can come increasingly to know their authentic self as a worker, and to accept and recognize individual strengths and weaknesses. Useful intimacy creates the possibility to feel connected at a deep level. At this level, each can hear the other's difference without feeling threatened, and are able to note their own mistakes and explore the consequences for the client without defensiveness. It is also very important to be able to be "in the moment", that is, able to respond flexibly to what *is*, not what is expected.

Negative intimacy, in contrast, could result in collusion, and creates the risk of failure to challenge when necessary, seeking too much closeness and comfort at the cost of useful open exploration or discomfort, and a necessary focus on the client.

It is a difficult task to keep a professional intimacy going while not spoiling the balance of the relationship by intrusiveness, or withdrawing for fear that the other will judge self-disclosure as weak or desperate. Some people cope with discomfort by avoidance or leaving. Deference makes many trainees put up with discomfort for fear of jeopardizing their success on the course.

I see the issue of boundaries as crucial here: boundaries that need to exist between the self and the other, and have to be appropriate for the two individuals, so no one feels trespassed upon, invaded, abandoned, or pushed around. Observation and checking out the responses of the other make for ease.

Does intimacy prevent or enable the necessary exercise of supervisory authority? Intimate relationships have both a potential for particularly robust exchanges, and a risk of collusion and avoidance of challenge. Intimacy implies the possibility of moving *beyond instrumentality* (using the other as a *thing* or a function) to a place of relationship where inner worlds are knowable and do matter and can be touched through attunement, in "moments of meeting" that have the potential for transformation.

Cognitive style and emotional preferences

There has been a lot of relevant work, largely in the USA, arising from applying the Myers–Briggs typology to supervision. Bernard and Goodyear (2004, pp. 102–107) provide a useful discussion that I refer to further in Chapter Seven, on supervisory style. They discuss authors who apply the Myers–Briggs ideas about extroversion (focus on the outer world of people and things) *vs.* introversion (directed towards the inner world of ideas); sensing *vs.* intuiting as ways to gather information; feeling *vs.* thinking, which distinguishes learning from subjective experiences or objective analysis; judging *vs.* perceiving, which explores methods of information management and retrieval.

They note that American supervisors, whether introvert or extrovert, tended to prefer "intuition" styles to "sensing", and thus were less interested in facts and details than in the bigger picture. Similarly they preferred "judging" to "perceiving" and so were more goal and outcome directed rather than adaptive and innovative.

Implications for relationships include frustration for a "thinking" supervisor with a "feeling" supervisee, or for a "judging" (i.e., well-organized) supervisor with a supervisee whose general approach to learning seems too random. Introvert trainees in one study expressed a need for gentle confrontation. It is important to emphasize that each style is, or might be, equally valuable and useful for a counsellor or supervisor. The issue lies in the ease of connecting between them through building a repertoire of styles.

Working in a cool style

What characterizes a cool supervisor or supervisee? It is an approach that does not normally include emotional expression, or a felt sense of "reaching out" to the other, but, rather, a cool and calm distanced availability. This could equate to a preference for thinking rather than feeling in the Myers–Briggs analysis, and thus some emotional reserve, (see Keirsey, 1998) or a dismissive and detached insecure attachment style (Main, Kaplan, & Cassidy, 1985). The rationality and analytical reflection, observation, judgement, and capacity to offer an overview, will be immensely valuable. Thinking and theorizing can be really exciting and productive.

One way of differentiating between more expressive and reserved people is to think about what charges their batteries: for expressive people (like extroverts) energy comes out of contact with others; for reserved people (like introverts) it is more likely to be solitary activity. Cool and reserved people might find supervision, perhaps particularly group supervision, too intrusive, and learn more from private reflection, journal keeping, note writing, reading or writing case studies.

Can two people meet coolly and still do useful supervision that addresses both tasks and process? Another American study examining cognitive style determined the type of supervision supervisees preferred. Supervisees (all trainee counsellors) who scored highly on intuiting, feeling, and perceiving (and low on sensing, thinking, and judging) preferred relationship orientated supervision, whereas those scoring high on sensing, thinking and judging prefer task orientated supervision (Lochner & Melchert, 1997).

I think that a cool relationship will have more focus on the monitoring and educational tasks of supervision and be more focused on analysis than on expressions of feeling. Thus, it might pay less attention to the overlap between the professional and personal needs of the counsellor. A cool supervisee might well prefer a cool supervisor. If both share this style, the normative or educational tasks of supervision could routinely take precedence over the restorative. Attachment theory would predict that they might manage emotional stress by denial, without exploring it routinely until it becomes extreme. This might have consequences for monitoring "fitness to practice", an important task of supervision encouraged by the ethical framework of our work.

A cool relationship can still be characterized by equality, and a "cool" supervisee might feel safer with a "cool" than with a "warm" supervisor, who may feel too intrusive. The relationship might offer calm, and, in this sense, a shared comfortable safe space for reflection. The focus might be more on casework supervision, on the *therapy* session and client's pathology, the strategies and interventions of the counsellor, transference issues, and the wider context, and less on the *felt experience of the relationship* of client and counsellor or counsellor and supervisor.

Another issue for research and reflection is whether or not the cool supervisor is as well able to contain anxiety. This is a key supervisory skill. If the supervisee is feeling shame or anxiety about the counselling work, s/he might not disclose or work with these feelings as part of the supervisory process. Creating understanding about the relationship between client and counsellor might be a route in to discussing these issues. However, some Adlerian theorists and practitioners argue that when a counsellor is "stuck" with a client, it is *always* because of some thing in their own history (Kopp & Robles, 1989; Shifron, 2007).

Warm supervision: sitting in the sunshine

I prefer a warm supervisor. I need to be in a warm relationship that feels underpinned by a sense of emotional connection, and has a quality of containment and encouragement. Even experienced and introverted practitioners sometimes need this, in the teeth of demanding and challenging client–counsellor relationships. It may be felt as relating with the fullness of humanity and even vulnerability: seeing and being seen "warts and all", as Oliver Cromwell said. Clearly, if the focus of the work were all based on feelings, the supervision would not perform essential reflective tasks. But, if the quality of the human connection is warm and accepting, the possibility of sharing what is felt to be shameful could be increased.

Person-centred supervisors might recognize "warmth" as bearing a close and partial relationship to Rogers' concept of "unconditional positive regard" (1977).

Rogers describes how warm therapeutic connection manifests itself "in speech, facial expression, gestures, ability to empathise, and general emotional tone" (1976, pp. 348–349). I am interested in the power of unconscious modelling in the supervisory relationship. Once more it is to Rogers I turned, and in the passage just quoted he described the power of a group leader's style to influence group members. He argued that this style affects group members who internalize attitudes and behaviour patterns that they observe, and this happens within educational settings very vividly (Rogers, 1983). I have not yet seen research about the degree to which supervisor style affects the supervisee's style as a counsellor or a supervisor, or whether any influence is greater in one-to-one or group supervisory relationships, but my own experience leads me to think it might do so, both consciously in following the style, and unconsciously from experiencing it.

So how do *I* describe supervisor warmth? It is that the supervisor conveys that they care about the supervisee as a person as well as a professional. I think that holding the overlap of the personal and the professional in mind is crucial to good supervision. This means that the person feels welcomed, remembered, and personal/professional themes and conversations are referred to. Some self-disclosure by the supervisor supports the working alliance. As in potentially transformative counselling, there is a sense at key times of "a moment of meeting" when the two individuals step briefly outside their roles to connect as individuals. In a fluffy phrase, the psychological contact is "heart to heart".

I found Rogers' original writing about non-possessive warmth (1977) by the therapist very striking in terms of parallels for the supervisor. His questions (*ibid.*, explored in pp. 50–53) are highly applicable, and a very productive basis for reflection about supervision.

Q1   Can I be expressive enough as a person that *what I am* will be communicated unambiguously? (Rogers calls this congruence.)

Q2   Can *I let myself experience* positive attitudes towards this other person, attitudes of warmth, caring, liking, interest, and respect?

Q3   Can I be strong enough as a person *to be separate* from the other? Can I be a sturdy respecter of my own feelings, my own needs, as well as his?

The third question links to a definition of psychological maturity, an ability to accept the separateness of the other. When the supervisee is encouraged to pursue their own development, unafraid of the envy or judgement of the supervisor, s/he can relate more authentically to clients. I see support for separateness as being equally likely and important from a warm or a cool supervisor, though it may be enacted and experienced differently.

If a relationship is warm, it does not necessarily imply that it is cosy or enmeshed, or lacking in task focus. As Egan (1990) said, a helping practitioner has to relate in a way that earns the right to challenge, and offer reality testing. When feeling connected, and with some trust in good will, the supervisee might be more likely to accept such interventions, because of some trust in the intentions of the supervisor. "Encouragement" is a process of "giving courage" to the supervisee to address issues (Millar, 2007), not simply giving praise that frames feedback within "a superiority–inferiority" dynamic in a relationship.

Warmth is a potent agent to create a sense of safety, mutuality, and equality, all elements that Weaks's research (2002) has shown is very important for good supervisory experiences when also combined with challenge. Some of Weaks's respondents emphasized the value of affirmation, and this had warmth as an essential element.

Warmth also has an impact on creativity. The relationship has to create the space between the supervisory pair where either is willing to show uncertainty, possibly even vulnerability, in the service of the work. "Play" promotes the work, and playfulness supports lateral thinking and imaginative exploration of supervisee's issues.

Bridging between styles

Are the most productive supervisory relationships those where supervisor and supervisee share similar emotional styles? Matched styles offer support and comfort. Mismatching may result in useful awareness of utterly different ways of being, but the relationship has to be earned more carefully. If the supervisor is cool and the supervisee is warm, the supervisee might feel exposed, too emotionally labile, messy, and possibly, therefore, uncontained. The supervisee might then imagine disapproval from the supervisor, or experience it in reality. Supervisees in these circumstances have spoken of feeling less "safe" as a practitioner, because they begin to hide parts of themselves that they are ashamed of (personal communications). The supervisor and supervisee then have to build a working alliance through careful contracting and a continuing willingness to review the effectiveness of the supervisory relationship, and give each other feedback to build the bridges which will end in trust of their difference, and the potential for relevant learning. After all, every counsellor also works with clients of different emotional styles from their own.

If the supervisor is warm and the supervisee is cool, the supervisee might experience the supervisor's interest in the personal–professional overlap as intrusive, too personal. It may feel smothering, not genuine, and uncomfortable. They might think, or ask, "Do I need to be taken care of this much?" They can negotiate for the focus of supervision to be more on casework and less on their resilience, but this angle cannot be abandoned. Both positive and critical feedback, then, need to be descriptive, detailed, and carefully timed, and interspersed with opportunities for the supervisee to comment, so that the supervisee can believe it and understand the implications of it for their practice.

Making feedback matter-of-fact involves balancing what the supervisee does effectively with feedback about what is not yet appropriate. Hawkins and Shohet's (2006, p. 134) CORBS model (CORBS stands for *clear, owned, regular, balanced,* and *specific*) is one example of a structure for feedback.

The challenges of group supervision

This discussion makes vivid the demands on the supervisor of groups. For *all* to feel that they are full members and be able to contribute, the facilitator has to be able to create a group structure and climate responsive to different styles. Once more the need for careful contracting is vivid, so that individuals can contribute at the pace and in the way that they best can learn. Groups do offer a place to hide as well as engage. Proctor (2008, p. 72) describes the different skills of a group supervisor in terms of behavioural flexibility, being able to move between active leadership, assertion, and receptivity. She also recommends letting go of some skills or styles from one-to-one work: long reflective pauses and offering undivided one-to-one attention are less productive in group supervision. Decisions about when to move to responsive leadership, trusting the group, can be more confidently made by a leader who can also calmly and assertively remind members of agreed contracts. The purpose of the group, the experience of its members, and their personal style preferences interact. Setting up predictable review and feedback systems so members can comment on their level of enjoyment as well as the usefulness of the space will allow members to calibrate their participation within their learning zone.

Reflections

Choice of a new supervisor, like any other significant relationship, needs to take personal chemistry into account. Meeting before agreeing a contract is important. For people allocated during training, or by an employer, to a supervisor with whom the chemistry is difficult, some strategies for bridging between different styles of relating are useful.

This chapter invites readers to consider the issue of whether there is any particularly productive emotional temperature for supervision; and to be aware of the consequences for people with different personal styles working together in supervision. Finding a match between cognitive and emotional styles to create an effective working alliance can also contribute to a counsellor's increased self-awareness and a more realistic self-appraisal as a practitioner.

CHAPTER FOUR

Encouraging resilience

"Life isn't about how to survive the storm, but how to dance in the rain"

(Anon)

R esilience is all about positive engagement with adversity and sustaining competence with consistency when under stress. It is about accessing the range of emotions being experienced, rather than denial. It is about learning to put attention on to positive emotions and to buffer the self from being over-whelmed by painful ones. Counsellors and supervisors take it for granted that they will be working in a context of high, even occasionally overwhelming, emotional demands. These demands can have an overwhelming quality because it is difficult to control the quantity of approaches from clients or supervisees on any one day in work settings designed to be responsive to needs. But that is not all. The quality of the interaction is very often draining, as people who are stuck, scared, angry, sad, or in pain come for aid. It is a truism that those of us who are drawn to work as therapists have our own shadow and pain to address as an important part of becoming and remaining able to do this work. I am interested in describing the supervisor's role with counsellors who are vulnerable, or might become stressed. I call on the wounded healer archetype explored further in the next chapter while discussing how to support and sustain maximum resilience through supervision that enables counsellors to stay in touch with self-esteem and make good use of this external social support.

The value of self-awareness through training, supervision, and continuing professional development (CPD)

Most professional counsellor training courses emphasize the necessity for self-awareness, and invite students to review their motivation to do the work. In particular, their personal family history is explored for issues which parallel the pains clients will bring, and they are encouraged to notice what triggers might push them into exchanges where they might be particularly vulnerable to soothing their own hurts projectively. For example, as a trainee counsellor, I saw a client who had been sent to boarding school much against her will, as I had. I felt I *knew* what she had suffered, and was willing to go out of my way to make her a "special" client, and help her to address her issues. In fact, I had not yet addressed my own, and supervision was essential to explore and identify this, and so was therapy to address the pains of it.

Motivation to do this work is affected positively and negatively by life experiences, and by attitudes and life stage. One major motivation to train as a counsellor can be having received counselling that was experienced as helpful. This can lend a messianic quality to the work, and an unhealthy focus on working with only one type of issue. This has struck me particularly among student social workers who wanted to work with abused clients and women, and with voluntary bereavement counsellors, and those in self-help groups organized around a shared problem. The relationship to the client can then be unduly focused around the client as a "victim" of this experience, rather than being on a *person* who has had this particular experience, among others, and who is still functioning sufficiently to come for help. This can parallel ways of thinking that distances a practitioner from the real perspective of the sufferer, like "the appendix in bed sixteen" approach for which doctors have been caricatured.

Potential for misuse of power is inherent in a counselling relationship, and new counsellors need to be alerted to this.

So, a review of motivation is essential for all professionals, and especially for those who are addicted to helping. Some might suffer an excess need to be needed (Beattie, 2001). The power imbalance and co-dependency patterns arising from such needs can be identified and worked with, ideally through therapy or personal development groups before counsellors are let loose on clients. Otherwise they may feel grandiose about what they can accomplish.

The ideas of Guggenbuhl-Craig (1971), Beattie (2001), and Coe (2008) are useful reading for all counsellors in their early years of practice. To spell out some key points from them: Guggenbuhl-Craig reminds us that helpers need to be aware that they can best help by having clear boundaries; by recognizing, and helping the client to recognize, their strengths and potential for coping; by acknowledging that family, economic, social, and political factors are a reality which may have limited options available to the client.

Coe (2008) brought recent developments on the issues about boundaries up to date with a summary of typical financial, psychological, and sexual boundary violations by therapists. He encouraged trainers and practitioners to notice small "boundary violations" where the patient is treated as "special", and clarified ways to discuss and resist bent or broken boundaries.

The exercise of power in the counselling exchange needs sensitive review. It is my belief that the counsellor's capacity to accept themselves "warts and all" is a more indicative predictor of their therapeutic efficacy than their *intention* to accept the client. We so often have harsher standards for ourselves than for our neighbours or dear friends. The biblical injunction to "love our neighbour *as ourselves*" bears this emphasis.

Emotional resilience

Emotional resilience is an important attribute for counsellors and supervisors. It is particularly significant when the counsellor is faced with either intense acute pain in one particular client, or with a number of clients living with similar chronic distress. Unless the counsellor can let go of the pain when the client has left, or shortly thereafter, and seek, in supervision, for connections that, in particular cases, make it difficult to let go, they are at risk of burnout either through overload or through a cynical hardening of the heart.

It is essential for the counsellor to identify a personal network of support. Some useful questions (Henderson, 2001) include:

"Where do you get your experience of unconditional loving?"
"On whom do you depend?"
"How do you allocate time to balance work, play, excitement and relaxation?"
"If a key element in your life were to be removed (Work? Partner? Children? A physical ability or sense?), what would change for you?"

These explorations help the counsellor to reflect on the balance of satisfactions in their lives, and the way they might use their clients inappropriately to sustain their own sense of being helpful, and thus their wellbeing, at a cost to the client.

The "Velcro" solution

I called "the Velcro solution" (Henderson, 2001) a process of viewing layers of emotional protection like an onion, and learning to add or remove them appropriately; removing them to be free to be empathic with clients, and walk accurately in their worlds, replacing some to be with more disturbing people, or colleagues, or others who require an assertive and determined form of interaction. Counsellors working empathically with clients need to be able to use their imagination and intuition sensitively. In a sense, they need to be able to take off layers of their own protective armour to be alongside the client. Such empathy was elaborated through something Adler noted as, "To see with the eyes of another, to hear with the ears of another, to feel with the heart of another . . ." (quoted by Millar, 2007).

Supervisors can help counsellors to think about the layers of self-protection necessary to their roles and resilience. Self and peer assessment can give a counsellor useful feedback about the balance to achieve between assertiveness and empathy. The supervisee can be helped to notice what works and be encouraged to experiment with doing more of it; and to identify what does not work and try something else and monitor what happens. Keeping a journal, monitoring energy, checking resilience, understanding stress management and burnout, and reviewing waiting lists and work pressures all play a part.

Keep a journal

Journal keeping develops habits of reflection (Progoff, 1975). A journal can mirror the reflective process a counsellor takes with a supervisor, too:

* notice what happens and / or how you feel about it;
* reflect on the meaning of this;
* try something new if necessary;
* have a safe place to tell the story of what happened;
* use the attention of another to help you reflect on it if it is not obvious;
* set the next goal or task, or continue to monitor what you have agreed to.

Scaife (2009) describes similar processes through "learning logs" and reflective diaries in supervision. Benefits include improved capacities to sustain curiosity, recording implications for practice, connecting learning that has come from different settings, clarifying thinking, expressing feelings, and acting as an aide memoire.

The energy monitor solution

Many Americans seem better than the British at feeling entitled to live a life characterized by well being. Maybe the constitutional entitlement to life, liberty, and the pursuit of happiness sets the expectation. In the caring professions in the UK, the Puritan ethic still commonly prevails: injunctions that I have found to be common among supervisees include "defer gratification", "dedicate your life to serving those who are more needy", and "use your talents to help the less fortunate". At an extreme, "Don't say no unless you are too ill to do it". These are worthwhile values, but they can prevent the professional from taking personal needs seriously. In the end, all the evidence shows that this leads to burnout (Glouberman, 2003). Yet, one of the potent influences we can offer our clients is that we model openness of heart, flexibility of thinking, and a capacity to enjoy life and expect it to be good, at least some of the time.

As I approached fifty, I decided to take a five-month sabbatical, one month for each decade of my life. I bought a round-the-world plane ticket that cost almost exactly the same amount as a year of therapy, and chose my stopping-off points to combine time with family and friends around the world, and to go to places I had always wanted to be. I faced my fears of totally unstructured time, went to places where I knew no one, or my way around the place. I stayed in many basic hostels, mostly with younger travellers who were very generous as we shared information and advice, and stories of our lives. I went to look for "the love in the world", and found abundance. I experienced bodily physical experiences of well being. I returned with a feeling of "deep rest" from spending time with loved ones, receiving many experiences of kindness from strangers, and turning my attention away from the pain and despair of client's stories. I keep a particular photo I took of a seaside where I can see it as I write, as just to look at it takes me back to that particular fresh morning. I was fed by the beauty of some of the places I went to. I was also hot, tired, uncomfortable, sad, and lonely some of the time, as one would expect, and was pleased to survive those times and discover my resilience to do so and capacity to accept the help of others. I wrote a journal of my travels, and many letters, and so have kept alive the joy of the experience and can call on it.

Keeping alive a connection to joy is important in our work. Looking for it, and recalling peak experiences long after the event stimulates endorphins (Bloom, 2001). Bloom explores the link between endorphins (a group of hormones produced naturally by the body), pleasure, and the experience of spiritual connection. He developed a method to enable people to produce endorphins to access higher states of consciousness even when exhausted or in crisis, linking current ideas of neuro-biology and spirituality.

The habits of mindfulness play a part every day. It is hard to stop and take in the smell of flowers, taste food, and attend to the signals of our bodies about need for physical exercise, rest, and pleasure in the weeks when we have scheduled too much to do for the time available. Getting the balance between planned and reactive work gets harder over time as more people seek to call on the practitioner's experience.

In my view, an essential survival skill for the counsellor and supervisor is to get into the *habit* of monitoring their energy levels, and of planning recuperative experiences when they plan demanding work into their diaries.

So, a personal review (solo in a journal, or with a supervisor) pays dividends. After writing about supervision and mental health (Henderson, 2001), I developed five sets of questions that focus on resilience. They are:

Resilience check:

1. HOW AM I USING MY ENERGY? (Excitement? Agitation? Task focus? Inertia?) In particular, is my energy blocked or flowing in the physical, intellectual, emotional, social or spiritual arena? (PIES is the acronym.) How much time am I allocating to each? How much satisfaction do I get from each? Are my intimate and social relationships mostly reciprocal?
2. HOW FAR DO I FEEL IN CONTROL OR POWERLESS? In relation to particular issues or to life in general at the moment, what needs to change to increase my sense of well-being in this regard? Does this sense of my "locus of control" fit with the reality of financial or social pressures?
3. HOW RIGID OR FLEXIBLE AM I IN MY THINKING? In relation to a particular issue or more generally, am I obsessing? Am I open to new ideas? Can I learn from my experience or others'? Are my explanations understandable to others in my milieu?
4. WHAT BODILY SENSATIONS AM I AWARE OF? How deeply am I breathing? How full of energy am I? Where do I feel pleasure or hurt? How much or how often am I aware of pleasure or pain?

5. WHAT FEELINGS AM I FREE TO NOTICE AND EXPRESS? Are there any I habitually express? Are there some I never notice myself feeling? Is this appropriate to my circumstances?

Understanding stress management and burnout

Stress has become a buzzword. "Burnout" is bandied about in the caring professions (Grosch & Olsen, 1994). One definition of burnout can be found in Schaufeli, Maslach, and Marek (1993, p. 17): "Burnout is a syndrome of emotional exhaustion, depersonalization and reduced personal accomplishment that can occur among individuals who do 'people work' of some kind".

Senior managers are required to acknowledge its existence, and have an organizational duty of care to staff. Yet, there is also a culture, especially amongst senior managers, that sees some fault or weakness in the individual who so succumbs to stress that the resulting inertia, anxiety, or depression prevents them from working, or significantly reduces their effectiveness for a while. Awareness and acknowledgement without stigma of the early signs and process of becoming stressed is overdue. Generally, it is only when politicians or celebrities leave office or write memoirs that the cost of their performance is laid bare.

It is now well accepted that stress is caused by a combination of external factors and the individual's inner dialogue. The external factors might be acute (accidents or trauma, illnesses or life events, including major structural change at work) or chronic (prolonged pain, chronic illness, uncertainty at work, or long-term abuse at home or work). How individuals construe these experiences, the expectations they put on themselves, and their awareness of the thoughts, feelings, sensations, willpower, and energy level they bring to the experience will determine their level of stress. The more powerless and trapped they feel, the less they can imagine a good outcome, and the more desperately stressed they become, often using physical illness to get them off the hook because illness is considered an acceptable excuse.

Veniga and Spradley's 1981 model of the five stages to burnout is instructive. They are as follows.

I   Eustress: Positive arousal and enjoyment when meeting challenges.

II Fuel Shortage: Feeling tired, bargaining with your body.
III Development of Symptoms: Beginning to feel ill.
IV Symptoms become acute or chronic: More symptoms, or a more acute symptom emerges.
V Hitting the Wall: Being unable to continue without professional help and time off.

The sequence is not inevitable. Individuals can and do recover good health even from level IV without external mental health interventions. But awareness that patterns laid down in stages I–III can undermine individual resilience in an unexpected crisis could encourage the practitioner to aim to stay within a healthy range, even under some difficult circumstances.

To take a positive message from an experience of burnout, read *The Joy of Burnout*, by Dina Glouberman (2003), for heartfelt descriptions and suggestions about creating a radical healing opportunity out of the experience, and restoring a love of life.

Workloads, and counsellor's caring roles

I am struck by the workloads that many counsellors are willing to undertake: some who work in two or three General Practice settings "hold in mind" dozens of clients at any one time, and schedule their workload with all the honest difficulties that arise as they manage a waiting list, emergency requests, returner's requests for follow-up sessions, and consultation. Busy colleagues who have learnt to trust the counsellor may lean heavily for informal professional, or sometimes personal, support.

A consequence for the supervisor is that s/he, too, holds in mind a great many clients described by her supervisees, and might be very aware of the numbers who are never brought to supervision.

How are we different from doctors, who are expected to provide a service for 2,000 patients? The work is more emotionally intense, and the counsellor has to remain willing to be "touched", but so does the doctor within his own role. Walking the line between being touched and being overwhelmed in this caring work becomes harder. Academics have traditionally earned their sabbaticals after seven years. Perhaps all professionals need them. Grosch and Olsen (1994) argue that psychotherapists are at risk of burnout after ten years of professional practice. I ask supervisees to reflect on the questions: is this costing me too much? Is it time to move on or take a break, or do something else for part of my working life? If so, what is my next step?

Many counsellors and supervisors manage pressure and avoid burnout by creating a portfolio of activities, involving themselves in some counselling, some training or supervision, some group work, or organizational consultation. Some keep a day a week for the self, to garden, paint, do pottery, or just catch up with admin or spend time with a friend or extended family members.

A supervisor may legitimately explore not only the number of hours of face-to-face counselling work their supervisees do in a week or a month, but also the number of clients it is wise for them to "carry" at this point in their development and life.

In Henderson (2001), I offered prompts for reflection about adequacy of supervision in periods of supervisee stress. I drew attention to the need to monitor the quality of psychological contact between the supervisee and her clients, and between supervisor and supervisee, to notice what balance of support and challenge is being modelled in the relationship, and the encouragement or inhibition being offered by the supervisor.

What facilitates resilience for the caring professional?

Interventions that I have found helpful to myself and others over the years include:

1. To *take stock regularly* of the counsellor's motivation to do the work, and the satisfactions and costs of doing it.
2. To explore the existence and support from *reciprocal relationships* with friends and family, to counterbalance the essentially dependent professional ones. It is really important that the counsellor allows herself to receive as well as give. If, because of geographical moves or family losses, there are no reciprocal relationships, as a supervisor I might encourage the counsellor to pay for therapy, for example, or massage. This provides support (Dass & Gorman, 1981; Hawkins & Shohet, 2006) but does not address an inability to choose and sustain relationships characterized by reciprocity.
3. To have had some *therapy*, or *personal development* in groups, and to seek out more if they need it. Some of the debate about this is

mentioned by Johns (1996), who reminds us that personal development within counsellor training is not primarily mechanistic,
but can also engage with "chaos, paradox and ecology". It is an
integrative and head and heart process, engaged with existential and ecological issues as well as internal worlds. It helps
trainees embrace the limitations of human control. Counsellors
have to attend to relationships and to systems and networks in
which these are embedded, and can bring understanding of
communication and emotional literacy garnered through personal development or therapy into their work.

4.   To discuss what else works for each to sustain their *emotional
resilience*, including reading or writing fiction, or absorption in
enjoyable hobbies and activities.

5.   *To explore boundaries and focus, limits, and priorities.* To discuss
what the counsellor will *not* do as well as what she will. This
might mean identifying what she will stop doing even if she is
good at it, and she likes doing it, with people she is fond of, in
order to focus, and keep work within limits that are manageable to the available energy of later life stages. And, in the
words of Estes (1992), it means being willing to be ruthless
enough about one's own creative or restorative activities to
have an actual or metaphorical notice on the door that says:

> "I am working here today and I am not receiving visitors. I
> know you do not think this is you because you are my banker,
> agent or best friend. But it does."

And then having the strength of will not to be distracted.

6.   To consider how far her *lifestyle*, and level of well being can be
a model to clients or not. So many of us bargain with our
bodies to last out until the next break. Some re-framing is
necessary, which is not to identify the "I" with will-power, not
to live the mind–body split, but to entitle the self to a well
balanced life with the power of the will exercised on behalf of
the body.

The contribution of the supervisor

If supervision is focused on accountability or case review and does
not ask, "What is it costing you to do this work?", and also, "What

are your joys, and feelings of satisfaction here?", an illusion is sustained that the individual who helps is not themselves a wounded healer. That illusion may be dangerous to the client and ourselves, since so many of us are. So, if supervision in an employing or training organization does not provide the restorative function, it is essential to find it through colleagues, friends, family, spirituality, or in the natural world.

For most of us, formal supervision is only a part of our strategy. We might seek a mentor. We might set up peer support and supervision arrangements. We might commit ourselves to continuing training. We might be determined about setting time aside to have relaxation and active recreation.

In the hard times created by the culture, society, economic crises, or external systems in which we work, we have to ask ourselves: "How far can I change the system I am experiencing as stressful, or change myself?"; "What will it cost me to continue as I am and hope to live with it?"; or "Should I leave?" Setting realistic goals and getting support from those who will not abuse a worker's vulnerability is crucial. Sharing decision-making, agreeing on common objectives with co-workers, creating a culture of mutual respect where "the other" does not have to be wrong just because they are different, all lays the basis for a balanced working team.

CHAPTER FIVE

Vulnerability

"It's not 'if', it's 'when' and 'how bad'!"

(Mountaineers' T-shirt slogan)

I t is essential to be able to speak about fear about vulnerability
as a practitioner, while also noticing one's resources, capabilities, and potential. Vulnerability arises from personal life events
and the meaning we attribute to them, and thus needs to be
mentioned in supervision, to discuss what is "really" happening in
relation to the counsellor's resilience. It is useful to routinely ask: Is
s/he blooming or wilting?

Shohet (2008) quotes Carroll (2001a, p. 77):

> It is possible that a supervisory attitude, viewing supervision as a
> reflective process that allows participants to think deeply and
> vulnerably about life and values, work and career, relationship and
> connections, might make an immense difference to how partici-
> pants live.

Good supervision does this, and values that attitude. It also
attends to the social and cultural context in relation to mental health

so that it does not pathologize the individual supervisee or client. In 2009, most counsellors, especially female trainees, are "time poor". If employed elsewhere while training, they might be subject to the fears of short-term contracts, work intensification, redundancy or job losses, working in institutions where counselling values are not shared, and training for a profession where more people are trained than there are jobs available. Doing triple shifts as a working parent who is also training creates practical, financial, and emotional demands and hurdles. Trainees and newly qualified counsellors face a long period of volunteering to "get hours", sometimes in highly exploitative contexts that do not employ them once they have become accredited, because organizational structures are based on volunteering. Some will also be preoccupied with global warming and the future of the planet, and Weaver (2005) describes how denial and splitting at many different levels can be explored in supervision in relation to engagement with interdependence and sustainable living.

The range of practitioner's personal vulnerability during a professional life mirrors the issues clients bring to us, and includes personal development issues, normal and abnormal ageing, health, finances, relationships, and crises. It is an easy list to write, as so many summaries are, so let me spell out what that has included for my supervisees and for me.

In my working life, spanning the years after I graduated from my first counselling training aged thirty-seven, the work went alongside periods of vibrant well being and draining difficulty, and all the levels of resilience in between. Staying steady to work, emotionally available, and hopeful is utterly different in the really hard times. Over many years I worked with different energy as I aged, and lived through the impacts on me of divorce, new relationship, friendships, money worries, house moves, car crash, moderate depressions, physical ill health, operations, children growing up and moving away, grand-parenting, dependent elders, ageing friends, and on and on. There were the inevitable gender related transitions, such as menopause. There were unique experiences of joy and sorrow, bereavements, disappointments, delights.

There were the pressures to balance income with outgoings, and unpaid work to support national professional organizations and governmental or local initiatives. There was further training and specialization that deepened the work and made me more committed to doing it, and that on occasion triggered re-experiencing of early hurts. There was the insight from my own therapies, from the deep peace of the long trip abroad described in the last chapter, and learning about living from dance and art. There was the slow development of increased capacity for self-care, something many counsellors and supervisors seem to struggle with. On any particular working day any of these would have some impact on how I met the clients or supervisees, and it was invaluable to be able to acknowledge it in my supervision

In the years of supervising colleagues, in addition to these sort of issues, they experienced bereavements, sometimes multiple over a short time, prolonged duress when a parent or a partner had Alzheimer's disease or became very frail, and did or did not die, their own feelings while working and coping with a partner's serious road traffic accident and its long aftermath, working despite a chronic health condition, fear as children grew up and as young adults took gap years or worked in dangerous environments abroad, money worries, debt or a credit crunch, the hazards of inadequate accountants and the Inland Revenue, isolation arising from sexual preferences, geographical moves or local house moves, and health and ageing issues.

This long list gives a much more vivid flavour of the necessity to monitor resilience and emphasize self-care during supervision.

I spell this out because, within the counsellor role, the personal impact of these life events is not normally expressed to clients, but sometimes does enter the thoughts of the counsellor. Momentary thoughts like, "and you think *you've* got problems", were sometimes articulated about the work during supervision.

I am particularly conscious of many occasions as a supervisor when I felt concerned about the levels of energy and emotional resilience of a supervisee. I have felt a pull to collude with some as they struggled with temporary or longer-term issues. My style as a supervisor has been to offer space to speak of personal issues, yet normally to limit my enquiry to how the supervisee was coping with it. This respects the autonomy of the supervisee and does not overstep the boundary between supervision and therapy. I found I sometimes failed to follow up with a supervisee who said what s/he would do to address it, but did not do it.

Many counsellors have written about health and the professional issues involved. Jeffries discusses self-disclosure when working after a cancer diagnosis (Jeffries, 2000a,b); Sanders names her personal and professional learning from facing a transplant (Sanders, 2006, 2008), and the parallels with a cognitive–behavioural therapy (CBT) approach; Rippere and Williams (1985) emphasize strongly that depression does not just arise from stress created by the work.

Etherington's powerful article (2000) on supervising counsellors who work with survivors of childhood sexual abuse also reminds us that if *early* life experiences were abusive, the supervisor and supervisee must carefully monitor and consider the supervisee's susceptibility to vicarious traumatization. This may arise from a variety of sources in physical or emotional resonances (also called countertransference reactions) to client reports of details of their abuse. She also described how such accounts affected her even more damagingly as a researcher about child sexual abuse, because no supervision of the process was offered in this role.

Personal experiences

Having stayed at work for periods of months when I was moderately depressed, I know how often I asked my peers and supervisors, "Am I doing harm when I feel so little hope for my own life?" "How much will clients 'catch' my mood and be harmed by it?" "How, and how much, can I help or heal from this place?" My answer for myself for these important questions was that as long as I was willing to keep asking the question and hearing the answers from others I trusted, and really acknowledged the energy I had for the work and what it cost me to do it, I could honourably and ethically continue to practise. Yet, as Bolen argues (1994) about depression and the "dark night of the soul", to work without any sense of play is depleting. She believes that unless their souls are nourished, men and women who work just for duty or the pay cheque often find themselves suffering from mid-life depressions. She thinks that depression masked as illness creates work characterized by lack of creativity. It is, thus, a significant ethical issue.

Manning (1994, p. 76) described similar calculations. On one occasion she went through *DSM IV*—the mental health manual more regularly used in the USA—with a patient and found that while the patient had five of the nine symptoms on the list, she had nine out of nine, qualifying for a diagnosis of a major depressive disorder. She adds,

> The rapport between us feels solid and workable. But I wonder to myself how someone who is nine for nine on the depression index can help someone who is "only" five for nine . . . I am rattled for the rest of the day. My therapist leaves a message on my machine asking me if I am interested in a referral. I can't believe it. Week after week he gets the blow-by-blow account about how lousy I feel . . . But knowing all of that he still refers me a patient. [*ibid.*]

These are powerful paradoxes. For a while, at one point, my sense of myself was of a fortress surrounded by a moat made up of my tears. I asked in supervision how big a portal for reparative intimacy this offered my clients, and if I came out of the fortress *only* to meet clients, from how rich and resilient a base could I practise? I took seriously the possibility that my bare availability for the experience of intimate relating at this time could put them at risk of an abusive relationship with me, so we monitored it carefully. Had I not been willing to self-disclose, clients might have been even more at risk.

I was in therapy when the fortress and moat image emerged, and this discussion reminds me of the necessity for "personal work" of some therapeutic kind. My mid-life depression entailed facing my history of loss, and my anxiety as I made choices to live life more authentically, and take the risk to work and parent and survive as best I could. Facing my fears became essential. I entered into my inner isolation and anxiety, and I am glad for the sake of my practice that I know that territory from the inside. It has made me unafraid to go there for and with my clients, and, in learning how to find my way out, has subsequently given me some optimism when working with them that they, too, can find their way. Supervisors in difficult times have both allowed me to be as I was and "seen" me there, and also engaged in "treasure hunting", looking for the jewels that I was not aware of in terms of my com-petence. I tend to call this a super-visory "bi-focal" vision, really seeing the vulnerability, and also the competence, too. It is a very precious gift in a hard time, and can be one reason why a longer-term supervisory relationship is valued.

Trust has been earned, and also shared memories of more optimistic or competent times can be recalled and leant on.

Colleagueship and friendship were essential to safe practice, and to adequate emotional resilience in those times. Supervision became very important, and I took much more of it than the required minimum. I trusted my capacity for assessment of my client's difficulties, as I was lucky enough to have a lot of permission, as I grew up, to think of myself as capable. What I did not fully trust without the essential support of supervision was that I was connecting psychologically in a way that was sufficiently therapeutic. Yet, clients stayed, and no one complained. I thought about the criteria by which a practitioner should judge the adequacy of their work. With a deeply depressed client whom I saw for five years, I felt I had made a deep and reparative connection, but we had not done what she came for: to lift her depression. Over a period of twenty years when she has bobbed back at irregular intervals into my professional ambit, she has developed insight, more courage, and stayed at work, moved to part-time work, and lived independently, and I salute her courage in these achievements. She remained preoccupied with her pain and social isolation.

I took an opportunity while in the USA to take some training with Steve de Shazer on solution-focused brief therapy, and met various Boston therapists also engaged in time effective therapies. Here was one solution for me: I liked the "making a difference" model more than the "cure" one. It fitted my own experience that even years of therapy with different and immensely capable therapists who had been very important to me had not reliably released me from that basic painful place to which I periodically returned. I could work to my strengths, and offer availability for deep connection, without having to sustain it over periods of years. I liked the contained nature of it.

Mental health workers' experiences

Rippere and Williams (1985) edited a very useful book, now out of print, that is a phenomenological account by nineteen mental health workers of their experiences of depression, their self help, and allowing themselves to receive lay or professional care. These are personal accounts of diagnosed and undiagnosed depression by a nurse, doctors, a consultant psychiatrist, academics, occupational therapists, and a psychotherapist. Although there is a list of authors, most chapters are not attributed to the author: a striking decision reflecting medical practitioners' fears about stigma.

It provides a rich description of the *experience* of affective disorders, contrasting this with the poverty of the labelling systems used by our profession, and arguing that

> an experience of depression can also be seen as a critical point on a trajectory through life, an object lesson in understanding the frailty and conditionality of human purposiveness. If used constructively it can be a growth point, a springboard for personal development: That is if the message conveyed by the depression to the self is heard and heeded. [*ibid.*, p. 3]

The editors note that one of the authors took her own life shortly after completing her chapter, reminding the reader that other depressions lead to despair and death.

They are keen to emphasize, however, that an episode of depression need not spell the end of a career, and that colleagues play a crucial role in co-creating a positive outcome. One had a visit in hospital from a supervisor, who came to reassure him that his job was safe: "She could not possibly sack all staff who suffered from depression or she would have no staff left" (*ibid.*, p. 180). Others faced indifference or, occasionally, overt hostility. The editors specifically enquired whether the authors' experiences did or did not improve their subsequent professional practice. Their choice of title indicated that, for many of them, it did, their rationale being that the practitioner's empathy, changed outlook, or interpersonal functioning was significant in this. This may not always be positive, and one author noted that depression was "an extravagantly wasteful means of forming character".

On page 6 they quote Bennet (1979):

> In many cultures it has been expected that the healer will also be the sufferer, and this is most vividly demonstrated in those societies where there are Shamans. These are people who are regarded as having a mixture of priestly and healing powers, but a requirement for the role is that they should posses some defect such as in

Western society would be regarded as an illness or a disability often of a spectacular kind like epilepsy, although it would be expected that they have mastered the condition or else somehow come to terms with it. In their own culture what might seem to Westerners as weakness was seen as evidence of the ability to communicate with the spirit world, and thus was conceptualised in positive terms. [pp. 185–186]

This may be too great a focus on spirit and vulnerability for some readers, though an emphasis on mastering difficulties is apposite. Contemporary mythologies of professionalism emphasize the importance of monitoring fitness to practise, so that individuals engage with their vulnerability and give priority to the needs of their clients and supervisees.

Discussing "fitness to practise"

Priority to protect clients is a key task entrusted to supervisors by the professional bodies. This has to be done when a supervisor comes to believe that the supervisee is not currently fit to practise, and should either take a break or else stop counselling altogether. Challengingly, it is on those occasions when the supervisee disagrees with this view, that the taking of supervisory authority is most complex, and the value of observation, description, and the clarity about behaviour or needs is crucial. Supervision of supervision is essential at this point; so is a genuine compassion, and a willingness to spell out the supervisor's concerns either for the well being and resilience of the supervisee or to protect clients. I have most often had these conversations when the supervisee had some ambiguous health issue, or a long-term responsibility to care for ailing dependents, or a bereavement, or relationship breakdown. If they become more cynical and less able to bear either the pain of their clients or the hassles of their employment, it can be very helpful to both supervisor and supervisee to have a chance to speak about it.

The supervisor needs to be specific about behaviour: what the supervisee is doing or avoiding which cannot continue for the supervisee's own sake, or their client's. There might be an honest difference of view about this. The supervisee might feel oppressed, or simply afraid of the financial implications of stopping work or changing employer. Some negotiation about the outcome, or the process of achieving the outcome might be possible, or sometimes it is not.

Harder still, but more common than is usually acknowledged, is the situation of the supervisee when the supervisor becomes unfit to practise. I have heard tales of those who fall asleep while supervising, allow a pet to intimidate a supervisee, or become very disorganized or forgetful. In a robust relationship, the supervisee would name the issue, but very few are able to do this. Many make an excuse and find another supervisor, or continue but lose respect for the supervisor. Where an employer or a training course allocates the supervisor, the supervisee might be afraid to comment on it, or confront the supervisor, in case there is a persecutory response. Research on bullying in supervision indicates that supervisors do not necessarily use their supervisory authority fairly (Rennie Peyton, 2004). However, this does not mean that the authority is inappropriate, only that the processes are challenging and difficult.

All practitioners need to monitor their professional resilience. For students, therapy or personal development groups in training courses can help them approach their work with more awareness of personal stories and the need for boundaries. It is not possible, in fact, to "inoculate" anyone against stress, particularly because so many people who are drawn to work in the caring professions, and who become outstanding workers, begin with unresolved issues from earlier years, and experience the impact of the wider context and the organizations for which they work through the lens of those experiences. In addition to the slow development of individual insight and change, it *is* possible—even essential— to alert them to strategies that will help them to recognize the stress which inevitably will arise, and manage it by taking responsibility for what it is within their control to understand and alter.

The British Association of Counselling and Psychotherapy (BACP)'s fitness to practise information sheet (2004b) offers a case study to demonstrate how a counsellor might continue to work when extremely upset, if sufficient collegial support is available:

Case study two

Uma is an experienced counsellor working in a large organisation. Recently, a client with whom she had been working for over six months committed suicide. This came as a total shock to Uma, who had not realised that the client had been potentially suicidal. Although she was extremely upset, she decided to carry on working. In part, her decision was made because she felt well supported by colleagues, management and supervisors. In addition, in a close scrutiny of her work, she had been reassured that she had probably done all she could. However, some of her clients noticed that she was looking weary. She considered telling them what was happening but decided that it was in their best interests (beneficence) if she did not. However, she did want to reassure them that she was able to be fully present. In the end, she decided to tell all her clients that she had had a bereavement, but to reassure them that she now felt ready and able to give them 100 per cent of her attention. Before doing this, she talked through the issues involved with her supervisor, in order to be quite sure that her motive for this kind of self-disclosure was in the interests of her clients (autonomy and beneficence) rather than in her own self interests (non-maleficence).

Taking seriously the need to be fit to practise, I used a new BACP information sheet and wrote this to show how it supported my decision-making and recovery at a stressful time.

Taking time off

I was impressed by the BACP information sheet: "Am I fit to practise?" which was first circulated in September 2002. It appeared in a period when I had been extremely fatigued and suffered considerable daily pain for some time, and had also had new family responsibilities that culminated in a sudden death.

So I took the sheet to my supervisor with my own "working through" of the issues. At first, as I only had a very small caseload of clients, I had thought I could manage to stay steady, and sustain my commitment to them.

First the sheet emphasises the practitioner's "duty to self". I declared I wanted to be "on light duties". As we explored what I meant by this, I named my wish to have a break from seeing clients for several months. I was surprised how, with his witnessing of me, that wish strengthened. It was not that there were many clients. It was that each one was potentially going to need me to dig deeper than I could at the time. I had headaches after each one. This was a clue!

Then we explored risks: I felt inefficient; my memory was not as usual; I was exhausted.

The ethical issue of "fidelity" to clients was important. We discussed current clients' needs and my counselling contracts with them and responsibilities for the process. Was I able reliably to be there for them? One had recently changed her appointment with me as I had an urgent dental need and her slot was the dentist's only space. I did not want to be asking favours of clients, though she "had not minded at all". I thought the dental story suggested I was "biting off more than I could chew".

Then, reviewing "Autonomy" reminded me of the client's right to choose, and my responsibility to declare conflicts of interest (or need) as soon as I am aware of them.

Beneficence, the commitment to promoting the client's best interest, led me to review *how* I was working, and to acknowledge my limited creativity and resilience in my current state.

Non-maleficence, the injunction to avoid harm, led me to consider if my own financial needs were too influential in the decision, and if I could manage without the income. I could, though it had consequences. There was also some risk of inappropriate self disclosure: they could see when I moved, got up and sat down, that I was in pain, and some were concerned and distracted by that, and a couple of clients knew of my bereavement because I had had to cancel a session at short notice. I had had an operation and some sessions were re-timetabled to give me ten days out.

Justice was not a problem. I decided to do the same for all.

Self-respect, the final ethical principle, focused my attention on my need for a break, to care for myself and enjoy my recovering energy and mobility.

So we discussed the details of how it could be managed for each client, and I booked four months without clients and told the relevant people. One hard part was saying "no" to an ex-client who rang with a new need, but the decision had been made, and I referred him to someone else.

The consequences were extraordinarily beneficial to me. I enjoyed the space to catch up with myself, and to rest, and write and think again. I had time to enjoy being with family and friends, and to be more relaxed with the teaching and supervising I continued to do. I had time to read some fiction and enjoy it. I spent hours poring over brochures for summer holidays. I had space to dream and plan for happy times to come. I was no longer exhausted.

Self-care

When Tholstrup and Shillito-Clarke (2005) recommended self-care for supervisors, they likened it to preparation for hill-walking: being physically and emotionally prepared beforehand, using the compass of self-awareness, and the country code of an ethical framework, being appropriately equipped, and bringing sufficient sustenance for the journey, and having agreed how we will walk (contract), and where (goal setting through supervision of supervision). They were surprised, when they offered the topic as a workshop for experienced supervisors, how many knew what they ought to do to take care of themselves, but did not do so consistently.

Accepting limits

As the years went by, and the workload in training, counselling, and supervision I was carrying affected me more, I wrestled more generally with the issues of how to schedule and limit what I did. I enjoyed each individual part, and needed a certain income. Conversations with peers indicated that this is common among counsellors and supervisors. I knew I also wanted some time for writing. One supervisee felt cruelly let down when I decided I would protect time for writing, and thus, after a transition period, would be stopping work for the agency he was volunteering in. I had struggled for years to put my own needs higher on my agenda, and to acknowledge when I was letting others down, and his reaction affected me so greatly that I almost changed my mind, but I did not.

Learning through dance and art, friendship and therapy that it was essential to consider and express my own needs and wants was transformative for me. Body psychotherapy had put me more in touch with awareness of my bodily responses. Now I choose to give myself more care. Preoccupied as I had been with being reliable and responsible, I released myself into giving more respect to considering my own needs for a better balance between work and life. I discovered that supervision is ·a space where, if the supervisee is vulnerable, this can be acknowledged and careful thought can explore the professional consequences.

CHAPTER SIX

Learning from supervision

One reason to have supervision throughout a professional working life is that it feeds the practitioners involved. Some supervision sessions are three-course meals, others a smorgasbord of possibilities. Some are too rich to digest immediately, and require a period of quiet reflection, or journal writing, or further work to assimilate. Some, inevitably, do not suit the digestion of the recipient, and go the way of all flesh. The possibility is there at every stage of improving the practitioner's understanding and offering a different perspective that frees the work. Both the supervisor and the supervisee should—in an ideal world—come away from each session having chewed over some dilemma, thought something new, or said something different, or understood something more clearly, or felt something more authentically. That is, they are changed, and can grow from the space to reflect and learn. This requires time for preparation beforehand, and time to consolidate afterwards, and the courage to meet, being willing to go where the process takes us.

I love being a learner. I get excited when I put together an experience and an idea, or release myself from rigid thinking. I can even cope with shame in the service of understanding what makes me work ineffectively, or be less than I hope to be. I have decided to take courage and offer real examples of my own limitations and learning, in part to help reduce the taboo on speaking about mistakes, or only speaking of the mistakes of others.

Because supervision functions as a form of ongoing professional development throughout a professional life, it changes to meet changing needs. The formative task is the one I think is most vividly marked by the stage of development of the supervisee.

Learning in supervision as a trainee counsellor

It is difficult, in advance, to convey the value of supervision to students in training, and so they tend not to appreciate it until they have had good experiences or have safely graduated from the course and no longer feel under the scrutiny of assessment. Counsellors seem to value a unique and carefully calibrated mix of support and challenge when they have developed enough trust to be open about their uncertainties and mistakes, and enough self-confidence to digest or spit out the guidance or criticism in a way that provides a useful basis for learning. While the supervisor is also an assessor, writing a report for the course that can affect pass or failure, the dynamics are more complex and potentially uncomfortable. The supervisor's power to fail a trainee counsellor can stop him or her from fulfilling the intentions that led to enrolment. When I trained at the beginning of the 1980s, this was not so, and supervisors' reports were not yet part of the process, so I did not avoid openness for fear of being failed.

As a trainee counsellor, my worry was that I did not *know* enough. I would come to supervision asking, "what are the issues?", when working with whatever anxiety-provoking content the client had brought, such as anger, bereavement, or relationships. I did not ask, "*How* am I—or how are we—in this relationship as we explore the issue?" Just as in the Stoltenberg and Delworth (1987) model at stage 1, I was preoccupied with "how am I doing?" I needed a lot of affirmation. I was used to feeling reasonably competent in my other work as an Open University tutor–counsellor. I knew that for everyday purposes my communication skills were adequate, but the burden of responsibility, the wish not to do harm, led to feelings of self conscious incompetence that were quite disabling of my confidence early on about relating therapeutically with clients. It did not stop me expecting that I could do it, though. I think this is a common mix: anxiety, and yet unawareness of limits of competence.

The personal growth demands of the training also led to turbulence in my private relationships, as it can do for many people. I began to reconnect with some avoided grief, and struggled to the point that a tutor told me, very lovingly, after one group that she was "worried about me". I was so touched to be seen and cared about enough for her to offer such a comment, and also invited to worry about myself, and review how I was functioning

My placement supervisor was from a different theoretical orientation, because she was the counsellor in the university counselling service I had elected to do practice in. When I was already struggling with a wobbly sense of competence, this was a complex experience, because our "taken for granted" psychological worlds and explanations were so different that it undermined my confidence further. Yet, we met well enough that I did feel contained by the regularity of the supervision, and her obvious experience of the. student group, and warm human connection. I admired her, too.

However, I was programmed to be such a care-taker that I could hardly bear to take her time to supervise me because she worked so hard that she was clearly exhausted. Unusually for a trainee, I did take a risk to comment about this, but when she insisted a little frostily that she was fine and looked forward to our time together as a change of role and developmental experience for her, too, there was no alternative but to defer. Walker, Ladany and Pate-Carolan (2007) researched such gender-related events in psychotherapy supervision from a female trainee perspective, seeing them in transference and countertransference perspectives.

Eichenbaum and Orbach's (1983) comments about women as clients of women counsellors are clearly echoed here. They say,

> We noted that a client would make attempts to reciprocate the care and attention of the therapist . . . in fact women strongly protected themselves from showing their dependency needs. The need to give and the difficulty in receiving was such a feature of each woman we encountered that we began to see it as central to women's psychology. [*ibid.*, p. 13]

Clearly this is a general gender issue worth further attention.

Habits of independent learning

What excitement there was in listening to the tapes of the counselling sessions and discovering in the transcribed detail of the exchanges, the pauses, the moments of felt connection, how I was being a counsellor. I was also, without awareness, taking my first steps to learn about internal supervision, and, as with many first steps, taking them from a position of unreflective assumptions. I was still preoccupied with thinking. I would sit and puzzle over the tapes, as I transcribed them, thinking about the interactions, wondering what I might have done differently, trying to work out what it all meant. An introduction to interpersonal process recall (IPR, see Glossary) on the course deepened my awareness of the interactive dance between myself and another, through exploring our responses to video recordings of an exchange and noticing feelings, body sensations, images, and reflections, as well as thoughts. (For a description of applying IPR to person-centred supervision, see Allen [2004].)

I was used to being independent, and it did not occur to me to ask for more from my placement supervisor. The magic of the counselling process entranced me. I had one-to-one course supervision, too, and felt very held and emotionally contained there. Initially, I had no idea that I might approach supervision in order to develop more awareness of my own intuition and sensing, rather than just relying on my intellect. I thought supervision was only about understanding the client, not myself as a practitioner. I think this and variants of this, working to extend trainee awareness from where they are initially comfortable and what they take for granted, are common experiences. It does highlight the importance of managing such enquiries well, though, to invite the supervisee into new ways of being with clients (more or less thinking, more or less intuition, more or less sensing). My course supervisor tried to introduce me to a neuro-linguistic (NLP) process, and, in retrospect, I think that was her way of moving me out of thinking to engage with other ways of understanding.

Learning from, and in, a peer group

Some years after training, I co-created a peer group that met regularly for thirteen years, all of whom had done the same counsellor training, though at different times. Structures that made a particular difference to the usefulness of the peer supervision group to us as individuals and as counsellors, and served as an apprenticeship in offering supervision, included the following.

1. We began with a check-in, to bring matters of current personal and family concern for peer support. Over the years we could do this economically, as we came to know about each other's life circumstances and personal styles. This was extremely significant in terms of personal and professional support, but we were also disciplined and focused on the supervision. Thus, we brought the support and the scrutiny from the personal to the professional clearly into the equation of the supervisory work.

    This created and sustained a professional "sisterhood". We noted at the end that four out of five of us had had brothers but not sisters. We were also mostly age-mates.

2. Management of equal time. At first we were all very hungry, sometimes almost desperately so, for supervision, and allocated the time equally—quite rigidly fairly—between ourselves. As we grew more experienced, and the amounts of other supervision we had waxed or waned, we grew more confident to ask for a specific amount of time, as little as ten minutes, as much as forty-five, as the need dictated. One person usually offered to keep time and remind us of its passing. We also became more able to say what we wanted from our time. There was a norm that all should have some time, but when it was scarce, or if someone did not have a pressing issue, the others got the opportunity to have more.

3. A robust tradition. One of the most useful developments was the group's capacity to grow and develop into full collegiality as people did further training and developed appreciative respect for each other's capacity for supervising. Several members had been in a dream group before this group began, and three embarked early on into a Gestalt psychotherapy training, and these traditions and habits led to a climate which encouraged reflective and robust, and sometimes personal as well as professional, responses to the material being brought. Any member could take a turn to comment in response to the

material being presented, rather than identifying one supervisor per slot. We were respectful about checking that the
"supervisee" was ready for another comment or a different
angle.

4. Leadership. Because of the "self-directing" traditions of our
    counsellor training and the personal styles we brought, it
    seemed very natural all to take turns in sharing the leadership
    tasks. Interestingly, there was little jostling for leadership,
    either. I wonder if this reflects the all female membership of the
    group, though I have been in plenty where being female was
    no hindrance to competitiveness. Our "supervisory authority"
    was very female in its expression and language: "wondering",
    "suggesting", "reacting", "imagining", "being reminded of
    other work or theoretical ideas".

A different style: developing intuition

The peer group was the main source of my supervision until I did
a further, "advanced" training that had a supervision group as a
significant part of the course. There, I learnt a lot more from a
highly intuitive supervisor, and from my peers, and from long
conversations en route with another student and fellow peer group
member as we reviewed the day's events and checked our differing
perceptions and constructions of what we had experienced. The
developmental training and supervision processes were largely, for
me, connecting to intuition and learning to trust my senses, and not
tune them out in favour of my habitual thinking approach.
However, I did find the intuitive power of the trainer very intimidating at the time. He would offer insights in a matter of fact way
that I had just barely come to in years of therapy. It reminds me how
powerfully magical intuition can seem.

Developing "sensing"

Supervision of my counselling work with traumatized clients led
me to become more aware of the information from my body as
a practitioner. As I empathized, I resonated with them bodily,

through "mirror neurons" (see Glossary). I was, on occasion, left with strong, usually painful, physical sensations. For me, they particularly connected to working with women who had been raped. I have not had such experiences, though it could be that issues of powerlessness were being triggered. I worked with one client of my age who had been raped in her own home, nearby. She was still in shock. For the next three nights I was gripped, as I went to bed, with uncharacteristic anxiety that I identified as vicarious traumatization. After considerable reflection on my own during these days, I asked a colleague, a local body psychotherapist to offer me a "body supervision", as I was clear this was not to do with my history; I had picked it up physiologically and could not dislodge it. One hour of telling the story and allowing associations to arise as she gently held her hand close to or on my belly and all my bedtime anxieties disappeared. Her description of the process involved is:

> I think that you had gone into experiencing the incident in the same way the client had. You had "caught" the incident physically and your system had gone into shock (re-traumatisation). In those days I would have thought "startle reflex". You were able to accept touch—I knew this based on prior knowledge and relationship. The touch in itself began to take you into the downswing of the cycle of regulation. Contact on the belly can also be soothing, although for some it is more arousing—mostly those who have not had much physical processing of experience. The talking was also expressive. I knew that you had the capacity to complete cycles physically based on all of your previous psychotherapy. I invited you to talk in a way that didn't re-traumatise you i.e. headlining that this was about rape—not going into an action replay of content, monitoring your well-being with the talk, especially arousal levels, mobilising how you/the client coped etc. The combination of talk and touch with someone you felt safe with enabled you to complete the unprocessed remnants in your system and to complete the emotion cycle (also called the vasomotoric cycle [Westland, 1997]).

The next week, when the client returned, the shock had worn off for her, too, and we continued without further symptoms being transmitted to me.

On another occasion, a client who had been gang raped conveyed one particular detail I could not erase from my mind, and

I took it to my supervisor. Our exploration did allow a memory to emerge, of giving birth and being stitched up under general anaesthetic, but I would never have accessed it by rationally searching for "similar experiences". Once more, when the unaware connection was brought into awareness, the power over me of the intrusive image and associated thoughts vanished.

As a supervisor, one particular experience stays with me because, again, it is an extreme example that taught me to pay attention to more subtle signals. A male supervisee had seen a particularly disturbing young person for a drop-in session. We met two days later for our routine fortnightly supervision. I was in a state of expansive and flowing well being after a good weekend on a dance workshop. As he spoke, I had a physical feeling of a flow of sensations and energy across the room from him to me, into my middle and up and out through my arms. I am not accustomed to such strong physical responses in supervision, and commented on it with curiosity to explore what was happening to him. At the end he felt better, and I felt completely undamaged. As I understood it, I had been a free-flowing conduit for release. It made me pay more attention to my own well being, too, as I could see so vividly how my own open state had contributed to the flow of his distress through me rather than getting clogged up with anything of mine. An unanticipated response was that I felt much more bonded, as the supervisory alliance had developed a maternal quality from the experience. It was so like a mother making an infant's inchoate experience manageable. Something had changed for the better from the experience for our future work as well as his present state. I later read Rose Cameron (2004), who discussed the value of much more everyday awareness of subtle energy and "contact" in supervision. This is the most vivid experience I have had of it as a form of release.

Westland (2008) recommends that personal experiences of trauma are explored in individual therapy by both supervisor and supervisee before undertaking trauma work. With that as a base, and sufficient theory and skills in place to do the work, then the development of body awareness and monitoring of arousal and the impact of empathy are essential. Pacing, slowing the work down to protect the client, supervisee, and supervisor from over and under arousal, is essential. Rothschild (2002) describes supervision of an emergency relief worker and notes the combination of personal resonances, the physical closeness created by the practical set up in the counselling room, and the counsellor's too ready imagining of the trauma as sources for vicarious traumatization that could be identified and then released in supervision and some further therapy. What is true for the extremes of trauma work also apply to the everyday: psychological contact, pacing, and self-awareness are all useful for supervision

Personal development as an experienced practitioner

I have developed recording habits that have stood me in good stead as a reflective practitioner. I am careful about note taking and keep them. For years, I e-mailed my supervisor between sessions, recording what I wanted to talk about next, and what, if anything, I had applied from the previous supervisions. One such e-mail ran like this:

> Re your comment about being desperate and doing harm, it's becoming clearer. I have arranged to finish with one supervisee whom I found irritating, and mishandled a challenge. I have also recently finished a peer supervision after an impasse arising from a mistake on my part that could not be overcome. In both, my inner critic seems to have been working overtime and inappropriately, at least in part, and the safety of the supervision space was compromised for the supervisee. I'd like to look at these e.g.s [sic] and see what there is to address and if I can do it. All other supervisions are going well . . .

I routinely reflected at the end of each year about what I had learned from supervision, and sent that piece of writing to the supervisor. This built up into a record of professional development.

As the years went by, I saw more clearly my major impact on the supervision, for good and ill. With the peer referred to in the e-mail above, my psychodynamic supervisor helped me to focus on my pathology in the situation. At the end of that year I recorded:

Learning from supervision: Date

1. Much of my learning in supervision arose from either parallels with clients' issues we discussed and my own patterns and

issues, or explorations of my own behaviour with clients and colleagues.

I am becoming more aware of my issues when I feel critical: that "difference" does not necessarily imply superiority/inferiority. I have grasped the value of expressing my view earlier and more straight [sic]. I see the connections with early shame, and issues of conditional loving.

I have been interested in destructive behaviour as a reaction to despair/desperation (clients and my own).

The following year, my summary with the same supervisor shows some further development as my understanding of my own behaviour moved from my head to an embodied grasp of the issue:

Learning from supervision: Date + 1 year

I have really "got it" that difference doesn't necessarily mean superior/inferior and that has been enormously helpful to me.

I have been helped to attend to and recognise hostility, anger and resentment much more readily, even when it is implicit and not expressed verbally.

The focus on supervision in the first three months has made me notice my own issues in the relationships, and encouraged me to be more direct in my communication with them, and state more clearly what I want in supervision as both supervisor and with you as supervisee.

Rich learning comes from mistakes, and I am heartened by Brigid Proctor, who wrote (2002),

We [she and Francesca Inskipp] believe that the counter-cultural expectation that we will open our work to colleagues—including our difficulties and failures—is a unique way of staying sensitive to the embarrassment, self-consciousness and vulnerability of clients; as well as to the fruitfulness of sensitive and useful challenge. [p. 37]

Nelson (2002) describes a valuable shared developmental journey between a female trainee counsellor and female supervisor in relation to work with a male client who cross-dressed and was preoccupied with secrets and lies and his masculine identity. They were aware of some gender issues, learned about gender identity and the many meanings of cross-dressing, and, through observation of details of their reactions, came to understand the challenges and learning in the work. The counsellor noted that she had begun to take particular care in what she chose to wear when seeing him, unconsciously expecting the client to be competitive. The supervisor felt protective of her. A question hung in the air: Who was woman enough for this work? A training event and supervision of supervision helped to reveal relevant issues, including those that the counsellor needed to take to her therapy. Rivalry, or restriction to mother–son relating, was avoided in the counselling, and both counsellor and supervisor benefited from the personal and professional development.

Learning from being an experienced practitioner

Latterly I have been involved in training for supervisors, and now have more coherent frameworks for thought as a result of teaching the supervisory ideas that could usefully have been my base earlier on. Using models (e.g., Hawkins & Shohet, 2006), I can navigate more purposefully between the counsellor–client system and the supervisor–supervisee one. By this, they mean that supervisory focus might be on the issues the client brings, and the interventions and relationship between the counsellor and client, or on the counsellor and her development, or on the supervisory relationship, and the supervisor's resonances and reaction to assist discussion of the counselling process and relationship.

I have a more vivid grasp of the needs of trainees and how these might relate to their personal and professional developmental stage. I am able to reflect about developmental issues, theirs and mine. There is something about age and over sixteen years of experience as a supervisor that allows me to take my authority in a more collegial way, with the benefits of having learnt from, and engaged with, that inner critic who has so dogged my more difficult supervisory relationships and my relationship to myself.

Supervision has been the place where much of my learning and development has taken place since I completed my Diploma. The regularity and predictability of the space, the choice of supervisor, the acceptance of imperfection and vulnerability in tandem with celebration of good work, the feeling of being held as I did the work, all contributed to my learning.

Reflections

My experiences as a supervisee mirror much of the writing about developmental stages of counsellors, though they are also unique because of my personal issues. My aim in describing them is to invite readers to consider their own changing perceptions of their supervision, and how they have sought different relationships and focused more on different tasks as their experience and work context and work load changed. I have never suffered an oppressive supervisory relationship, and my supervisors have variously modelled ways of being that influenced my work with clients and my own supervisees greatly to my benefit. Only as a trainee did I consciously defer to my supervisor, knowing that I could not raise the issue of her exhaustion with her further. I have been gripped as a supervisor by an inability to address an issue in a relationship that took me several months to name so that the supervisee would take it on.

CHAPTER SEVEN

Developing a supervisory style

"It is not possible to be intimate without also relinquishing the desire to control or being controlled—yet issues of control and power dominate our inner and outer lives—and are configured at the heart of our individuality. If control is more important than the desire for connection, you may only connect with those to whom you feel superior"

(Dowrick, 1992, p. 196)

The components of a supervisory style are complex in origin and subtle in expression. Most people are highly influenced by the style of their early supervisors, and if these people were helpful and encouraging, this can provide powerful modelling of how to be as a supervisor. When the relationship is damaging, the supervisee might make reactive resolutions about how not to be. Trainers and colleagues on counsellor or supervisor training courses may also be taken as models, so students who are treated ethically and with respect learn by this experience. It is particularly useful to observe others offering "live supervision" at conferences or during group supervision. DVD and video resources are rare, but, where they exist, also hold opportunities to see how others do the work.

The introductory quotation directs the reader to the twin issues of intimacy and control. This chapter considers the intertwining of personal and professional development into unique roles and relationships as supervisor and supervisee. The supervisory pair have to honour professional traditions while staying flexible and continuing to learn and develop in ways that best suit them now.

Supervisory style refers to the *relationship* style preferred by the supervisor (see Chapter Three on relationship climates) and competence in undertaking the roles and tasks of supervision. The core element of a professional style probably emerges from individual personality, personal and professional preferences in relating, identification with, and imitation of, people who are influential models, and through the norms developed in training.

Bernard and Goodyear (2004, pp. 105–106) summarize Kitzrow (2001), who created a model of supervisory style based on psychological type. This discussion focuses on cognitive styles and variations in ways of processing information, and identifies the developmental hurdles for each "personality type" of supervisor. Issues of pace, preference for action or reflection, preference for tradition or novelty and flexibility, attention to detail, balancing the theoretical and the practical, and moving between the larger view and small detail all arise in part from personality. The capacity to move skilfully in the world of another who does things differently needs practice.

Style also influences the choices by a supervisor of where to focus in supervision. Interest and engagement in the supervisory work and relationship will have a powerful impact on the supervisee. It is essential for the supervisor to accept the level of relating that is within the supervisee's capabilities, and this means being sensitive to developmental issues, both personal and professional.

Choice of style also arises from preferred theoretical orientation, and the assumptive world of the practitioner. Bernard and Goodyear usefully depict the impact of supervisor style, as it influences role, which influences strategy, focus, and method (Bernard & Goodyear, 2004, p. 75).

"Supervision is partly a process of socialization into professional identity and practice" (*ibid.*, p. 119). Supervision includes modelling, but either party might not notice this is happening, or what is being learnt. It is crucial to become aware of assumptions and style taken in from previous supervisors, and to understand how difficult it can be to sustain relationships that honour differences while supporting socialization into the accepted norms of professional identity and style. The trouble with developing a supervisory style from being supervised without specific training in the role might be that accident or circumstances will determine whether or not the new supervisor develops a conceptual frame that includes all the tasks, or a model for dealing with difficulties.

Reflection processes consider patterns of behaviour and learning preferences as a supervisor.

- What's my most typical intervention in supervision?
- What was my most unusual intervention in supervision?
- What new technology would I like to use more?
- On my first meeting with a supervisee the most important thing to me is . . .
- How would a supervisee describe me as a supervisor?
- What do I think are my strengths as a supervisor?
- What is my most familiar feeling about supervision?

Awareness of your personal style at work

It is useful to be aware of your own personal style preferences for any professional role. Gilmore and Fraleigh (1983) usefully analyse personal communication style as it pertains to work. They identify variations in the following elements.

1. Relationship or task focus as a preference: this reminds us that, under pressure, some of us prioritize relationships whereas others prioritize goals.
2. Risk-taking: some people thrive on taking risks whereas others prefer a more careful conservatism.
3. Pace: quick intelligence is different from slower reflection, but people with one style can find the other very frustrating or intimidating.

4. Comfort with emotional expression: this is contrasted with a preference for cool or more rational connection.
5. Preference for solo or teamwork: this clearly links with items 1–3. By the nature of the counselling task much of it is solo, but a number of practitioners choose the context they work in so that they have colleagueship. Group supervision can be delightful to some, a nightmare to others.
6. Need to respect the person in authority and believe enough in the rightness of the system: this is particularly necessary for counsellors working in multi-disciplinary settings such as the National Health Service or an Employee Assistance Programme (EAP) where the dominant culture does not share the same values.

It is likely that we are drawn to particular theoretical modalities by these personal preferences. Gilmore and Fraleigh identify four distinct styles around these elements. Their interesting idea is that some people can call on all four styles, which creates the advantage of flexibility of response, but can be experienced as confusing or unpredictable by those around them, whereas many people have a preference for one or two styles. This may make them more predictable, and also more rigid in responding. The differing factors that those who most prefer each style will find stressful are described, and the typical reactions that they have to being stressed. Gilmore and Fraleigh are clear that every style has strengths and integral or "allowable" weaknesses, a view also expressed by other management and teamwork consultants (e.g., Belbin, 1981). Supervisor development will aim to identify preferred styles and invite new supervisors to extend their range of styles of relating further.

Responsive supervisory relationships

Page and Wosket (2001) note that supervisors need to acquire a *range* of styles and approaches in order to adapt sensitively and appropriately to the individual needs of each counsellor as s/he moves through a sequence of developmental stages. Successful supervisors, according to supervisees, are "insight-orientated' or "feelings-orientated" in their way of relating and their focus with the supervisee (Rowan, 1989).

Crick (1991) also emphasizes flexibility, as she summarizes supervisory style from the literature as,

> using all sorts of evocative metaphors: The supervisor as potter, moulding crude clay into serviceable containers; the supervisor as gardener, pruning and watering the tender shoots; the "jug-versus-spectacles" methods; and so on. [p. 241]

From her experience as a supervisee, she highlights the dialectical versus the didactic styles, asking which is better, the dialectical that contains primitive anxieties, or the didactic that offers a sense of a firm frame. She decides that a good supervisor can move between the two to meet the needs of the supervisee.

Self-disclosure

The degree to which a supervisor is willing to be open with supervisees about their own working experiences seems to predict the beneficial quality of the supervisory alliance. Gilbert and Evans (2000) explore supervisory style and self disclosure. Bernard and Goodyear's (2004) discussion of Friedlander and Ward's supervisory styles inventory (p. 149) distinguishes three styles to predict the strength of the supervisory alliance: attractive (consultant), interpersonally sensitive (counsellor), and task orientated (teacher). Both the interpersonally sensitive style and the attractive one predicted levels of supervisor self-disclosure about personal issues, neutral counselling experiences, and counselling struggles, and these then positively predicted the strength of the supervisory alliance in the supervision of trainees.

Bernard and Goodyear (*ibid.*, p. 164) note how much the supervisor can ameliorate the impact of shame, first by offering consistent support to create a climate of safety and then by describing embarrassing moments in their own work. Kottler and Carlson (2003) interviewed successful American therapists about their worst mistake in therapy and what they had learned from it, with the intention of opening the debate about the inevitability of making mistakes, and the importance of learning from them.

I have taken the risk on numerous occasions to speak to super-visees and write of my embarrassing moments. I created a series of "practice notes" framed around my various lapses for a local, small circulation therapists' magazine. One in particular described seeing a client in my night-clothes, and has been a basis for frequent delighted and relieved feedback about how reassuring it has been to readers. I reproduce the piece below.

In a casual conversation with another counsellor, we were talking about embarrassing moments in our work. I recalled a time when I had a regular client every Wednesday night at 8.00 p.m. She came to my house, and had been coming for over a year.

On one particular day, I had spent the day teaching a particularly tiring all-day workshop, and came home and sank into a long hot bath at 6.30 p.m. Completely forgetting that it was Wednesday, I got out of the bath and into a nightdress and dressing gown, made myself some supper, and settled down to watch some television.

When the doorbell rang at 8.00 p.m., I went to answer it without the ghost of any anxiety about my state, wondering idly who might be there. As soon as I set eyes on her, embarrassment washed over me. In a split second I took in her look of appalled embarrassment, and her concern, as she thought I must be ill. Hastily I reassured her that I was not ill, but that I had indeed forgotten that she was coming. I insisted that I was perfectly capable of giving her the session. I showed her into the counselling room.

My dilemma continued. Should I leave her there and quickly climb into some clothes? She was a woman of my own age; another coun-sellor, a woman who herself understood about the times when one gets into night-clothes before the sun goes down, and we had been meeting for more than a year. I checked whether she had a prefer-ence. She was keen to get on with her session. We did the session with me in my night-clothes. I don't remember having any diffi-culty in concentrating, or it affecting the content of the session directly. She was a little wary when she turned up the following week, but finding me ready and appropriately clad, didn't refer to it again.

In order to write this piece and get her permission to use the episode, I contacted her through a mutual friend. Her version of the session and the impact it had on her went like this:

"When my counsellor contacted me and reminded me of the above session, I took some time recollecting the experience. It was a long while ago, but surprisingly, I found I could relive the session.

"I always liked to keep exactly to the time of the session so if I arrived early I would sit in the car until the correct time. I regarded my counsellor with some awe in that I felt she represented the epitome of professionalism, and to some extent I felt she set a standard for me to achieve. My immediate response when she answered the door in her dressing gown, obviously not expecting me, was to assume that I had made a mistake and that it was the wrong day. It was easier for me to assume my fallibility than that she might have got it wrong. My next thought was that she might be ill and unable to work with me. Because she told me exactly what had happened, and that the mistake was hers, and also the way in which she offered to continue with the session regardless, I felt reassured and keen then to minimise the impact of the circumstances. I did not find the nightwear a distraction, and once we got underway [sic], the strangeness of the situation faded. After the session, I reflected on the impact of this experience for my own practice. The fact that she had been open and direct about her mistake, that she had been able to display her fallibility in an honest way, had a very positive effect on me as a client. Even though she had initially "forgotten about me", the way she dealt with this benefited our working relationship, and was a very useful learning point for my own practice."

In my written piece, I invited readers to consider what their comments would have been to me had they been my supervisor.

Deference and idealization

This episode reminds me of the habits of deference among clients and supervisees. Often, this is explored in relation to gender and supervisory relationships, but it could also be a sign that the supervisor is exercising appropriate authority that the supervisee accepts. The need to idealize the counsellor or the supervisor has been extensively discussed in the literature, and Burton,

Henderson, and Curtis Jenkins (1998), among others, have expressed concerns about the meaning of this idealization of supervisors. My point here is specifically about the related potential to avoid giving negative feedback to a supervisor (or counsellor), or take risks in the relationship to reveal difficulties in the counselling work.

Rosenblatt and Mayer (1975) explored "spurious compliance" when faced with an unpalatable supervisory style. Any of us with experiences of rebelliousness in our youth can identify with this solution, but it fails to meet the basis of a working alliance.

Cultural background, power, and life experiences

Supervisory style is unique to each practitioner, though some shared elements have been described in research. One significant component is the way the supervisor uses power in supervision, and especially in relation to difference. I will use cultural difference as an example.

I am aware of research that asserts that too few practitioners at a later, supervisory stage of their career have been exposed to current ideas about trans-cultural relationships, and that even fewer have developed supervisory ideas that respect non Anglo-European values (Coleman, 1999; Ryde, 2006),

There is a lot of research evidence now that where there are differences of race, gender, or sexuality between supervisor and supervisee, especially when the latter is a trainee, the supervisor is unaware of the degree to which they are missing cues (Bernard & Goodyear, 2004, pp. 119–135). I believe that no one is culturally neutral, and every client, counsellor, and supervisor has cultural experiences that determine their assumptions, world view, and expectations. It is important to me not to privilege my own frames of mind as "normal", and be willing to notice and find out about and work with those of others. I have wrestled with the paradox that any limits and prejudice of which I am unconscious cannot be addressed by exploring my conscious assumptions. This is one value of self-disclosing conversations: I am brought to realize what I have taken for granted because of what others might say from a different base.

Group supervision plays a very useful role in relation to this.

I am interested to notice and explore differing ways of thinking: the ways of seeing the world and framing experiences, the emotional ground that attends them, and the patterns of feeling that shape the making of meaning. I want supervisees, and supervisors, to think how to co-exist with different values that have very vivid practice consequences, and how to be inclusive, and create safety and belonging in supervisory relationships. I want them to be interested in what to do with *feelings* about difference: e.g., shock, disgust, superiority, or shame. I am interested in motivational roots: the fundamental aspirations that drive our choices.

Coleman's transcendentalist ideas (1999), which emphasize the *interaction* of cultural, familial, and personal factors, fit my assumptions. His argument that cultural identity should *routinely* be addressed in supervision fits with my interest in socialization into professional values, and my emphasis on having an ethical base routinely available to supervisors and supervisees. Attention to language is always important, especially when tuning in to metaphors or idiomatic phrases of significance from one language or culture to another.

Seneviratne (2004) deconstructs ideas about culture and race, and quotes Littlewood to highlight the specifically *dynamic* re-creation of culture by each generation, and the historical, social, and personal interplay of expectations and experiences. Her chapter offers valuable insight through her own experience of the dynamic of race within supervision. Instead of learning some specifics about other cultures in a search for "knowing", she recommends the development of an ability to be comfortable about "not knowing", and sufficiently at ease in the relationship to explore the difficult places that race and racism (or other significant differences) force us to encounter. I am influenced by this emphasis on dynamism, and endorse the "not knowing" stance generally in supervision. My wish is to consider my potential responses to many differences without disrespect, and to enable the supervisee to explore pain arising from difference that it is often hard to articulate, and which, to the inexperienced, might seem to be a vulnerable overreaction to hostile events.

Drawing on Lago and Thompson's list (1997, p. 121) in relation to cultural difference, relevant differences may include:

- thought and belief;
- use of language, non-verbal cues, cultural assumptions;
- use of kinship support systems in therapy;
- philosophies of life;
- patterns of child rearing;
- roles of men and women;
- attitudes about time;
- polite behaviour;
- what constitutes a problem;
- methods of helping,

Understanding identity development in relation to race, ethnicity, age, religion, and also sexuality, class, and other significant differences, is highly relevant.

I think it is especially important to encourage supervisees to attend to their intuition and information from their senses in order to increase their attunement to others, and be aware of the potential for "parallel process" to emerge in the supervision. Awareness of parallel process in general forms a base from which to pick up particular shifts in expectations or relationship, and note adaptive or compliant responses to the expectations of others. This is specifically useful in alerting them to difficulties arising from difference.

An aim for supervision is to increase awareness of self and others and connect this to consequent choices. Specifically, to emphasize that sensitivity to uniqueness of the individual in a collegial relationship is combined with awareness that we exist in a country where institutionalized oppression can pervade many working contexts for clients, supervisees, and supervisors alike.

Seneviratne (2004) describes the importance of having confidence about your own identity so that issues of difference do not intimidate supervisors, and they can accept others and themselves in all their complexity, and yet can stay conscious of the broader context within which triangles of difference are played out. This includes awareness of our own *internalised* racism, sexism, homophobia, disablement, ageism, classism, and the other assumptions of inferiority–superiority.

Bernard and Goodyear (2004, p. 135) assert that *reflection* on identity development, in relation to race, sexuality, or gender, seems to be more important for supervision than *identification* with any particular group, and that it is the supervisor's development which will *dictate* (their italics) whether the supervisory experience will be positive. Although "dictate" may be an optimistic word, it is clear that it is often up to the supervisor to initiate explorations about difference, especially when there are difficulties. The power that is inherent in the supervisor's status and role greatly affects this.

CHAPTER EIGHT

Developing the "internal supervisor"

"We don't see things as they are, we see them as we are"

(Nin, quoted in Epstein, 1999, p. 834)

The phrase "internal supervisor" is Patrick Casement's (1985). However, there are roots and connections to the ideas of Schon (1983, 1987), Bolton (2001), and many others who have developed the ideas of reflective practice. There is a value in monitoring our experience during the counselling session, taking time to reflect afterwards, using a variety of methods to increase personal sensitivity in the work. The supervisor's role is to assist supervisees to develop, with awareness, an internal encouraging voice that is also disciplined and rigorous about looking at practice.

It is essential to recall that many, if not most, counselling sessions are never discussed in supervision after training is complete, except where people have tiny caseloads. Thus, the development of the "internal supervisor" of the counsellor is essential for ethical work. Reflective practice is at the heart of our profession, and it behoves us all to take time to think about every client for ourselves. I find early morning swimming useful, as I sink into the rhythmical activity and my mind is free to process the work of the previous day. Others speak of walking the dog, watering the garden, and cycling to work as offering a similar space. Working lives are so pressured these days that the discipline of protecting a reflective space can be very hard to sustain, especially in the early years of work when building a practice.

Interpersonal process recall (IPR), developed by Kagan and Kagan (1991) in the USA, originally to help teachers become more aware of what was affecting their work, has been recommended for the development of the internal supervisor (Allen, 2004; Inskipp, 1999; Inskipp & Proctor, 1993). It draws the practitioner's attention to process, to what they were thinking, feeling, sensing, and intuiting, as they observe a videotaped recording of a session. Support for the process is offered by someone in an "enquirer" role, who invites reflection on the experience through a series of questions. Afterwards, further questions about satisfactions and dissatisfactions, learning and reflection on what was useful, complete the experiential learning process.

Driver offers a useful metaphor when she writes of the supervisor as navigator of the internal supervisor of the supervisee,

> who points out the co-ordinates and constituents of the work, so as to enable the supervisee to define the transferences, counter-transference and projections and to make links to the internal states from which the patient is relating. [Driver & Martin, 2002, p. 55]

She is clearly highlighting the role of supervision for helping the supervisee take responsibility for their practice, and become more actively responsive to their own internal supervisor.

Levels of self-awareness are at the heart of the process, in that it is essential that all responses in the therapist—or supervisor—are available for reflection, and not blotted out of awareness because they are uncomfortable. Thinking is important, too, in the process of noting and connecting significant themes and tangents for the client as they emerge through dreams or stories of life events. Weaving a texture of significance with a quality of *narrative truth*, that makes something coherent and useful for the client that was obscure, may be part of a run of the mill process, or arise from a more sudden resonance or clarity in the counsellor.

For internal reflection during a session, I have had to find a way to access the useful resources I have in the moment when I realize something different needs to happen in the counselling session. Within this unique relationship and this specific setting, in a split second, the practitioner, like a computer, needs to find relevant information, while, unlike a computer, simultaneously checking his or her physiology and body symptoms, intuition, empathy, and imagination, and the temperature of the relationship with the client and other influences on the session. Computing and such artistry are complex bedfellows. When we add to this the anxiety that competing philosophical models of disease generate, we create a "hall of mirrors" in the relationship, where many explanations and responses are possible. Probably, most counsellors feel impelled to check their own reactions because of an experience of disruption of flow in relating, a sense of "dis-ease". Strong sudden impulses or small niggles, reactions arising from experiences resonating from earlier life, might all form a relevant spur to reflection within a session.

I think this felt sense of disruption can become the useful trigger to reflection-in-action, and a description indicates the complexity of the process.

As I have experienced it, I begin with a felt sense of interruption of relationship or flow, or some other prompt to shift my attention: shocked feelings, or sleepiness, for instance. I move into thought and possibly memory or intuitive processes, splitting my attention to take some awareness away from the immediate process in order to reflect and, if necessary, change tack. At the same time, I still have to sustain the therapeutic relationship in a moment of risk to it, and then decide whether or not to say or do something with immediacy to acknowledge the process.

These are moments of potential to respond with more attuned intimacy. Merry (2003) reminds us of Roger's ideas about the core conditions for relating. "Rogers suggested counsellors are better equipped to facilitate change if they can be empathic, experience unconditional positive regard, and remain congruent in their relationships with clients" (p. 175). Merry comments that such theory may allow for real encounter, because of the *discipline* that lets idiosyncrasy and authentic relating flourish.

Another issue is that options for action and alternative ideas may arise from a theoretical base or from experience, or a combination of the two. A potential intervention might be newly learnt, from a recent experience that was powerful in personal therapy, from books, courses, or conversations with colleagues; or it may be part of a taken for granted repertoire, unexamined, a reflex.

Reflection

Reflection is a process that requires courage, and is best supported by habit. Bolton calls reflection, "The hawk in your mind, constantly circling over your head, watching and advising on your actions—while you are practising" (2001, p. 15). Some supervisees jib at making it a hawk, and substitute a softer image like an angel, or a more technical one like a helicopter. Bolton describes learning to attend to tiny details as being like the film *Blow-up*, where it is only when a photo is greatly enlarged that a detail to resolve a murder is to be seen. She encourages people to note that no detail is potentially too trivial to write, think, and talk about. Learning reflexivity may come through internal processes such as note-taking after a session, journal-keeping, or creative writing (Sugg, 2008) as a part of supervision. Painting and drawing can serve a similar function (Bell, 2007), and bring out thoughts and feelings that are just out of awareness. Creative methods that use metaphor or imagery are particularly helpful to some reflection (see Chapter Nine on creativity). Morrell (2003) proposes routines of ten minutes before and ten minutes after sessions (whether of counselling or supervising) to be still and allow material to emerge into awareness. Activists might find this much more of a difficult discipline than Reflectors (see Chapter Two), but this could mean that they benefit most from it. However, there are many employment contexts these days that do not allow for such spacious scheduling. The time is used up in answering e-mails instead!

Habits of self-questioning, of aiming to think from different angles, are built by experience of supervision, and can then become routine for the internal supervisor. New perspectives can be habitually sought through a post session reverie that invites wondering, such as:

• What would the client's nearest and dearest think about what happened today?

- What might my supervisor say?
- What might a counsellor working from another theoretical modality think?
- What did I say or do that I am proud/anxious/ashamed about?
- Will I tell my supervisor about this?

Casement (1985) refers to learning to watch oneself as a therapist, and to "an island of intellectual contemplation" that the new therapist has to learn how to attain with the patient, to look together at issues arising from the transference. The therapist's own experiences of therapy might mean he has empathy and insight, and this facilitates "trial identification" with the patient, especially about their relationship to the therapist.

The Johari window (Luft & Ingham, 1955) has been popular in training. It is usually drawn as a four-paned window. (On the Internet, Google "Johari window" for many versions.) It drew attention to elements of the self the person is aware of and shares with others, those s/he does not share, and to the blind spots others know, but s/he does not. The fourth pane contains elements that no one is aware of yet. Supervision can make it possible to share elements not usually acknowledged, and to discuss observations of the blind spots.

One issue is that inexperienced practitioners need to learn when to trust their internal supervisor, and how to judge whether an impulse to authentic but idiosyncratic practice is sound or not. Self-disclosure is a particularly sensitive issue. Occasionally, it is powerfully releasing for the client to hear that the counsellor has had some similar experience, thought, or feeling. Normally it is not, and injunctions not to self-disclose are there for good reasons. Experienced practitioners have a huge advantage here because they will have more experiences to call on, and, if well taught and well supported, may have been encouraged to monitor closely the consequences of their interventions. I have had both good and bad experiences in this regard, and some examples highlight the difficulties, in particular, and the skills required to survive strong reactions to inappropriate disclosures.

When self-disclosure worked well as a counsellor

Most counsellors will be able to recall times when some comment about what is happening in the room is useful to the client. An example of the value of this use of reflection in action occurred when I decided to comment on my sudden, overwhelming sleepiness with a client, noting that I had been wide awake before we began, and wondering what she made of that. Many writers reflect on the meaning of sleepiness, connecting it to empathy or parallel process, and consider it might imply that some feeling is being avoided, so I was wondering if there was something she aware of. I offered this as a possibility. There was, and we then talked about it, whereupon my sleepiness vanished and she engaged with an issue she found difficult, but useful to explore.

On another occasion, I was working within an organizational setting, and a regular client waited in the corridor as I overran into our time slightly with the previous person. A colleague was chatting to her as she waited, and the colleague was in tears as I came out. It was coming up to the first anniversary of the death of the client's partner, and, as the session went along, with her describing in a very matter-of-fact way how she was planning to spend the day, I found tears rolling out of *my* eyes. I said, "I do not think these tears are mine. What are you doing with yours just now?" She replied that she was unable to cry and let go, and that her bereavement was leading to a loss of faith in her world view, a sense that the partner was "leaving her" and becoming very far away, rather than waiting for her in the afterlife, as they had promised each other. From that session on, she began to show more of her feelings, and, over a further period of some months, became able to listen to music again, and came to accept her own sadness and anger, and to a softer way of being. Eventually, she made another partnership.

When self-disclosure provoked a cruel response

On one occasion, a young client of whom I was fond made some cruel comments that made me weep in a final session after three years of work together. He was angry about a self-disclosure by me in the previous session, when I had tried to describe some recent experiences of my own that seemed to me to be parallel to his. He did not accept the parallels, but did not show it at the time. In the final session, he was contemptuous of me and of counselling. I felt hurt and surprised, to the point that tears rolled down my cheeks. He turned the knife with unusual overt hostility: "It's good for it to be you who are crying and sweating rather than me for a change." He added that he thought this sort of conversation was more real than therapy. I said therapy was a discipline, and he had just been very angry because we had spent time on my issues. He saw what I meant. This was a turning point in a difficult session, which ended soon after some more sharing of his recent distresses, and with a sense of some reconnection that made it good enough, though he "forgot" to pay as he left.

Immediacy re-created enough sense of psychological contact for me to be able to offer a genuinely warm farewell. Yet, I had to accept that I was very vulnerable at this point, and my mistaken self-disclosure, intended to increase psychological contact, had had an opposite effect. My supervisor invited me to reflect on the impulse to self-disclose. We also discussed my fitness to practise while so emotionally labile, and whether and how to seek payment for the fee he had not paid as he left. This was all helpful, but, more than the actual supervision, I could feel an internal shift out of the experience that would make me much more careful in a future session about impulses to self-disclose.

I value my willingness to be vulnerable with another person, client, or supervisee, but do not wish as therapist or supervisor to be out of control so that the feelings flow uncontrolled from me because of my needs, history, and expectations. Mollon (1989, p. 113) described the "narcissistic perils" for the counsellor faced with a client whose hostility arose from criticism for not being made well. A counsellor might not disclose such details to a supervisor, for fear of disapproval, but cannot hide from the experience, and can choose to reflect and take learning from it.

Reflections

The supervisor's role in the maturation of a supervisee's *internal* supervisor is best when it is a respectful one, with the developmental focus explicitly agreed between them. Ideally, it is one that encourages each supervisee to develop their own artistry as a practitioner, to trust their impulse to co-create a relationship that is useful to the client. Yet it also provides discipline by requiring an account of the process.

Supervision with a supervisor adds an extra layer, another world and perspective, and theoretical frames and chains of inferences arising from them may inform questions as well. This is a chance to review assumptions, schemas of thought, understanding of parallel process, or how the situation was misunderstood, if that is what happened. Any new perspective has to be offered from a point of view that begins with appreciation of the perspective of the actors. When there are conflicting views of the same situation, facts or judgements will not often help them resolve what best to do next, but the dialogue allows new ideas to emerge and be considered that the counsellor might not have thought of alone. All theoretical orientations concur that trainees cannot be taught to "do counselling", they can only be helped to learn it for themselves.

CHAPTER NINE

Creative supervision

"After all, Creativity is the flame of life"

(Lahad, 2000, p. 119)

This chapter is a marker of a major journey for me as a counsellor and supervisor. I nearly did not include it in this book, because I had a view of myself as handicapped in expressing my creativity in artistic ways by my education and personal style. My confidence increased as I understood that creative issues and approaches relate to ideas about the right side of the brain, and affect many processes, such as understanding metaphors, reading faces, expressing and reading emotions, music, and global holistic processing. These approaches free the juices. They bring liveliness and enjoyment to supervision. They create opportunities to engage imaginatively with the client. They also facilitate the therapeutic task within supervision, as many creative methods focus primarily on the reactions of the supervisee. A bedrock of careful contracting and respectful awareness of the supervisee's privacy and safety are the core to this way of working.

Since I have admired the work of Inskipp and Proctor (1995), Houston (1995), Lahad (2000), and Ryan (2004) on creativity, learnt a lot from them, and changed my practice substantially as a result, I felt I had little new to add to their work. However, when I began writing this chapter, I checked a couple of American textbooks (Bernard & Goodyear, 2004; Bradley & Ladany, 2001) and I found no references to creativity—or humour—in supervision. I am sure there are many supervisors in the USA writing about this topic, but I know only of Kopp and Roble's work on using early memories in supervision (1989). This led me to think about the role of creativity in UK supervision and the importance of it for professional development work.

Humour and creativity

"I see nobody on the road," said Alice.

"I only wish I had such eyes," the King remarked in a fretful tone. "To be able to see nobody! And at that distance too! Why it's as much as I can do to see real people, by this light!" [Carroll, 1871]

American writing about supervision research is so dominated by supervision of trainees that their tradition does not seem to emphasize the value of play, intuition, sense awareness, or humour. It might be that British supervision is not very playful with trainee counsellors, either. Under the pressures of beginning a practice, coming to terms with a placement, and integrating new theory with new practice, are we also very serious? If so, this is regrettable, but I recognize that such assumptions have affected my work, too. When I am invited to hold the expert role, presumed to know answers, required to assess, this creates a different relationship from that of two professionals united in exploring "not-knowing", who are willing to find out. As Matthias Sell said in a British Association Supervision Practice and Research (BASPR) conference, "You cannot be intuitive if you try to be right" (Sell, 2000). Humour creates space for new connections to emerge, and unsettles fixity and "either/or" thinking.

Ideas about professional developmental stages (Stoltenberg & Delworth, 1987) are also pertinent. At first, trainee and newly qualified counsellors are often preoccupied with anxiety and "what do I do *now*?" Sensitivity is needed to introduce stories or play without appearing patronizing. It is only when the supervisee begins to think, "I am somehow getting in the way because of my own issues", that process-centred supervision of this sort comes into its own. If the supervisor believes that the counsellor and his or her client are essentially able and capable, then distressed or damaging feelings, thoughts, or behaviour can surface more safely to be explored further.

Learning by doing

I began, as many untrained supervisors do, by using methods that linked with my counselling approach. Metaphor, imagery, and visualization fitted with supervisory tasks as I understood them. "Conversations" between supervisees and their clients, role-plays, and physical exercises made sense to me. On occasion I invited a supervisee to hold out her arms while I piled cushions into them to represent different current responsibilities until she refused to carry more in the interests of self-care. I was greatly influenced by my supervisor, who had some smooth pebbles and beautiful shells available in a basket. I always need to "do" for myself before I can "do with others". "Speaking as an object", noticing relative sizes, and where I placed items, exploring "what if" I take one item out or move things about, habituated me to the possibilities. Then I did some reading and felt yet more inspired.

A contrast between the kinds of questions it is equally possible to ask shows different ways to encourage the counsellor—or supervisor—to notice her own needs. In a review or workload overview, she can be invited to pay attention to her immediate responses to feelings, and to think about them in relation to direct questions like:

Who do I look forward to working with?
Who bores me, and why?
Who tires me, and why?

Or she can be invited by direct questions with more vivid language embedded in them:

Who do I have to gird my loins before meeting?
Who lights up the room, joins in, and has fun?
Does he hide his light under a bushel or shine?

At a conference, when I facilitated a workshop about creative approaches to the supervision relationship, we simply responded to some creative prompts. Members completed the options silently and then compared notes. We discovered that we were more able to notice qualities about the supervisory relationship through this playful means:

"If I was an animal in my last supervision session what sort of an animal might I have been?" "What would my supervisor have been?"
"If I were a firework, what sort of a firework would I be?"
"To get the most from my next supervision session, what colour might I be?"

The first of these prompts was enough to provoke an hour of exploration in a small group of supervisors. This reminded me of the value of including some more enlivening exploration within a focused process like a review of supervision, and that hearing from the other what their perceptions are, or their playful images imply, can be quite surprising.

The value of using creative methods

An explicit and mutually agreed contract for this sort of experience, and for the specific technique to be used, might include the possibility of teaching about the metaphoric way of thinking to introduce new perspectives and possibilities. Fears of being overexposed, or expected to disclose or reveal too much are pertinent, and need to be discussed. Almost always, instructions are crucial to success, in that they need to be both very structured and also open-ended. The supervisor needs to be able to build sensitively on a response, too. When s/he works regularly from the same room, these resources can be kept at hand and available for the moment of use to arise in the natural course of a session. Small shells or pebbles or buttons can be brought in a little pot to enliven any environment.

Ryan (2004) quotes Elektra Tselikas-Portman:

In a culture that bases professional activity on rational thinking, that believes in and propagates the power of reflection for the gaining of insight and growth, the question arises: In which way does such a process help the professional cope with the demands of her professional situations? (p. 27) . . . The artistic creation . . . allows a contact with the depths, a sounding that expands perception, puts us in contact with imagination and allows us to feed the soul, see with many eyes, speak with many languages, particularly those which are beyond linguistic constructions. [Ryan, 2004, p. 14]

I find this moving, and a persuasive frame to think about creativity and its value in supervision.

Ryan (2004) also quotes Estes (1992), to remind readers of the value of giving expression to many aspects of practice or of the self:

To create one must be able to respond. Creativity is the ability to respond to all that goes on around us, to choose from the hundred possibilities of thought, feeling, action and reaction and put them together in a unique response, expression, or message that carries momentum, passion and meaning. In this sense, loss of our creative milieu means finding ourselves limited to only one choice, divested of, suppressing or censoring feelings and thoughts, not acting, not saying, doing or being. [Ryan, 2004, p. 88]

Experienced practitioners and play

My research in progress with experienced practitioners gives an impression that they "play" more. Feeling confident and collegial, aware that difficulties are often connected with personal and developmental issues, experienced practitioners may have more optimism and courage that such play will reap rewards for the counsellor as well as the client. Especially where issues of difference and diversity are creating difficulties, representing difference through colour, size, shape, or objects makes it more possible to explore them by externalizing the difference visually and handling it kinaesthetically.

What is clear to me is that experienced practitioners from many theoretical modalities play a lot in supervision, and find it highly purposeful and significant. In my experience, I have used creative methods more with peers than with paying supervisees, which might signal my own limits about introducing these approaches with new supervisees at an initial contracting stage. I have come across them more within group supervision and at conferences, courses, and team-building events, where there is a rich tradition of using experiential exercises as a basis for learning.

Group work and team building

Because group supervision is too complex for purely cognitive work (Proctor, 2008), creativity contributes through heightening imagination, intuition, and sensory awareness. I have found it useful and a quick way into some insight. It requires careful contracting so that the supervisee consents to using a proposed method or approach, and attention to "de-roleing" people and even objects at the end.

Thinking about the members of a supervision group as different instruments of an orchestra can be a playful way to consider the impact of each member on the work of the group as a whole, and a useful way of emphasizing the value to the overall work of individual difference. If I am temperamentally a French horn, can I take the role of a piccolo or a cello or timpani? Or is there someone else who can do it for me in a particular group?

Creative methods have served me well in consultative team building, and the application to supervision, and supervision of supervision, is clear.

It is helpful to use systemic ideas to move participants out of any thinking about blame and into curiosity about difference. For instance, participants may choose an image for themselves, or develop one from an offered category. The supervisor might ask: if this team (or group) were a family, circus, or car, What sort of family, circus, or car would it be? This is good for finding a common, non-judgemental language to discuss how they behave (Wilmot, 1987).

The supervisor can use images to heighten contrasts, following up with a series of Socratic questions that build on the answers to the previous prompt. For example, if the supervisee describes herself as a pony, questions might include: "What sort of pony are you? Pit pony? Clydesdale? Shetland pony?", or "What sort or colour of car are you? Is there a driver? Who are the passengers? What happens when the driver accelerates or slows down?"

Or, to look at how a family or a team or a supervision group works, the supervisor might use a sporting analogue: are you more interdependent like a football team? Or working in separate units like a Davis cup team in tennis? Or a relay team, needing to hand over the baton of information between shifts? What do you need to be like to get the job done?

Sometimes, it is helpful to begin with encouragement to view the work of a group positively: "Imagine your agency has given a cup for the best group and you have won it this year . . . what would the message be about why it had been given to you?"

If a group is denying strong feelings, a simple way to approach feelings is through objects like buttons, pebbles, or shells. With one group, the admired leader was about to take a secondment. She was full of feelings of abandoning her colleagues, and anxiety about the continuing well being of people and success of the project in her absence. The members were being very rational, though their issues were an amalgam of excitement about opportunities and fears of the impact of her absence. Each chose a button, and placed them in relation to each other until all were satisfied, to represent the situation before the sabbatical. The leader was absolutely central. As group facilitator, I asked who would like to move the button from the centre. No one did and faces paled. With one simple movement, when the button was removed the group moved from an intellectual discussion about a change of major significance to all of the group members, to an emotionally charged reportage of the impact of the absence, and the plans necessary to meet their needs. It became more real.

Carroll (2001b) encourages supervisors to explore language, gender, individual and systemic issues within organizations, where, he asserts, supervisory skills are badly needed.

Understanding the process

Inskipp and Proctor make a major and relevant contribution to understanding the value of creative, that is, "more than talk", supervision (2001, pp. 156–160). They describe the process as accessing any or all of the senses with an invitation into a "focused state", similar to the light trance induced by watching TV, or reverie. They note that we can tell ourselves things not accessible to our reasoning self. Bollas (1987) calls this accessing "the unthought known".

Inskipp and Proctor quote Perls to make a highly significant distinction. Creative processes may be about being in direct contact with subjective internal experience, or through sensing, with the external world. Creativity can do either or both. The internal focus "invites someone in" through imagery, metaphor, or expressive materials into their subjective awareness. For instance, an intense internal felt response might arise in relation to objects chosen:

"I am big and spiky, she is round and small and very delicate.
"Oh, she is heavier than I thought.
"If I say 'she is heavy', how do I feel about that?"

In contrast, the external processes "invite someone out" by methods that create some distance from the experience: watching others role play or sculpt, writing, using Play-Doh or objects to stand for a person or situation. Broughton (2006) describes the existential experience of applying Hellinger's constellations approach to supervision (Hellinger, Weber, & Beaumont, 1999), emphasizing the systemic insights from setting up a physical representation of a client's internal sense of an issue, using other people in a group or objects.

A supervisee wrote to me in the context of reading another chapter I sent her, about her learning from our supervision:

Oh, do you want to know the one thing that I often "quote" from what I learned with you? I will tell you anyway . . . you pointed out to me that underneath and amongst the large shells on the beach there are small, tiny, shells—each one beautiful but often overlooked. This comes with me to my work and features in my research, it is now part of my being. Thank you.

It can be anarchic and is unpredictable. It needs responsive facilitation, clear structures and direction, and agreed time boundaries, especially to move from the experience into debriefing, and then to reflective analysis of the significance of what has been experienced and how to use it to change the counselling work.

Expressive supervision

Bell (2007) illustrates beautifully the value of using expressive supervision. She describes a responsive contractual process, where focus may be on process or content. It is especially relevant if the supervisee is also using expressive methods with clients.

> If we move between one non-verbal mode to another non-verbal mode, our self-awareness seems to deepen significantly. We seem able to access deeper layers of consciousness, and bring them into verbal awareness and expression. [*ibid.*, p. 60]

She describes its power to "loosen" the therapist's feelings about the client, and the process itself, e.g., pressing hard on paper, as reconnecting the counsellor with the experience of a session. A description of three drawings done in one hour of supervision to convey four years' work with a client illustrates how economical, vivid, and restorative such a process can be. Her three pictures to convey her understanding of supervisory models show how a practitioner can explore a theoretical construct expressively, and thus internalize it and make it real, but also generate further thoughts and questions. She notes the colours that Inskipp and Proctor's three functions create for her, and the *mélange* that results as she imagines putting their ideas in to her practice. On the Hawkins and Shohet model of supervision process (2006), for instance, she adds an extra line, going two ways to point up the mutuality that connects the *interventions* of the supervisor and the supervisee.

Scaife (2009) has a useful and systematic chapter on creative methods, particularly productive about symbolic use and arrangement of objects in visual supervision. Whatever the sizes or shapes, it is important that objects can be moved around so they can be viewed from different perspectives and in changing relationships to each other. Such materials support real connections to internal experiences and provide structures for externalizing problems.

Adlerian contributions

Several Adlerian supervisors have made a major contribution to exploring the use of early memories as metaphors for change when there is resistance in therapy. Here the *counsellor's* early experiences connect and resonate with those of the client. Adlerians are interested in the "life style" (see Glossary) of a supervisee. Since these are developed early in life, Adlerians explore early memories known as "early recollections" (ERs) to suggest the roots of the person's life style (Newbauer & Shifron, 2004; Shifron, 2007).

Kopp and Robles (1989) were the first to recommend using ERs for supervision of resistance. They describe the process they developed in the USA. This requests vivid details of an early memory from the supervisee, with the key moment recalled as if it is a snapshot, to gain maximum recall of senses and feelings. The supervisee is then invited to change this memory into what would have been ideal, and then to tell it "as if" it had happened that way. Again, the snapshot of sense and feelings is encouraged.

Only when this supervisee memory work is complete does the focus return to the work with the client to explore the parallels between the counsellor's and the client's ERs and the supervisee's issues in the counselling situation. Supervisor and supervisee can then formulate interventions using the original ER and the idealized ER as metaphors for change.

Shifron's approach (2007) builds on Kopp and Robles. In her work, she also uses ERs in a similar way to work with the stuck feelings of the supervisee through use of memory as metaphor. Her focus is a classic Adlerian contribution through focus on identifying the *unacknowledged strengths* of the client and the supervisee. She also identifies strengths the therapist is *overusing*, because they parallel those of the client and get in the way of the therapeutic process. Her work clarifies how a supervisor can work respectfully and contractually on personal issues with a supervisee with a clear focus on the professional development of the supervisee and the promotion of the work with the client. Indeed, in more recent work as yet unpublished, she also uses the ER of the client to signify the client's implicit wish for how the therapeutic relationship should be.

A key idea of the method is that exploration of each ER can reveal hidden creative abilities that the person is using in order to survive and to cope with life, and of which they are often not consciously or fully aware. It is the therapist's role to point out to the client his/her strengths, as it is the supervisor's role to show, through the use of ERs, the supervisee's strengths.

Supervision which attends to both the client's and the therapist's Life Style is very productive. It assists effective supervision by identifying the place where the therapy is stuck because of the overlap of the inner worlds of client and therapist. [Shifron, 2007]

Two Israeli contributions

Both Shifron (2006) and Lahad (2000) are Israeli, and I wonder what, in the professional traditions there, has supported the development of creativity in supervision, or if this has been an innovation arising from work with very traumatized people. Perhaps it comes more easily, as Lahad describes, from schooling, or an upbringing like his that is pervaded with storytelling, support for the imagination, and unconditional love. He describes the value of attending to inner reality for self-nurturing, by focusing on specific experiences of feeling loved.

Lahad recommends readers to use his book "gently, keeping in mind the boundaries of others as well as yourself, and allowing your own supportive nature, warmth and playfulness to be present" (Lahad, 2000, p. 8). He has a background in existential and Gestalt traditions, and emphasizes the value of time and patience in relation to work with "resistance", both of the client and the counsellor. As many writers have noted, resistance is the client's unique way of co-operating (de Shazer, 1989).

Lahad argues that, in supervision, "when you share your fantasies, dreams and images, they are mostly used to help you learn about your countertransference" (2000, p. 12). A bridge can be built between left and right hemispheres of the brain to connect logic, creativity, and fantasy through increased awareness of the therapist's imagination, feelings, and senses. It goes without saying, I hope, that the supervisor has to take the stance of being of service to the supervisee, and not the judge.

Lahad's approach includes assessment and diagnosis, storytelling and play, and is designed for the times that Kopp and Shifron described, when the supervisee comes feeling stuck with the client, or where the supervisee is stuck in too rational an approach. Imaginative exercises, like having a character from a film as a co-therapist, are also used as vehicles for generating release, optimism, and new perspectives.

Lahad also describes using films, cards, objects and artefacts, free writing, fairy stories, psycho-dramatic exercises, art materials, plasticine or clay, a poem, a postcard, or a picture of an item belonging to the supervisee, as well as metaphors and images. He says that interpretation is almost never useful. Rather, listening, investigating the object, lateral reactions, and reflection work well. For instance, one supervisee describes herself *vis-à-vis* her client as a "snail", and asks, "What can a snail do? . . . so slow, so fragile" (*ibid.*, p. 29). She is then invited to consider other aspects of herself until she discovers her resourceful self through playing with ideas about colours to signify different relationships, and is ready to visualize herself in relation to the client more productively, trusting her work again and with some new internal resource or strength to do difficult work.

CHAPTER TEN

Taking supervisory authority

"On the one hand the supervisor is working within a process that enables discovery, and on the other, is needing to maintain their own observing ego and hold an authority that emanates from experience and expertise. As in all balancing acts there is a danger of collapse to either extreme. . . . A working alliance, therefore depends as much on the internal attitude of the supervisor as it does on the supervisee."

(Driver & Martin, 2002, pp. 54–55)

The central value of supervision is about creating a trusting working alliance. It requires courage and skill to take an authoritative stance. "Taking supervisory authority" involves learning to take authority without being authoritarian. This applies normally in relation to boundaries and a frame for the work, and in the more unusual, emotionally charged experiences when something is going wrong.

Challenge can create feelings of shame and exposure for the supervisee, or anxiety for the supervisor. The exploration of unconscious processes can mean that the supervisee feels that they lack control over what is seen by the supervisor, even when they are intending to take control over what they bring.

Examples of the *relationship* qualities required are subtle to convey, and supervisee's assumptions greatly affect how they respond to the issue. It might include many ways to relate that require immediacy, might be uncomfortable, or that simply take more active initiative than is normal in many counselling relationships.

Routine examples include:

- making contracts for the work
- taking and sharing responsibility for allocating time during the supervision;
- coping with ethical dilemmas;
- giving feedback about the skills or approach of the supervisee;
- writing reports or references;
- requesting a list of current caseloads to consider those clients not yet—or ever—brought to supervision;
- containing difficult feelings in the supervisory relationship, and being willing to name and explore them;
- assessing "fitness to practise" together when the supervisee is facing difficult life events or health problems.

Less regular and predictable examples include:

- failing a trainee on the practice component of a course;
- inviting a supervisee to stop practising;
- informing an employer or professional body about a serious ethical breach;
- being persistent in giving positive feedback to a less confident supervisee about her effective skills and practice.

This is an opportunity to identify and explore an issue, take appropriate responsibility, and exercise the skills involved to seek a positive outcome.

Supervisors assessing trainees

Especially when supervising trainee counsellors, there is a significant power differential arising from the tasks the supervisor has to undertake. This must be openly acknowledged rather than denied or minimized. Assessment and giving feedback are core tasks for the supervisor, so these tasks need to be done within honest exchanges, sensitively, and, where possible, without attacking the self worth of the supervisee.

There is also a responsibility issue: the supervisor is overseeing work with a third party, the client, whom s/he will not normally meet. Somehow, the supervisor is expected to protect the client from serious consequences and from major problems resulting from the normal stumbles and uncertainties of beginning in practice. S/he is also trusted to support the development of the trainee. Wigram (2002) describes the value of group supervision for trainees, who can learn from each other as well as the supervisor. She argues that fairness in the assessment process means that the supervisor should assess herself as well as the trainee. She concludes,

> Assessment is essential to protect the patient and the possible trainee; in doing so we must be careful not to lose the delicate arts of insight and intuition which are such an essential part of the talking cure. [p. 30]

Power inequalities should not be denied with trainees. Some courses *do* invite supervisees formally to assess their supervisor, but without prior experience a supervisee might not realize supervision could be more enabling, and accept minor invalidations and difficult dynamics deferentially, assuming the fault must lie with him or her. Chapter Two describes some of my experiences in this regard.

Criteria for good practice

As I have thought about the issues, I have tried to develop criteria for good practice for myself in relation to supervisory authority, and I think they include five distinct elements.

First, counsellor supervisors need to teach and encourage their supervisees to take responsibility for preparation and for what they want in their supervision time, so that they do not ascribe control and initiative totally to the supervisor. Too few counselling courses succeed in convincing trainee counsellors of the importance of preparation, and indeed it is difficult while they are unsure about the relevance of what they need to bring. Slowly, people get better at it, if encouraged, but often it takes until counsellors decide to train as supervisors for them to become fully aware of the value of preparation to present their work.

Second, supervisors need to develop their own views about the purpose of supervision, issues of power and authority, the development of an ethical stance, and an awareness of the importance of ethical principles and frameworks to approach supervisory dilemmas. That is, supervisors need to become clear when they *must* act, and how those times differ from those where they *might* or *can*. Inskipp and Proctor (1995) have described this clearly.

Third, they need to understand about interpersonal dynamics in relation to feelings of inferiority and superiority (the inferiority–superiority dynamic, see Glossary) and how to sustain a commitment to equality and mutual respect, especially when difficult things are to be said. This includes a capacity to bear being disliked or hated in the fallout of having to fail a trainee or recommend that a volunteer or employee or freelance counsellor consider taking a break from work or stop working. Timing is important. Reviews can support supervisee development of awareness that s/he is relating as if to a parent, or a judge.

Fourth, they need to become aware of the bases for the exercise of legitimate authority. These might include expertise, role, charisma, and the professional body's expectation of a gate-keeping role, so that supervisors keep a watchful eye on practice for the sake of the profession.

Fifth, they need to accept that the person undertaking the supervisory role has a right and a duty as part of the role to help to identify bad or inadequate practice and enquire about "fitness to practise". With this criterion comes the expectation that the supervisor should develop the skills and attitudes to exercise this right while minimizing assault on the sense of worth of the recipient. Ideally, as a supervisor, my role is to model the skills involved, and also to engage in equally respectful relationships, even when offering feedback that I can predict will be painful or disappointing to receive. I also must be willing to receive uncomfortable and upsetting feedback in my turn, and look at it with the supervisee carefully to discover what has gone wrong that may arise from my—and our—way of being. I aim to model, for instance, putting the relationship first, not ducking the responsibility to be clear about standards or expectations, aiming to be aware of and value differing styles that may be equally effective even though I do not work like that, and being willing to share some of my own struggles to practise professionally.

Contracting

Making the contract sets the tone for the relationship. Clarifying skills are crucial, and negotiation about the focus on particular tasks (Proctor, 1997).

Some questions indicating relevant issues for reviewing a contract follow.

- Is it a basis for a working alliance?
- Is it comprehensive or sloppy or so informal as to be actually or almost invisible?
- What leeway is there for meeting the unique needs of this supervisee as well as this supervisor?
- Does the supervisor feel entitled to be clear about her or his own needs, such as adequate payment, or notice for missed sessions?
- Does the supervisee feel entitled to be clear, too, to be able to request help without having to hide vulnerability or skill?
- Can s/he be accepted and understood at the current stage of development?
- Is there clarity about who is responsible for what?

Contracts are crucial at the start of the supervisory relationship, and also at the start of each session, especially when the supervisee has a big agenda. The contract conveys that this purposeful relationship can be negotiated, monitored, and reviewed by both parties regularly enough to allow uncomfortable matters to be discussed before they become impossible to speak about. Routine reviews at the end of a supervision allow each to identify useful exchanges, or what each may be taking away.

Managing the time during sessions is a shared responsibility. If the agenda is big, supervisor and supervisee can decide the order of topics, and renegotiate when some elements take longer than anticipated. Invitations to creativity and to focus on a specific question for supervision under each heading can invite the supervisee into healthy habits of preparation for supervision, and build their internal supervisor in the process.

This sort of contracting and preparation should not squeeze out immediacy and shifts in focus arising from what is happening in the moment. On the contrary, these become clearer through contracting, and the gains and losses of moving from the plan in response to interest and need can be talked about, too. One danger is that a supervisor might have a "bright spot", an area of current interest that could lead her to follow up a passing remark beyond usefulness to the supervisee.

Power and the taking of authority

Power issues need to be explored. Ways to address supervisees' expectations can be identified. In practice, the supervisee may feel professionally "adolescent" (Crick, 1991) while in training, or frozen by feelings of incompetence. They might feel almost "fully grown" as a trainee, but still not yet have passed the course and thus are not yet entitled to take a full identity as a counsellor. Yet, some may have many years of voluntary experience or have skills to transfer from another profession. Crick gives a vivid description of the pains and sense of being de-skilled she felt when she was learning to be a therapist, and the powerful discomforts of her dependence on the good opinion of her supervisor, specifically because of the process of assessment impinging on the relationship. She also notes that she valued the supervisor's style towards her changing as she became more confident and experienced.

When a supervisee feels inferior, fears failure, and pervades the dialogue with anxiety and excuses, blaming or complaining, the power dynamic can be discussed, and the supervisee can be invited to express their concerns, and to take responsibility for their part in the interaction. This is honestly very difficult. Preoccupation with defensiveness or superiority in either role might correlate with an evaluative focus on *how* either party is doing, rather than a more descriptive one on *what* they are doing. Thus, direct communication of difficult matters may help form a paradigm for other relationships, and could model authentic relating that the supervisee may take back into their relationships with their clients. Sensitivity is required, and sometimes it cannot be made all right.

Either party needs to be able to say that the relationship is not working, and propose an ending, but, in particular, the supervisor has responsibility to be monitoring the efficacy of the relationship and the work coming out of supervision. The review might have risks of oppressive practice. The supervisor might take too much control, or fail to create a space for a genuine negotiation, be grandiose or selfish, assume the supervisor's needs should take precedence, or else the reverse, engage in an over-protective, potentially patronizing "care taking" which fails to encourage the supervisee to bring their needs and abilities fully to the negotiation. Supervision of supervision can usefully explore such risks and difficulties. It is important to emphasize that supervisors need to stay open to learning, too, and that the supervisor is not necessarily right. Some are envious of their trainees, or idealize them unhelpfully, or are unaware of their own need to control.

Schon (1987, p. 222) quotes Karl Weik's story as a parable of the movement from objectivism to constructionism and expressions of power. This story is about three umpires, and also reflects attitudes to power and beliefs. He writes,

"The first says, " I calls 'em like they *is*!",
the second, "I calls 'em like I *sees* them!";
and the third: "There ain't nothing *there* until I calls 'em!"

Minikin (2002) described often leaving supervision feeling "stupid" as a trainee, until slowly she developed a capacity to hold on to herself, stay alert, and ask for what she wanted within a relationship she recognized as being about her own development. Holding the tension between feeling shamed and stupid, and yet accepted by her supervisor, allowed her to shift her personal issues around exposure and being seen. I have left supervision with a supervisor from another orientation feeling less confident, because our frames of thought were so different. Sometimes, the difficulty lies in the vulnerability of the supervisee to shame, and the best a supervisor can do is to be watchful about this, and be much more explicit about identifying what the supervisee is doing that seems effective, and that the supervisor accepts and values the supervisee and is on her side.

Engaging with ethical dilemmas

Ethical dilemmas come in at least two different forms: those that the supervisee has identified but does not know how to manage, and those that the supervisor identifies which the supervisee had not. The latter, like any "mistake", has potential to raise feelings of inferiority and shame for the supervisee, and possibly for high anxiety or superiority for the supervisor (see Chapters Eleven and Twelve, on ethical dilemmas and mistakes, respectively). Yet, if the discomforts can be faced, not fudged, learning can take place, and the supervisory relationship may even be enhanced. Some novice supervisors need a lot of encouragement to discuss and set boundaries, or exercise initiative as supervisors, yet these are the occupational tasks that come with the role, whatever the theoretical orientation. Specifically, some supervisees and many new supervisors might conflate "taking authority" with "being authoritarian", a style they do not wish to implement because it would undermine a core supervisory value about collegiality and equality.

The value of feedback

Giving feedback, especially to supervisees when written reports are also required, raises all the power dynamics associated with being judged. Good practice requires exchanges that tap into the courage of the recipient, and acknowledge strengths with equal enthusiasm to naming learning edges. Feedback is best on a very regular basis, based on preparation and self-assessment, including feedback from each to the other. This could be a particularly complex process, because the seniority of the supervisor does mean that they are likely to have more experience, yet they might not be more experienced, or even right, in a specific circumstance. Especially with trainees, the "awe of the knowledge and skills of the supervisor" (Minikin, 2002) can make any challenge bruising, and tap into vulnerable fears of not being good enough. Yet, this does not mean that the supervisor is necessarily right in any individual situation. It is important that each can state a view, and each can then decide how they will act on the insights gained.

I had one supervisee who said, "What's the point of coming to supervision if we discuss something, disagree, and then you encourage me to do what I was going to do anyway?"

To that, I replied that he was the one in relationship with the client and what we were doing was airing possibilities and other perspectives, but, as a professional, he was in charge of his own practice. Thus, rather than abnegating my responsibility to set him straight, as he saw it, I aimed to explore ideas, facilitate insight, and honour his reflections.

Ideally, thinking differently does not indicate that the "OK-ness" of either party is compromised. Supervisors need to learn how to combine giving information and validation to the supervisee with feedback about what has been missed, not handled in a productive way, or what must change, e.g., if the supervisee is not preparing adequately for supervision.

Carroll and Gilbert (2005, p. 55) describe the importance of understanding the supervisee you are giving feedback to in terms of five specific elements:

1. His/her preferred way of learning: emotional, intellectual, etc.
2. How much time does he/she need to talk through the issue, in order to hear the message?
3. Is he/she able not to be defensive when receiving feedback?
4. How able is he/she to be in touch with themselves?
5. How am I perceived and experienced by the other person?

Taking supervisory authority within this feedback task is, of course, likely to be pervaded by anxiety for both parties when uncomfortable things need to be said. This could be compounded when there is potential for misunderstanding arising from differences or diversity issues, and feelings of oppression felt by either, particularly the supervisee, since their future might rest on getting a good report, reference, or accreditation recommendation.

Scaife (2009, pp. 326–333) is particularly useful about giving feedback about impaired, incompetent, or unethical practice.

Unique elements of authority in peer supervision

A peer group has to share supervisory authority, roles and tasks, and may decide to do this formally or informally. It is useful to have a mental checklist of what needs to be monitored. The lessons of my experience in peer groups suggest the following.

- Expect commitment and join up only with those for whom you feel respect. This enables you to share sufficient values for any differences or difficulties to be expressed full-heartedly. Recommit to the group, possibly annually, or if regularity of attendance becomes an issue.
- Allow time for "check-in", that is, for each individual to say how they are and tell any story necessary about current pressures or joys in their life. Bringing the personal alongside the professional enriches both, and it also allows peers to make enquiries from a position of knowing the personal context. It gives information, too, to use when monitoring resilience. It is an element of using supervisory authority to address the personal and professional overlap between the members of the peer group so that the supervision work is not compromised by relationship strains between members arising from dual relationships. It is also important not to let the group become a place where the personal takes over and the other casework supervision is squeezed by it.
- When personal and professional connections change, and people start or stop working in the same agency, for instance, discuss it in the group to identify how it is affecting the supervisory process, and the personal relationships, and review the contract. Decide whether or not to work in the same establishment at the start, and if you do, explore the consequences for those who do and for the group process as a whole.
- Take time to review process matters in the group, and to evaluate the usefulness of the work at the end of each session. Without someone taking the formal leadership role, such tasks

can be avoided, especially when the group is working least well and they are most needed.

It is important to expect that there will be "shadows". Talk about them, especially when the shadows are organizational as well as personal.

Reflections

Supervision is a fundamentally collegial relationship that also has a bottom line of potentially lonely responsibility for protection of clients and of working colleagues who come for supervision, and some responsibility for the good name of the profession as a whole. *Supervising Counsellors: Issues of Responsibility*, edited by Wheeler and King (2001), remains the best source of ideas and commentary about these issues. Where there is trust and safety built up from the initial contracting, many difficulties can be worked through to the benefit and learning of both parties. Where there is a habit of regular reviews, a routine context is created for feedback, when emotions are not running high. But when the supervisee lacks insight, and the supervisor has checked out his or her concerns through consultation, difficult decisions need to be initiated. It is important to be willing to hear the supervisees' responses and views, and yet take the authority implicit in the role if that is really required. The supervisor cannot normally actually stop a supervisee working once s/he is qualified, but she can stop supervising the person, and, *in extremis*, convey to an employer or professional body the concerns s/he has.

These supervisory skills requiring more initiative have few parallels in the counselling role. The challenges can be acutely uncomfortable for both the supervisor and supervisee. The aim of learning to take supervisory authority is to create a supervision climate in which ethical concerns can congruently be expressed and explored. Feedback that is offered from a position that accepts and values difference, considers the outcomes of supervisee behaviour, and builds the supervisees' capacity for reflective practice is potentially transformative, and very respectful. Then the conversation can focus on what the supervisee is doing, rather than offer a generally negative view that creates feelings of inferiority and shame.

Supervision needs to give priority to naming issues, and helping supervisees explore and address their behaviour when it is problematic, without attacking the self-worth of the person. This is easier said than done, but practice means that it can be done, and that is a very valuable achievement for the individuals and the profession.

CHAPTER ELEVEN

Coping with ethical dilemmas

"Our duty is to do what is *right*; but as a practical matter, we would just as soon have things turn out as *well* as possible"

(www.friesian.com/dilemma.html)

W e do not speak often enough about how counselling can do harm. It can, and Lambert's research (2005) suggested that 8% of clients in his USA study got worse as a result of a counselling experience. Whatever the actual number in an individual's workload, engaging with the possibility of doing harm means that the supervisor has a role to help with this issue. This can occur through discussions about assessment to help identify clients at risk, and through reflection on practice to share the monitoring of the counsellor's work and resilience, and the client's process and outcome, as far as these can be reasonably known without ever meeting the client.

The normative function of supervision (Inskipp & Proctor, 1995) derives from these ethical or managerial responsibilities. The aim is to protect the client from malpractice and poor practice, to protect the reputation of the profession, and to aid the supervisee in processes of reflection and self-care. This might sound dull and dutiful, but in many ways it is the most interesting and challenging part of the work of a supervisor, as each party wrestles with ethical dilemmas without obvious or easy solutions.

When poor practice is exposed, the core dilemma of the normative task is revealed: how to sustain a safe relationship so that the counsellor will disclose information despite the fact that this could show that their practice is not up to standard, and there might be uncomfortable consequences to face (Henderson, 2002). The pull within the relationship might be to protect the counsellor when s/he is vulnerable. The push of normative tasks is to confront the issue as sensitively and skilfully as possible, but not to duck the responsibility to do so.

I think that the personal qualities most needed to undertake the normative tasks as a supervisor are courage, rigorous thinking, and intuition. It takes courage to articulate reservations and concerns honestly, and in a timely way, and most supervisors who have worked for some years can identify a moment when they had to say something significant and difficult to a supervisee who did not want to hear it. For many, this is the rite of passage that moves them to consider themselves experienced, once they have survived the process.

Bollas (1987) uses a musical analogy, describing supervision as being like reading a musical score or attending a musical event. This caught my imagination, and I thought of times I have attended to the overall impact of the music, or to the music behind the words, or sometimes to the bass notes of the underpinning ethical base. The metaphor could take us to reflection on the many levels of conscious and unconscious interactions to attend to for supporting safe, creative, and ethical practice.

This chapter is designed to spell out the balancing act between the excitement of exploring gritty dilemmas, and the rigorous thinking and consultation required. It describes some ethical dilemmas and ways to cope with them. Ethical problem-solving structures are now widely known (British Association for Counselling and Psychotherapy, 2004a), and there are matters of interest to consider about sustaining collegiality while articulating standards. A professional ethical framework plays a hugely educational and containing role (British Association for Counselling and Psychotherapy, 2005).

Pragmatics, too, are an important focus: considering the counsellor's workload, and examining not just the hours a supervisee works, but also the complexity of need and the emotional demands of the people being seen. Fitness to practise discussions need to be routine, so that counsellors get used to monitoring their own resilience; more painfully, these discussions might need to be initiated by the supervisor when the counsellor is denying their declining health, or energy depletion (British Association for Counselling and Psychotherapy, 2004b).

What are ethical dilemmas?

Ethical dilemmas come in a variety of sizes and difficulty, and they invite us to exercise our "internal supervisor" muscles. Most counsellors face minor ethical decisions, such as small boundary pressures from a client on a regular and frequent basis, but resolve them confidently because of experience, theoretical guidance, or a developed capacity for ethical problem-solving. Few people will practise for long without coming up against some taxing ones. Because of the potential for serious consequences for the client and the counsellor, supervisors and counsellors need to be really familiar with a professional framework or code, and to practise thinking about ethical dilemmas.

The supervisor is often the first port of call for worried counsellors, who might make contact between sessions to calm their anxiety and talk through options to act or refrain from acting. Legal helplines and professional bodies also advise, as do experienced practitioner networks. The British Association for Counselling and Psychotherapy (BACP), with a membership of 29,000 in 2008, had an average of two hundred calls per month from members who were seeking guidance about practice issues from an ethical perspective (BACP internal document, 2007). These calls are more than normally complex, and can often take considerable skill and time to explore possible options in a wide variety of settings and contexts. When the counsellor becomes fearful and anxious, their self-confidence and clear thinking can be affected. An important skill for both counsellor and supervisor is to learn to slow down and reflect, rather than give in to the pull to take urgent action.

The first task is to recognize that the counsellor is facing an ethical dilemma. This is where Szecody's (1990, p. 250) concept of blind spots and dumb spots, those matters we fail to notice in our own pathology, is particularly useful. Ethical practice is also a matter of becoming socialized into the norms of the profession, about boundaries, confidentiality, dual relationships, fitness to practise, and similar knots. Not all psychological practitioners share the same ethics, though the core values are common to most professions.

A mnemonic to remember the BACP ethical principles was invented by a colleague, Libby Wattis: "Frigid Aardvarks Believe Nothing Justifies Sex." (fidelity, autonomy, beneficence, non-maleficence, justice, self care.)

Ethical decision-making

The specifics of reflecting on particular experiences, and rigorously monitoring the potential of doing harm are instructive (Gilbert & Evans, 2000, p. 136). For instance, one supervisee, who worked for many years in a small rural town, described one day how she had walked around the market square, knowing the names of sexual abusers described by her clients. She also knew one person concerned by sight. She felt that she was being a bystander, and that "something more should be done", and felt furious that it could not. She had an impulse to action, although not sure what that might entail. She brought the issue to supervision. Is there anything she could or should do? We discussed whether she does normally act if there is any direct evidence of a child being currently at risk at home or school or youth group, because she is required to do this by her terms of employment. I caught her indignation and helplessness, which resonated with my feelings about people who "get away with it" and about sexual abusers, especially of children and vulnerable people. I had to decide what to do with these resonating feelings: was it useful to her to articulate them? There is no point in a collusive moan about how awful people or abusers are. I also wondered "why this is coming up now", and explored that with her. Is this an issue about burnout and overload? Do we need a restorative focus? Is there a normative issue? There are a number of possible areas such a pair could explore, and it is up to them jointly to agree a focus.

Carroll (1996) discussed monitoring professional/ethical issues as a supervision task, and describes his research with BAC recognized supervisors as indicating that most supervisors of *trainees* wait for the issues to arise in practice, considering that basic teaching should be done by courses. Using his method for ethical problem solving (pp. 160–165), if this pair considers the issue above they can reflect from four different angles.

1. *Ethical sensitivity.* They could think about her values, and how exposure to so many similar stories is affecting her. They could consider the power issues, the wish to punish the perpetrators who have not been dealt with by the judicial system. They could think through the implications of behaviour for all others involved in the issue. In particular, the necessary habit of creating "thoughtful delays" (Pryor, 1989, p. 303) so that the practitioner considers all aspects before taking any action.

2. *Formulating a moral course for action.* Consulting an ethical framework, and discussing personal moral imperatives and motivation is a base for this element. They could identify the source of conflict in her personal value system, and in mine, and explore some gender issues in relation to it. In thinking about the possible outcomes, they could review the implications for clients. They could also consider the consequences of doing nothing. Each may need to let off steam about the limits to their capacity to change a social ill.

3. *Implementing an ethical decision.* Here, the bystander issue raises its head. It is easier *not* to act, sometimes, when one should. How to decide if inaction arises from cowardice, pragmatism, or wisdom? Self-interest, protection of the clients, the issues of employment, are all relevant to inaction. Is there any element that prescribes action? The protection of vulnerable children could give them thought.

4. *Living with the ambiguities of the decision.* Because a difficult situation provokes anxiety, and competing ethical principles are so often pertinent, anxiety about the correctness of the decision might continue.

In the end, she and I decided that the priority of client confidentiality was greater than the impulse to act, but that it was worth continuing to think about it, and notice if and how her feelings about the issue continue to affect her.

Peluso (2003) created a useful resource tool, the ethical genogram, for practitioners to review parental and early life approaches to difficult dilemmas and the impact of these on their later professional ethical decision making. This is best used as a resource for training or private reflection, but is helpful to identify sometimes unexpected and taken for granted personal values.

Facing fear in an ethical dilemma

Many supervisors and counsellors will recall a dilemma that resonated with them, or was in some way unsatisfactorily resolved to the extent that it becomes a developmental marker for them, possibly one they continue to think about for a long period.

I still reflect about my decision-making process about one ethical dilemma I faced as a counsellor more than ten years ago, even though the outcome was, by chance, as good as possible.

I was counselling a very actively suicidal sixteen-year-old, who was very able academically, but troubled by psychosomatic complaints and depression. Overtly self-confident and dismissive of adults' attempts to help him, he subtly conveyed despair and vulnerability, but, if it was alluded to, vehemently denied it.

He had accepted antidepressants from his GP, but when a psychiatrist changed the prescription to one with more side effects, he refused to take either prescription, or to return to the psychiatrist, or confide further in the GP. I was the only adult he was confiding in at the time, according to him. (Consider the traps arising from feeling special!)

Meanwhile, reminding me of my commitment to confidentiality, he disclosed a plan to use an open-dated ticket he already had to go abroad by himself, without prior warning to his already anxious parents, and to turn up at the address of someone with whom he had made a close Internet relationship. He did not intend to tell the person that he was coming.

I made an arrangement to see him before his planned travel date, and sought immediate supervision. Not convinced by my supervisor's view that he was testing me to see if I would hold my promise of confidentiality, and that he would not act on his plan, I asked a peer for her views. Inevitably, I received contradictory advice as I wrestled with the issues. The peer thought that he was implicitly begging me to do the obvious, and stop him, and that was my duty of care. My fear was that if I betrayed his confidence he would immediately reject further contact with me, too, but not turn to other adults who were available. He was already self-harming, impulsively. I was very concerned.

Sometimes, fate is kind. In this case, the travel agent unwittingly revealed his plans to the parents by phoning and leaving a message, and all was revealed and worked with in the family. However, he did refuse further meetings with me, and I never saw him again. I often wonder how he is when I cycle past their house.

From recall of the feelings within the relationship with the client, I needed to disentangle at least four conflicting ethical imperatives. There was fidelity and autonomy in relation to a client's insistence on confidentiality, non-maleficence in the teeth of predictably dangerous outcomes, and my own self-respect, which was greatly affected by what I would have wished a counsellor seeing an offspring of mine to do under the circumstances. Although his parents were not my clients, they had begged me for help for him, and I was influenced by their anxiety about him.

Helping others to discover their limits

One issue is about people who are trained on poor courses, and thus do not know their limits, or have not done enough personal development or therapy themselves. When one had also been asked seductively, while still a trainee on a Diploma, to start teaching on the organization's certificate course, alarm bells rang for me. These usually able and well-intentioned people may well have an excellent grasp of appropriate theory. Except in very unusual career patterns, they seldom have enough practice experience to underpin their theoretical understanding.

The interaction of personal and professional elements

The overlap between the personal and the professional for counsellors and supervisors is not sufficiently discussed in relation to ethical anxieties, but, for good and ill, it is highly relevant to good counselling and supervisory work. So is the practitioner's capacity to undertake the role without doing harm to the recipient or becoming more vulnerable to falling into ethical traps because of their own life circumstances or health. This book has many reflections on the issues of self-care. My own experience as supervisor and supervisee has taught me how crucial the supervisor role is in relation to this at every stage of a working life.

I have had several supervisees who carried heavy caseloads exceeding sixty clients at any one time within GP settings. Whether it was debt or the need to be useful that drove them, it took many years to make significant headway in getting them to reduce their caseload and increase their self-care. My supervisory role was to keep monitoring and mentioning the issue, and inviting them to consider the cost to them of these choices. They would make themselves available out of hours for emergencies, too, in ways parallel to the GPs with whom they worked, so there was a combination of the professional pressures of the working culture and context, and individual style and pathology. In practice, once a counsellor is qualified, few supervisors will *insist* that they stop work, though many may *suggest* a break.

Acting on impulse

Too ready empathy leading to a breach of confidentiality can be harmful to the client. Once, as a counsellor, I impulsively breached a suicidal client's confidence, having sat with her in her despair. I rang her GP because I was worried that he might give her medication that she would then use to kill herself. It turned out that the GP was also a family friend, knew her circumstances, and would not do any such thing, but was very relieved to be sharing a feeling of burden of care with me. The client had scared me by being very actively suicidal. In principle, I would have said I believe that every one is autonomous and has the right to make what decisions they choose about their life. However, as a counsellor in relationship with a desperately miserable client who had dependent children, and who was grieving for her husband, I wanted to make sure that she was being explicit to the GP about how she felt so that at least he would not inadvertently prescribe the means to kill herself. It was an overreaction, and it spoiled our very tentative therapeutic relationship. My supervisor was uncharacteristically firm with me: I should tell the client what I had done in order to convey that I *was* in connection with her, and was worried about her. I did so in the next session. She immediately stormed out of the session, refusing to discuss it further or to return. Some weeks later, she wrote to me in response to a routine feedback form, saying she had forgiven me, and although she still felt no better, she did understand why I had done it and was in regular touch with her GP.

Confidentiality

The BACP information sheet G2 (2008) about seeking client permission to breach confidentiality or to refer on, offers a useful disclosure checklist (p. 7) that also refers to relevant legislation:

> It may help therapists in the decision making process about sharing information to consider these points:
>
> Is this information regulated by the Data Protection Act 1998 (DPA) or the Freedom of Information Act 2000 (FOIA); (for example, do the records comprise client-identifiable sensitive personal data held on computer or in a relevant filing system?)
>
> Were the notes made by a professional working for a public body in health, education or social care?
>
> What are the relevant rights of the person concerned under the Human Rights Act 1998?
>
> If working in the health community, is disclosure compliant with the Caldicott principles and guidance? [See Glossary.]
>
> Is there a legitimate requirement to share this information: e.g. statutory duty or a court order?
>
> What is the purpose of sharing the information?
>
> If the information concerns a child, young person, or vulnerable adult, is sharing it in their best interests?
>
> Is the information confidential? If so, do you have consent to share it?

If consent is refused, or there are good reasons not to seek consent, does the public interest necessitate sharing the information?

Is the decision and rationale for sharing the information recorded?

What is the most appropriate way to share this information?

Bond and Mitchels (2008) have provided a thoughtful book on confidentiality and record-keeping that explores legal and ethical issues and responsibilities as they affect practice in much more detail. It is designed to inform practitioners of essential matters and includes case studies to demonstrate that poor record-keeping can incur legal liabilities. There are useful chapters on developing agency policy, and on supervision, audit, and research.

When the supervisor behaves badly

Supervisors, too, can do harm and be damaging. Supervisors differ on their normal level of basic trust or mistrust with colleagues in ways that are embedded deep in their personalities, and their normal responses might be disturbed and disturbing when they become highly anxious about an issue.

Supervisor ethical breaches have been studied in the USA by Ladany, Lehrman-Waterman, Molinaro, and Wolgast (1999). Their definitions include minor infringements such as allowing interruptions of supervision sessions, but include disrespectful treatment, issues around confidentiality, and supervision boundaries.

In the UK, Rennie Peyton (2004) looked at bullying in supervision. She described examples of supervisors labelling trainees: "Well of course you would do that—it's your lack of experience", or refusals to hear critical feedback to the supervisor, labelling it as negative transference. Bullying is very much in the ear of the receiver, and tone of voice can alter the impact of a comment greatly. In an e-mail to me, following publication of that article, one counsellor wrote:

> In another setting I had group supervision, 3 of us. The supervisor got really cross with a supervisee and called her "a fat cow". I can hardly believe I heard this and on reflection I so wish I had taken comments like these to our boss or BACP but in my infancy as a counsellor, I did not feel I had a right to complain.

The emotional arousal that is engendered by such inappropriate and hostile comments makes individuals feel humiliated, unsafe, if not also angry, and inhibits the clarity of thought necessary to the supervisee to make good use of a supervisory space.

Crick (1991), writing while still a student, notes the discomforts of being assessed, and quotes a psychoanalytical psychotherapy student in training who was told: "Well, whatever else is going on, it's certainly not psychoanalytical psychotherapy", commenting that such a style of feedback strikes at the heart of the lack of confidence of a trainee. It takes confidence for a trainee to make complaints about such behaviour.

Keeping the supervisory relationship straight

In Chapter Ten, I wrote about the courage required to take supervisory authority. Here, I also want to mention the professional and human tensions in the relationship when ethical dilemmas are being explored. Working with a defensive and frightened supervisee can be exhausting, and require a sensitive balance of support and challenge. An experienced supervisee, recently bereaved, who wants to continue working when it is clear she is white-faced and strained, might pull me two ways. My investment as supervisor in *this* relationship pulls me to want to advise or guide, but I cannot insist if she is reluctant to take some space. After all, without being there or having evidence on tape, I do not *know* how she is working with similarly bereaved clients, or with the whole range of the client group. Maybe she is showing me her suffering in supervision precisely so that she can hold herself together in the counsellor role (Walker & Jacobs, 2004, pp. 98–102). Yet, professionally, I must hold the needs of the client group in mind, so we have to keep monitoring it together. I could offer flexible or extra supervision. She could reduce the caseload, or not take new referrals for a while. Clarity about the counsellor's autonomous responsibility for her own work is essential. As Walker and Jacobs say, quoting Winnicott, sometimes the client is more helped by the counsellor continuing even if she cannot do more than "keep alive, keep well and keep awake" and leave clever interventions aside (*ibid.*, p. 101).

Other examples of relationship issues that might result in ethical difficulties include the practitioner whose inner critic is so harsh the supervisor does not want to give it more ammunition, or who collapses under any comment construed as critical; the practitioner who hides in a group, avoiding presenting, or individually who fills up the whole time with detailed content reports, making it difficult for the supervisor to get in and comment; the practitioner who requests cushioning after a prior difficult supervisory relationship, who may say or imply, "I need you to be nice to me", and the ethical supervisor has to reply, "What then do I do with any concerns I may have for you or your client?"

Some strains arise from gender, and might particularly affect counsellors and supervisors within higher education settings. Two Canadian women academics wrote about the stresses of their working lives in a paper entitled: "Doing good and feeling bad: the work of women university teachers" (Acker & Feuerverger, 1996). They described the strains of relating to colleagues and students. They competed with male colleagues, took a more female role in pastoral care of students, and stretched themselves to the limit to include their research and writing, teaching, and family life. As they tried to live up to contrary prescriptions for "caring women" and "productive academics", while also often taking roles as a token woman on many administrative committees, they described anxiety and perfectionism and dissatisfaction when caring roles did not attract promotion in the way that research did. They looked at their roles through the lens of minorities and outsiders, and in the context of rapid change in their institutions. It reminds me that the context of the work and ambition is a crucial variable to discuss in supervision.

I have not seen other writing about attunement to a supervisee who is bringing heavy stories when the supervisor has just been having a lovely time, and is full of a sense of well being. In the midst of a love affair, after an enjoyable weekend, having just been in beautiful places or with congenial people, surely others have struggled to sit still and contain their joy. That place of inner abundance is possibly more useful to the work than duty and responsibility and modelling how to cope.

Reflections

The taxi driver, in Waskett's (2006) metaphor for supervision, has to let the supervisee set the direction of travel. The supervisor needs to knows the Highway Code (or, in our case, the ethical code) and anticipate the ethical potholes; be able to take some short cuts, yet know where the blockages and road works are; and help keep the cab and its occupants safely on the road. Each contributes differently, but both assist the supervisory enterprise to get to the desired destination. The supervisor is in the driving seat, as there are the realities of a power differential to engage with. Yet, it is important to drive at a pace and in a way that makes the process of the journey as important as where we arrive, and that reduces the anxiety of the passenger. My learning about ethical practice in supervision is to remember to enjoy the thinking process, to notice the anxiety in myself or the supervisee as I see potholes ahead, to ensure the supervisee feels safe to ask for help, and to consult others for another perspective, and then take courage and responsibility to wait or to drive on, knowing I might have to give an account of my route map to others.

CHAPTER TWELVE

Mistakes and complaints

"Mistakes and failures are integral to the practice of psychotherapy and counselling because they are integral to life. In both life and therapy, mistakes are invaluable because they bring us up against reality—force us to recognise what is real rather than what we imagine, fear or hope for"

(Totton, 1997, p. 319)

This chapter has understanding of shame and fear at the core, and encourages both counsellors and supervisors to explore mistakes in supervision, whether these are made intentionally, unintentionally, or unconsciously. The uncomfortable work required to rebuild a working alliance after the exploration of a major mistake asks a lot from both parties. *Fear* of complaint has an impact on practice, and the consequent risks of defensive practice can affect every practitioner at some moments. Some useful fear is instilled by training, which sets out boundaries and appropriate behaviour, and during the transition from a trainee status to taking full responsibility for our own practice. We tread the line between being rule bounded and, therefore, sometimes being less genuine in our relationships to avoid risk of offence, or doing our best at the time, and trusting inner wisdom with awareness that it could lead us astray.

Professional accountability is achieved when successes or failures that arise from the (counselling) process are shared with a fellow professional, who assists with self-monitoring (O'Neill, 2002). Essentially, professional autonomy and responsibility lies with the counsellor, not the supervisor (Wheeler & King, 2001). Both supervisor and supervisee need to be willing to identify, acknowledge, and explore their professional mistakes and learn from them to protect the client. It is difficult for most supervisees to articulate their concerns about their own practice, never mind speaking of any discomfort created by their supervisor's. Especially in the early stages, it is a brave trainee who would do so. This means that supervision of supervision, and time spent in reflection by the supervisor, are important sources of information about human and professional failings in supervisory practice.

Weaks (2002) investigated how experienced counsellors characterized good supervision. Responses indicated that supervisory relationships based on equality, safety, and challenge were deemed to be the best. To feel safe, supervisees in her sample wanted permission to discuss all aspects of client work without having to protect themselves, feeling neither threatened nor judged. They wanted challenge that promotes awareness and insight, within an essentially collegial relationship.

This has the potential to work well when the mistakes are minor and the supervisee is willing to learn. Minor mistakes by counsellors and supervisors are normal, inevitable, and common, and are likely to be a feature of practice at all career stages. For writing that is based in research and complaints practice, readers are referred to Daniels (2000) and Palmer Barnes (1998). Palmer Barnes offers a useful base for analysis that distinguishes between mistakes, poor practice, negligence, and malpractice, the latter being work that intentionally and preferentially meets the financial, emotional, physical, or sexual needs of the therapist. In contrast, she defines a mistake as "an unintended slip in good practice", for example, a practitioner forgetting a session.

Many counsellors accept that some failings are a response to the client in just the way they need to be failed for something to be resolved. Poor practice is different. The supervisee might not recognize a mistake until the supervisor identifies it or subsequent events highlight it.

As a supervisor, I normally trust the competence and resource-fulness of an experienced supervisee. When a supervisee reveals a major mistake, especially if s/he has not recognized it, I might feel shocked (Henderson, 2002) and explore the issues using the BACP ethical framework. Supervision must explore what happened, and give priority to ways to reduce or repair damage to the client. We both need to communicate clearly and honestly and remain open to feedback when feeling "disturbed" by information that changes established views of each other. Both need to express our thoughts, feelings, and interpretations. However, embarrassment and shame affect trust and safety, and, without mutual goodwill, a vicious circle of misunderstandings and hurt can be created. If either fails to fully speak their truth about the impact on the supervisory rela-tionship, a further shift occurs that results in either collusion or an advance towards further authentic relationship.

I have experienced this sort of big shift four times in sixteen years of supervision, and only once did the supervisory relation-ship survive intact. It raised profound issues for both of us, as the language in the account below conveys.

The supervisee had broken a boundary in a relationship with a client, and casually "ran it past me" just to check it was not a prob-lem. I said I was shocked that she had done this, and she said much later that my use of the word "shocked" had "stabbed" her, as it felt punitive and attacking and she had felt childlike shame, and fear that I would send her away. This felt too much for her at the time, feeling that she had disappointed me. In such circumstances there are often echoes of analogous early experiences of rejection. She was under considerable personal pressure at the time, and this had contributed to a slippage of her own internal supervision. She was angry with me for interpreting her behaviour differently from the way she had seen it. Previously, I had trusted her judgement, and this shock and surprise led me to wonder whether this trust had been well founded, so her anxious response was appropriate: I was jolted into being judgemental, and thus the safety of the relation-ship was initially compromised.

My supervisor helped me to sort out my thoughts and feelings. Then my supervisee and I wrestled openly with the ethical dilemmas and their implications, including her *feeling* about being discussed in supervision. (She had always known intellectually that this would happen, and only her first name was used, so she was not identified to him.) We scanned the ethical framework together to help us think about it. As we reached the end of an intense series of exchanges, we both felt that we had learnt a lot, and the process had enhanced our relationship, and then she repaired hers with her client.

Supervisor mistakes

Supervisor mistakes and shortcomings are highly relevant to the success of a supervisory relationship. A correspondent wrote to me (after an article I wrote) and described her experience of her supervisor's mistakes in empathy, understanding, and respect, arising from envy, as follows.

> I was in my early stages of counselling, post diploma, after two years, and I engaged with a supervisor, which had disastrous results. She undermined my ability quite openly. She asked how much I charged private clients. When I told her, she was annoyed and dismayed. In our next meeting, she said, with regards to what I was charging she was putting up my fee and all her client's fees!

> I had another supervisor who opened the door to her cleaner in the middle of our session, never remembered her diary for future appointments, was not empathic towards my clients (or me!) and gave me a sense of "can't wait till the end of session".

Crick (1991) describes the impact on a student of supervisors who cancel many sessions, show boredom, demonstrated by "resting their eyes", or intersperse dozing off with having no compunction in saying that they find a case dull, with an occasional burst of active interest and enthusiasm.

Some supervisors fail to be encouraging or reveal positive reactions to supervisees. Ladany, Lehrman-Waterman, Molinaro, and Wolgast (1999) described some examples of positive reactions to supervisees' counselling and professional performance from his research in the USA with supervisors and trainees. Supervisors articulated these when asked by a researcher, *but had failed to say them to the supervisee.*

His examples included:

"She's doing a great job as a new professional."

"I don't think I was nearly as comfortable asserting myself."

"How enjoyable it is to work with the Supervisee."

Shame

Thomas Shroeder researches shame and how shame triggers a wish to cover up or conceal mistakes in therapy and in supervision. At a conference in 2007, he said that shame inhibits reflection and leaves practitioners unsupported, so if supervision is to be an effective part of clinical governance as well as professional development, shame must be minimized.

He argued that we need three components to address shame in supervision: a theoretical framework for making sense of shame experiences; a climate of enquiry and curiosity which mitigates shame; and, very importantly, a capacity to be compassionate towards our own struggles.

His four-part theoretical framework differentiates therapists' experiences of guilt from humiliation, and internal and external shame.

Guilt leads the therapist to be concerned about the possibility of having caused harm to another. Feelings of regret, sadness, remorse, or sorrow focus the therapist's attention on the consequences of his/her conduct and on ways to undo the damage or make reparation.

Humiliation leads the therapist to be concerned about being unjustly denigrated by another (especially the patient) as inferior, inadequate, or bad. Reactions may involve feeling contemptuous, or vengeful towards the other, possibly leading to a desire for retaliation or an impulse to defend the self.

Internal shame leads the therapist to be concerned about a private negative evaluation of self as inferior, inadequate, or bad. Reactions may involve feelings of anger, disgust, or contempt towards oneself and possibly wishing to shrink away from this notion.

External shame leads the therapist to be concerned about being viewed as inferior, inadequate, or bad by an actually present other, usually the patient. Reactions may involve fearing exposure to anger, contempt, ridicule, or disregard, and wishing to appease, cover up, or hide. If feeling shamed by an important, but currently *absent* other, reactions may also include wishing to conform or comply.

Counselling is eager to establish its position and reputation as a profession. It has key values about personal development, human fallibility, and the potential for growth that arises from errors. Yet, complaints or law-suits might arise from any mistake. Complaints may provide a spur to personal or professional development, if the person complained against is supported appropriately. The feelings are overwhelmingly strong, often combining some mix of shame, shock, anger, self-blame, outrage, fear, hurt, self-doubt, confusion, or guilt. It is one thing to explore "how I might have done something differently" if there are no fears attached to the process of exploring; quite another if the repercussions are dire for a professional reputation or employment.

Complaints

The working context has changed significantly over my working lifetime in the last thirty years, with a culture of complaints and litigation becoming more intrusive. Professional organizations have responded in part by clarifying ethical frameworks, tightening up complaints procedures, and writing information sheets. BACP offers some that relate to the potential for complaints and lay down the legal and professional bases for practice. In 2008 these included *Confidentiality, Counselling and the Law* (G2), *Access to Counsellor Records* (G1), *Making Notes of Counselling and Psychotherapy Sessions* (P12), *Confidential Guidelines for Reporting Child Abuse* (E6), *Making a Contract for Counselling and Psychotherapy* (P11), and *Contingency Plans if Personal Crises Impact on Independent Practice* (P14). Professional organizations and professional liability insurers offer legal and professional help-lines to advise members.

I see at least five circumstances or stages of a professional life when a practitioner might feel particularly vulnerable to experiencing a fear of complaints. These are listed below.

- When in training or inexperienced, and therefore having some difficulty in identifying ethical dilemmas or whether the client is too complex for this stage of development.
- When working beyond competence at any stage of development, for reasons of ignorance, arrogance, theoretical blinkers, organizational or financial pressure.
- Working when too vulnerable. This risk has been exhaustively explored.
- When offering new methodologies learned recently, without appropriate supervision or thoughtful integration into existing practice and approaches. Specifically, after attending short courses, or reading about new ways to work, working in a new way without fully appreciating necessary safeguards or seeking specialist supervision within that framework (Jeffrey, 2008).
- Working when too old or too professionally isolated. Being out of professional networks can lead to failure to keep up to date with current practice imperatives, norms, or changing contexts. Not reading journals or participating in professional meetings may all contribute to isolation. Fears of one's own existential state can mean continuing to see clients or supervisees to hang on to a familiar sense of identity past the point when it might be wiser to stop.

All of the five circumstances above share similar themes. The practitioner is not aware of his or her lack of knowledge, skill, or ability to create and sustain an appropriate, boundaried, therapeutic alliance. In one sense, we are all only a hair's breadth away from a complaint, and most that occur arise because of these sorts of difficulties rather than malign intentions to malpractice.

For both supervisors and counsellors, the early years of practice are when they most need containment from experienced colleagues, often on the hoof or down the phone at the point a difficulty is identified. If they work in private practice at this stage, they might have the advantages of setting up more easily than by finding employment, but, being young in the role, they might not seek or get sufficient informal support.

Accounts about complaints

Hewson (2008, pp. 37–39) writes about her experience as a supervisor when a supervisee was complained about. She valued her supervision of supervision to get a new perspective on the issues involved, and then realized she and the supervisee had been unaware of protectively colluding, the supervisee with one member of the couple being seen, Hewson with her supervisee. Reflecting on the grain of truth in the complaint through her supervision then enabled her to help the supervisee to approach the complaints procedure less defensively.

Daniels' research (2000) was based on seven semi-structured interviews with supervisors. She raised useful issues about ambiguities in supervisor accountability, and how a supervisor and the profession can deal with mistakes. She was writing before the current BACP ethical framework was developed, but reminded readers that in theory any mistake can be the subject of a complaint.

Traynor (2007) provides a practice-based, person-centred review of complaints and the supervisor's potential to support the person complained against. The supervisory focus might be on thinking or feeling, or how they are interacting during the ups and downs of long drawn out, debilitating, and time-consuming processes. Modelling of the person-centred approach is important to Traynor. She contrasts the adversarial process of complaints with what the supervisor can offer through open and non-defensive exploration of the personal and professional issues involved to elicit the professional development potential of the experience. Pragmatic arrangements for greater supervisor availability might be needed, and supervision could provide a space to review and think through possibly competing guidance from multiple sources. Her description of "thinking whilst feeling under emotional siege and a professional cloud" captures the process well. Power issues can include feeling misjudged by people from other theoretical modalities.

Injustice and feeling unfairly pursued

A group of Australian women psychologists met regularly to examine narratives they had written about memories of gender differences (Crawford, Kippax, Onyx, Gault, & Benton, 1992). I was most struck by their chapter entitled "Saying sorry and being sorry". In it, they recall childhood experiences of being required to "say sorry", and, to their surprise, they discovered that every one of them had felt that the requirement to apologize was unfair because it had been based on implicit rules of which they had not been aware. They explored inadvertent social transgressions, for which saying sorry appeared to be the necessary step to restoring the existing web of social relationships. Exploring stories of these transgressions further, they discovered early stories that involved two patterns: defiance about injustice, or mortification, shame, and guilt. Punishment was by chastisement or public shaming. Some accepted the punishment and introjected the rule; some accepted the punishment but did not feel guilt. Some rejected the punishment and the adult's definition of their actions and felt angry and misunderstood. This is a rich exploration that provokes thought about the parallel ways that counselling practitioners respond to complaints as professionals, and the role that feelings such as shame, guilt, or indignation about being falsely accused can play when practitioners face complaints.

Casemore (1999) described feedback to the BAC complaints panel that their procedure was perceived principally as punitive by members, and asked, "Why can't we own our mistakes when an apology is really what many complainants seek". That might suffice in relation to mistakes, and even poor practice, if not for negligence or malpractice. He reminded readers that possibly the professional indemnity insurers might have had a role in discouraging admissions of fault. His book (2001) is useful in relation to complaints and professional bodies.

Complaints against supervisors

A recent audit by BACP of 142 complaints over a ten-year period (1996–2006) (Khele, Symons, & Wheeler, 2008) found eighty-four went to full hearings, twelve of which were about supervisors (Figure 1).

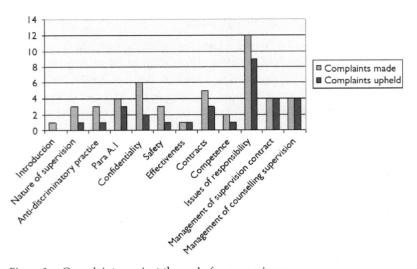

Figure 1. Complaints against the code for supervisors.

In general, more men were complained against, but the authors did not identify the gender of the supervisors involved in this review. During this period, the original BAC codes of ethics were in use.

> As with the Code of Counsellors, the greatest number of complaints (12, representing 25%) were made under "issues of responsibility". These clauses include requirements that supervisors help their supervisees to reflect critically upon their work, help their supervisees recognise when their work might be impaired due to personal difficulties, and take responsibility for setting and maintaining the boundaries between the supervisory relationship and any other professional relationships. The greatest proportion of upheld complaints were in the broad area of "management of work", where all complaints brought were upheld. These clauses include the requirements for supervisors to make explicit arrangements regarding fees and frequency of contact and for supervisees to acknowledge their individual responsibility for ongoing professional development. [p. 128]

Complaints procedures and supervisor responsibility

Angry clients may easily frighten a counsellor that they might complain. Reports of complaints proceedings and their impact on the individuals involved make clear that it is an onerous business for all participants. On the two occasions when I have heard complaints on behalf of BACP, I have been clear in my own mind that inexperienced practitioners were working beyond their competence and that the supervisor involved had been influential and complicit in the decisions about what to do, but had totally escaped the formal process of the complaint. This did not seem fair to me. Indeed, paradoxically, the more conscientious a student or recent graduate was in keeping notes and transcripts, the more data was revealed about the limits of their competence. Yet, in the early stages, few practitioners are fully aware of what is too difficult for them. Conversations between experienced practitioners looking back on their early days are almost always accompanied by the feeling that they were lucky not to have had a complaint made by some client. One nub seems to be how to support counsellors in their early work without too much or too little interference. Skills in assessment, habits of audio-taping, and live supervision could all play a part, but often do not.

I recommend that readers look at the BACP information sheet P12 (2008e), on making notes of counselling and psychotherapy sessions, that quotes ethical and legal requirements, and some problematic issues in note-taking.

Supervisor notes and records

I write notes *during* supervision, to help me keep clear about the points being made, and emerging themes. These are always available to the supervisee. I review them periodically to consider the whole piece of work reported with a long-term client, or in preparation for reviews. This was essential when I was taking memory impairing painkillers, because it ensured that, although my functioning was impaired, the jottings brought back more detailed recall from one session to the next and over a period of months.

My format is simple:

Date of supervision	Supervisee name	Clients or themes and supervisory comments

Walker and Jacobs (2004) have a very clear section (pp. 69–74) outlining differing formats for supervisor notes, based on a running log of specific clients discussed. In every case they separate "material presented" and "issues addressed". They also propose a structure for notes to be brought by the supervisee. For group supervision, this is to be copied for all present. This records the date the client was first seen, the contract, presenting issues, how the client relates in sessions, significant relationships and life events, and when presented for supervision. There is also a column for supervisor's remarks, thus encouraging the supervisee to record anything she finds useful from the supervisory exchange.

Issues about ownership of such records when a supervisor is working for an agency are complex. In my view, *process* records are always the property of the person who has made them, and they do not form part of an official file. If specific clients or patients of an agency are discussed, it is important for the supervisor *not* to record the person's name or full initials, so that they are not accessible under the Data Protection Act, or access to personal records processes. As far as the supervisee may be concerned, if he or she is also an employee of the same agency, there may well be legitimate requirements for the organization to check that the person is attending supervision, and the supervisor can send in to the administration a summary of dates of meetings, but that is all that is required. The notes may serve to construct an appraisal report, but the notes themselves should not, I think, be available to anyone except the participants involved, except after careful and explicit negotiated agreement.

Release of notes to other bodies

Most counsellors and supervisors are reluctant to release notes to courts without seeking all possible alternatives. Most do so very rarely, and only at the client's explicit request, with prior consent and review. Some send in a report, to the criminal injuries compensation board, for instance, or a housing department.

I have worked with counsellors in primary care about how to summarize their work for the patient's file, and each comes to their own conclusion, but all agree it needs to attend to the competing demands of being appropriate to the client's difficulties, useful to the GP or other colleagues, sensitive to the personality and trustworthiness of those with legitimate access to it, and minimally revealing of personal detail. Technically, I believe patients should be informed of what goes on to their health record. Temporarily, some counsellors will put a Post-it note into the patient's file when they are actively suicidal, so that any colleague involved in contact between counselling sessions will know of the patient's state, and this can then be taken off the file by the counsellor when the period of extreme distress has passed, with no permanent record to influence future medical or insurance reports.

Supervisor responsibility

Counsellor training courses have a responsibility to prepare students for supervision, and ensure that all students who pass are *able* and, at least in principle, willing to reflect on themselves and their work in supervision.

The supervisor needs to be explicit about what responsibility s/he takes for the work of the counsellor, and this may depend on stage of supervisee development, employment contracts, and the context for the work. However, there is also the supervisor's "duty of care" to the supervisee (Jenkins, 2006). Good supervision is an emotional, as well as an intellectual, process.

Supervisor training courses need to give a priority to helping trainee supervisors to make thorough and well-negotiated initial contracts with supervisees, to articulate boundaries, and to learn about how to discuss supervisee behaviour when it is problematic, without attacking the self-worth of the person. This is easier said than done, and requires some attention to increased professional self-awareness so that the "internal supervisor" of the novice supervisor can increase sensitivity to the impact of their supervisory style on different supervisees.

As the BACP ethical framework indicates, there are rarely clearcut answers to ethical dilemmas. Supervisors and supervisees need compassion, courage, openness, knowledge, and experience to confront mistakes, and good communication skills to survive them. Every time a supervisee faces a complaint, the supervisor needs to consider what his or her role might have been that contributed to the problem. Then, laying that shame or guilt aside, consider what role is most useful to support the supervisee to learn from the painful process.

CHAPTER THIRTEEN

Giving references and writing reports

"It takes a diplomatic use of language to indicate that a strength may also be a weakness, and an intuitive ability is absolutely essential to foresee the development of potential into actuality, or what is commonly called the blossoming factor"

(Mander, 2002, p. 43)

It is not easy to form a fair view of an individual that takes into account interactions of their confidence and competence, and the standards required of them at each stage of their development and working practice. Some issues of power and collegiality, transparency and integrity are implicit in the processes of writing about supervisees. A report writer can choose to be either explicit or ambiguous. Putting pen to paper on behalf of another is an opportunity to endorse their work wholeheartedly, or face moral dilemmas about how honest and specific to be about reservations.

Supervisors complete many references and reports for trainees, or those about to undertake further training, seek a job, or apply for accreditation or, until recently, re-accreditation. In reality, referring clients to a supervisee is also an active form of reference, reflecting a good opinion of their practice. Some organizations involve supervisors in annual appraisals of supervisees that are then used within the organization for planning training or considering the future of the counsellor and the organization. Writing a letter of support when a supervisee has been complained against is also an invitation to contribute to accountability in the profession. I have been surprised to discover that some supervisors charge for many of these reports. It seems to me to be part of the core role of the supervisor to supply such written feedback to and about the supervisee when requested.

Even in peer groups, occasions arise that require references, and there are unique dilemmas here because of differences in the nature of the relationships.

The sociological concept of "sponsored mobility", where a patron or mentor promotes progress and provides opportunities for development, is relevant. Some people seek supervision from a locally well-established supervisor, or one who works on a training course so that the likelihood of getting clients from him or her is increased, and the supervisor's reputation can be used to imply approval of the counsellor.

It is good practice to show any reference to the supervisee, either before sending it, or at least when they next meet. Even better, invite the supervisee to write a self appraisal that can be used as a basis for discussion about their readiness to practise, to be accredited, to join a training, and so on. This increases collegiality, and supports the autonomy required of practitioners. At least in an ideal world, either party can discuss any differences of perception identified in this process, and each should be able to identify examples from which they can ground their comments.

Reports about trainees

A supervisor of a trainee has to offer fairness and optimism about development, to encourage the trainee as their competence and confidence develops, and yet also aim to protect clients from unaware disastrous practice if possible. Thus, a report has to identify what the trainee can already do well enough, and what s/he needs to develop further in order to pass the practice element of a qualifying or post qualification training. It refers to previously identified criteria for practice if the course has supplied any. Reports referring to micro-skills analysis, and feedback about observed practice, have most weight because they can be specific, and especially with tapes of sessions, particular exchanges can be reviewed for comment. Feedback can then form a basis for agreed targets or aims for development. I find trainees generally are not good at identifying what their next steps may be, so some form of summary of expected skills and competences offers useful prompts. More complex issues arise as trainers or supervisors wrestle to find words to give feedback about trainees' professional development issues arising from a lack of capacity to recover from training experiences that create a splitting response, and threaten their sense of internal stability.

Page and Wosket (2001) advocate the writing of a "joint learning statement", negotiated between both supervisor and supervisee to mirror the collegiality of the relationship, and to make a summative report arise from a formative series of points of review. Where a difference of opinion is not resolvable, either party can add a note to this effect. They describe a supervisor working with a trainee who found it difficult to bear client distress, and the form of words that allowed a respectful but clear boundary to be set that either the trainee engage in some personal counselling, or that he should not do counselling work that required catharsis. By being specific and descriptive, a report pointed the way for future development and signposted the alternatives for the course to consider at the end of the training if there were no change.

Conveying supervisor observations by naming an issue as a developmental edge is an encouraging option. Another is to acknowledge some mismatch of personality or style and share the responsibility for a difficulty in creating a working alliance.

Inskipp and Proctor (1995) offer the following list as an example of what a trainee might be expected to do: make an appropriate contract with the client; develop and maintain a counselling relationship; do the work; develop self awareness; manage their own values and professional and personal development; understand how to work in an agency or as a freelance counsellor; develop referral processes and an information bank; and convey their capacity to give an account of their work and monitor, record, and evaluate it (p. 110). This list reminds me how much there is to grasp early on. It is like riding a bike; once one can do something, it is really easy to forget the developmental steps necessary to master the skills.

Wheeler (2001) describes development of practice through feedback on a course from course staff, peers, clients, or trainees themselves, as well as the supervisor. Obviously, the supervisor can benefit from exploring the supervisee's self-assessment in a supervision session, as they have a shared experience to call on. Wheeler provides an example of the form for supervisor evaluation of student performance used by the University of Birmingham (pp. 141–143). This covers clinical insight, clinical practice, and counsellor self-development. Each item within a section is marked from one to ten and an overall score is computed with a required pass mark. Scoring systems are transparent, but seem difficult to calibrate fairly between assessors in such subjective interpersonal assessments. Somehow, numbers seem harsher to me than words, so I would jib against them and be glad of the supervisor's comments that accompany them. That course used a trial run of the form half-way through the year, so there was an opportunity for formative assessment and to get to grips with it.

Robiner, Saltzman, Hoberman, Semrud-Clikeman, and Schirvar (1997) noted tendencies for individual supervisors idiosyncratically to demonstrate a leniency bias, strictness bias, or a central tendency bias (not to use the whole numerical range) on ratings of trainees. Strictness bias tends to indicate problems with the supervisor's unrealistic standards or displaced personal frustrations. Their discussion of the role of the supervisor in assessing personal and professional development of the supervisee (pp. 83–84) notes the importance of the supervisee's openness and their capacity for self care rather than defensiveness. The supervisee inspires more confidence when "their personal issues that can block their understanding or communication with others are available for exploration".

Reports can also help trainees to create shared intentions for focus and further reflection in supervision. A trainee can experience such reports as enabling, or as a warning about barely adequate practice. It behoves the supervisor to clarify their intentions, and if a big signpost or "shot across the bows" is intended, that it can be offered with additional information about how to work more effectively in the future. If it is more than that, and the supervisor has come to think that the trainee should not pass a course, it is important to take courage, bite the bullet, and initiate discussions with the supervisee and the course or placement at as early a stage as is fair. Being human, it is often only at the point at which a review or appraisal takes place against given criteria that nagging doubts crystallize, and the supervisor faces the reality of what they have to say and do.

Some counsellor training courses allow for extra experience, perhaps supervised by a different supervisor in order for the trainee to reach an adequate standard, and this seems fair if there have been problems in gaining a range of experience, or there are professional developmental problems or difficulties in the supervisory relationship. The hardest task comes when, at each yearly review, the trainee is given feedback about what they have to achieve to pass, and they *just* do so, but do not sustain it, or develop further. I think that the supervisor should not be left to carry the decision to fail a trainee alone.

Accreditation references

A request to give a reference for counsellor accreditation is more like a job reference, in that it needs to cover specified criteria. An example from my files shows how a relationship of mutual respect is conveyed pragmatically with many specifics:

> I have been C's supervisor since 1994, and we have met twice monthly to 6 weekly in that time, depending on her other commitments and supervisory support and mine.
>
> Criterion 7.1 and 10.1: I was her supervisor whilst she completed her post qualifying Diploma in Counselling at X University. I am aware she is currently undertaking supervision training with Y.
>
> Criterion 4: She has worked in primary care as a counsellor throughout this period. Initially she worked as a counsellor in X practices. Now as initiator of a managed counselling service, she provides counselling herself and introduces and supervises others in several practices. She has also sustained her private practice throughout this period.

Criterion 8: She works effectively as a primary care counsellor. She is willing to make flexible contracts, which work to the averages and norms of 6 sessions in primary care, but with the support of the GPs she often provides long term counselling support to people for whom no other available local service exists. She has been very creative in developing structures such as regular but infrequent counselling after initial work, which assist people with major difficulties to continue to cope. She manages a big waiting list effectively, and is willing, should clients wish for it, to liaise with the GPs in the client's interest or to provide an integrated package of care. The local Community Mental Health team and psychiatric service work collaboratively with her, and often refer patients back to her.

Her case study demonstrates how she works, and I confirm that it represents her work to my knowledge. I have heard a tape of her counselling, some years ago when she was on the course, and confirm that her description of her work fitted with the tape. She offers an unusual mix of client-centredness with strong use of imagery and a capacity to reflect on it afterwards using a variety of theoretical insights. She is highly approachable, and works in depth to good effect.

Criterion 9: She makes positive use of supervision. Her openness to it allows her to take learning into her client work and her working context. We have discussed many ethical dilemmas over the years, and she is willing to explore mistakes or difficulties and to take action if necessary and possible. Recently we discussed the issues arising from police pressure to provide her counselling notes for a court case.

I think she is a sound and accreditable practitioner, and recommend her.

What this reference does not confront is that this practitioner routinely overworked. I decided not to introduce this as a reservation to an accreditation document because there was no specific invitation to comment on counsellor self-care. It was not something we ducked in supervision. Along with a number of other supervisees, it was constantly on the agenda, and their practice habits slowly shifted with age and health and an acknowledgement that they were doing themselves too much harm. In retrospect, I think mine may be a common protective response, and one that makes the tasks of accreditation much more difficult for the professional body. It is always difficult to be sure when a supervisee uses supervision to "collapse" and to focus on what is not going well, that their work is indeed still of an adequate standard. My own standard is that I ask myself three questions.

Would I send a loved one to this person?
What would they get from this counsellor?
What might my reservations be?

If I would not send a loved one to them as they normally function, I do not wish to supervise them, or refer clients to them.

What the request implies about the relationship

When a reference is requested, it implies that the supervisee believes the supervisor will support the endeavour that requires the reference, or that the supervisee is required by a system to ask this supervisor. If the latter, the reference can cause a widening split if the two do not get on and it contributes to a disappointing outcome. A number of trainees have sought informal help from BACP about course supervisors or placement practice supervisors whom they felt have been unfair to them. It can be very difficult for the trainee to feel they have a fair hearing on a course when other staff will not engage and offer help with their difficult relationships with a tutor or supervisor. Course or professional organization complaints procedures do not always suffice. This is when the hierarchy and potential for abuse of power can be painfully experienced. The other side of this is that those trainees who lack insight about their own personal difficulties might avoid or refuse to accept the feedback they consider inaccurate or persecutory, even when it comes from more than one person. The bottom line is that the formal system has the final word.

What the request demands in terms of honesty and plain speaking

The writing of reports is a major developmental step for many new supervisors, and relates to their capacity to take their authority in the relationship and hold clear and explicit standards of practice in a matter of fact way. The skills of speaking and writing plainly and descriptively about what is uncomfortable are required. This gets harder as the supervisee becomes more experienced, and the supervisory pair or group meet for longer, because the collegial nature of the relationship can at times make it more difficult to express ambivalence and reservations.

When there are *no* reservations, there may be some laziness or mutual idealization, since, for the most part, people have strengths and weaknesses, and those strengths that are overdone may well create problematic practice at times.

When there are reservations, it is important that the reference is not the first time that these are expressed. The request is often a prompt to have a conversation that needed to be had anyway. One example of a reference I gave that triggered a difficulty arose because I had not spoken of my discomfort earlier on when a colleague withdrew from work she had undertaken to do. I later put mixed messages into a reference, and compounded this by sending it off before showing it to her first, and this greatly upset her. I realized when we disentangled our feelings and opinions later that we had differing perceptions about her withdrawal from the work, and that this had upset my view of her as very reliable. My acting out is undesirable, and suggests I had a lot to learn about confronting difficulties. I am not alone in this. I discuss the impact of my own emerging learning on this through supervision in Chapter Six.

Offering affirmation and useful encouragement

Some supervisees only really believe that their supervisor has a good opinion of them when they see it written down for the purposes of accreditation, a reference, or a course application. When they lack self-confidence, it can be a useful vehicle for discussion to write such a report as part of an annual review, whether or not any outside person wishes to see it. Ideally, the supervisee should prepare a self-report, too, so that the exchange of information can identify points of agreement and differences of perception. A supervisor could use the same opportunity to *seek* feedback on what needs to change to make the supervision more useful. I have had few supervisors who have routinely remembered to ask me for feedback, and very few supervisees who offered it unasked.

One supervisee asked me to write her a general reference when I retired, and I found myself thinking about what I had gained from the relationship, and wanting to add that into the equation explicitly like this:

> Our supervision has been a huge source of learning for me too. I initially supported her after previous supervision bordering on professional malpractice, and she came very slowly into a fuller awareness of her ability as a skilful practitioner. We both learned through the challenges and support needed around her practice and ethical issues. We learned "to speak the unspoken" in this supervisory relationship to our mutual benefit, and developed the use of creative methods in supervision.
>
> She has been an enthusiastic companion to my development, too, usually willing to try out or respond to my latest enthusiasms, with the specific exception of my preferred administrative systems to underpin supervision.

Even very experienced, capable, and confident people benefit from affirmation and feedback about how they are seen by colleagues. Our profession is a lonely one, and working with diffi-cult emotions and stuck feelings can engender anxiety about compe-tence in all of us, however experienced. The encouragement of a detailed review can contribute to clarity about skills or abilities the supervisee might take for granted, or be unaware that they possess.

One respondent in my current research with experienced prac-titioners noted:

> Latterly as part of a research project I have received very direct feedback on my work and its impact anonymously, both from clients and colleagues and this has had an uplifting and affirming effect, which has been unexpectedly gratifying and validating of what is otherwise often lonely work.

Conveying ambivalent feelings or active concerns

Courage is required to say uncomfortable things, and it is the mark of an experienced supervisor that they neither avoid the issue nor put it off.

Cultural sensitivity and awareness of difference is crucial. Opportunities to behave oppressively peak under these circumstances. Generosity is also useful, and I eventually learned to notice when my compassion or general acceptance wore thin, and used this as a trigger for reflection, supervision, and exploration with the supervisee prior to taking any action.

Giving references as a member of a peer group

It might not be obvious which member of a peer group should write a report. Alliances need to be acknowledged, and ideally the applicant and all the members might brainstorm what might go in. However, it can be that dual relationships locally create extra complications.

In the peer group I was in for thirteen years, there was, at times, some uncomfortable awkwardness when one member was applying for work in the domain of another. One was interviewed by her peer and rejected initially for a job share post, and accepted later for another, both for clear reasons, but none the less uncomfortable for the individuals. It says a lot for the commitment of all members, and especially of the two caught up in the recruitment processes, that this degree of discomfort could be tolerated and endured for the sake of the benefits of the group as a whole without either member feeling she had to leave, or with the rest of us splitting on one "side" or the other, even though one other group member had supplied a reference. It says a lot, too, for the applicant that she expressed no resentment when the job share plan was not successful, though she did express disappointment within the group. Of course, it meant that some things could not be brought to the group in these times, particularly for the interviewing member, so other supervision for her was very important.

At various times, we gave references for each other, and in one case one member was eventually line-managed by another. In the end, this did mean there were both extra intimacies for some pairs and some difficulties and things that could not be said. In such circumstances, it is very important to attend to the underlying feelings, and give space to talk about and review the assumptions people are making, and the perceptions about behaviour or alliances that need to be confirmed or clarified. These sorts of dual relationships can be more common when counsellors seek peer supervision as they are becoming more experienced practitioners in their local area. Outside the big cities, there are relatively few counselling jobs available, so competition arises or complications occur.

Reflections

As this book demonstrates, habits of recording are very useful for later reflection. Notes need to be full enough to serve the purpose. In general, as an independent supervisor, I think of the notes I keep as my baseline resource for references, appraisals, re-accreditation submissions, and our shared reviews. Thus, they form the *aide memoire* to recall what we have discussed, and, as I always look at them before a session, they prompt some key points of preparation between one session and another.

CHAPTER FOURTEEN

Becoming more experienced as a supervisor

"Then she began to tell me a story about an old man who is walking along a beach at low tide, picking up starfish drying in the sun and gently throwing them back into the ocean. He has been doing this for some time when a jogger overtakes him and asks him what he is doing. The old man explains that the starfish will die in the sun and so he is throwing them back into the ocean. Astounded, the young man begins to laugh: 'Why, old fellow, don't waste your time. Can't you see there are hundreds and hundreds of starfish on this beach? And thousands of beaches in this world? And another low tide tomorrow? What makes you think you can make a difference?' And still laughing, he runs on down the beach.

The old man looks after him for a long while. Then he walks on and before long passes another starfish. Stooping, he picks it up and looks at it thoughtfully. Then, gently, he throws it back into the ocean. 'Made a difference to that one,' he says to himself"

(Remen, 2000, pp. 273–274)

Supervisors advertise themselves as experienced after supervising for between three years and twenty, according to experienced supervisors participating in a workshop about the topic. Many people survive a critical incident, and at this point claim to be experienced because they have learnt from it. Within this span of years, some common career developments occur. The balance of time spent on supervising may change, as more people seek supervision with a supervisor who develops a reputation. There may be extensions of experience from one-to-one to group supervision, or between supervising, training, or consulting. Special interests and expertise may emerge, about a context, a client group, a problem, or a modality. With experience and confidence might come more clarity about role, task, functions, and boundaries. Increasingly, as more post-graduate courses have become available, some experienced practitioners will now decide to take a further degree, and do some research in the process. Invitations to be part of working groups in a professional body or a local context might increase.

A self-concept as a senior practitioner emerges. If intending to work beyond 2011 s/he might have sought accreditation as a counsellor to prepare for the requirements of regulation. Some also are accredited as supervisors, though this makes no difference to freedom to practise in the role, as there are no regulatory plans in prospect in 2009 to make supervision a designated term. S/he also has to learn to monitor energy levels and accept that these might decline with age, though some people continue to practise well into their eighties, or, more rarely, into their nineties. Specifically, s/he has to decide how she will make a difference in the working time that is left.

Balancing the workload between counselling and supervising

Little has been published about average caseloads for supervisors, and there are big differences depending whether the work is one-to-one or in groups, and depending on the balance of work between counselling, supervising, training, and consulting. Half of the eighty respondents so far in my research about the work and careers of experienced practitioners see supervisees for nine hours or less per month, and a quarter work as supervisors for over twenty hours. I did not ask them to differentiate between one-to-one and group supervision. Group supervisors will hold in mind many supervisees, and their clients.

Between my third and tenth year as a supervisor, I saw ten to twelve supervisees individually, and supervised some over many years. I saw most monthly, and a few fortnightly. For agencies, I would mentally set a limit of fifty sessions that, meeting fortnightly, would offer a supervisory relationship for two years, or, if meeting monthly, for four. A change of supervisor after two years was desirable for them and for me at that stage, as these were generally inexperienced counsellors at the start, getting hours towards accreditation, and I wanted them to have varying experiences of supervision. Some agencies required or pressed for a change every two years.

Latterly, I have combined some training for supervisors, some supervision of supervision groups for graduates of this training, and a tiny practice one-to-one. The balance has shifted because I wanted to work less regularly, and also because I became more interested in the potential for creative work within group supervision.

Long-term supervisory relationships

In my private practice, I had a small number of women who stayed with me for more than ten years. I think significant age and gender issues created this pattern. They liked my style, my relational emphasis, my patterns of thought, my more established interest in brief therapy and primary health care, and my knowledge of local contexts.

In the experienced practitioners research, I have discovered that long supervisory relationships are by no means unusual. The longest described so far has lasted for twenty-two years, and more than ten years is quite common. Many experienced practitioners stay with the same supervisor or same peer group because there are few options in rural areas and small towns, and, as years go by, few are more experienced than they are. This is satisfying and delightful, of course, but it means these practitioners are not exposing their work to supervision by more recently trained supervisors, who might well be more aware of equality and diversity thinking, for instance, and the pressures of current working contexts.

Developing specific expertise

As interests develop, reputations grow around these. I capitalized on my initial training as a sociologist, and the outline curriculum I developed for counselling in primary care (Henderson, 2006), to develop my thinking and understanding about attending to the organizational context and culture. Because I then had five supervisees working in nine different GP surgeries, I had a lot of direct experience to base this on (Henderson, 1997). When I wrote a chapter about supervising in medical settings, relatively few supervisors of counsellors had direct experience of this context. Few had knowledge or skills in time-limited therapy. The norm was to attend in supervision to casework and not to contextual or "managerial" elements such as the waiting list or multi-disciplinary team relationships, or the "sink or swim" culture of most medical settings (Curtis Jenkins, 2001).

Under the aegis of the Counselling in Primary Care Trust, I also organized a research project to connect supervision in primary care to the generic research base of supervision (Burton, Henderson, & Curtis Jenkins, 1998; Curtis Jenkins, 2001). Mary Burton, who did the bibliographic base work in 1996, discovered sixty books and 161 articles and book chapters, but she only considered sixteen items relevant to primary care, and most were American, where medicine operates under different organizational models.

This bibliographic summary thus had similar lessons to the two scoping research summaries later prepared by Wheeler (2003) and Wheeler and Richards (2007) about supervision research: much research has been done, largely in the USA, but the methodology and application to practice is problematic.

A conference for invited supervisors experienced in primary care supervision met to debate the results of Burton and her colleagues' research, and this led to a booklet with contributions by participants. The booklet was designed to offer a new model, describe the research, propose suitable contracts for supervision in primary care, consider the impact of the context, propose specialist training, and publish the research bibliography (Curtis Jenkins & Henderson, 1997). Within ten years, one participant had co-created another specialist professional organization that offered, among many other elements, a specialist training for supervisors in primary care. Graham Curtis Jenkins had the energy and vision to support these developments, and the funding that the Counselling in Primary Care Trust supplied through the Artemis Trust enabled the work to happen in a time when other funds were unavailable. Such patrons and mentors are rare jewels.

Some development towards more authentic practice

Deciding *not* to take on a supervisee is a rite of passage. At first, most novice supervisors are hungry enough that they take on those who approach them who seem within their competence as supervisors. As confidence develops and the pressures for more experience reduce, the supervisor's needs and preferences can come more into play. Standards and ethics loom large, too. It is always worrying to supervise work by a practitioner whom the supervisor does not trust.

Over the years, two people have begun with me, as counsellors in private practice, whose training or practice I felt too anxious about to continue to supervise. One was the product of a poor local training. He had not been well trained about appropriate boundaries and dual roles, or the current limits of his competence, and was seeking his clients inappropriately from his other work role. I told him in our second session that I did not want to continue beyond our next session. He listened well and was hurt, but responded congruently in a way I did find reassuring, but not enough to change my mind. My increasing experience and courage in owning my own feelings and perceptions without blame paid some dividends in our exchange. With the benefit of hindsight, and more experience, I could have worked with him, because he was willing to come half-way to meet me.

I came to acknowledge that my tolerance for disorganized supervisees was too low to make it useful for me to work with them. If people forgot to come, forgot to bring diaries or to pay, on more than a few occasions, I would become too irritated to be generous in my responses. I would enquire what it might be signalling about our relationship or point out implications for their approach to their clients, and either they would change, fail to make further arrangements, or we would agree to end.

Becoming interested in triangles of difference

As individuals with unique characteristics and personal histories, client, counsellor, and supervisor will bring salient differences, and, in any particular circumstance, one member of the triangle might feel "ganged up on" by the other two. The supervisor's position, based on a combination of sources of power, means that most of us behave oppressively at times, and so all of us have to be willing to talk about difference and our own mistakes. Hawkins and Shohet (2006) describe the accumulated power of the supervisor arising from role, culture, and personality. It could include role and status, experience and expertise, the values and beliefs of the dominant culture or organizational sub-culture, and personality or charisma.

Because of supervisee deference and the power imbalance between supervisor and supervisee, many factors of diversity or membership of the dominant majority in terms of race and culture can *combine* to create potential for oppressive behaviour. In supervisor training, it becomes clear that the meaning of the differences to each party is revealed only when differences between supervisor and supervisee are named and the potential implications discussed. Attitudes to difference are so pervaded by the superiority–inferiority dynamic that useful risk and safety in supervision are compromised without such conversations. Research (e.g., Granello, 1996) about differing conversational styles of men and women suggests potential complications and misunderstandings as men and women may give instructions or feedback with differing emphasis.

Becoming more cross-culturally aware

American research (Bernard & Goodyear, 2004) shocked me into more coherent reflection by reporting that experienced supervisors are likely to be less aware of important difference and diversity issues than more recently trained supervisees. I also had to think this through because I was offering training in supervision. I needed to read and reflect a great deal about the issues, examining roots of my assumptions and beliefs in my own development of identity (Henderson, 2008).

For supervision of every supervisee, and especially if the supervisor thinks s/he is a member of any oppressed group, Gautney's injunction (1994) is sound:

> The advice I am about to give is strictly from the perspective of a lesbian supervisee to supervisors: bring it up. Talk about it. Whether your supervisee or her clients are heterosexual or homosexual, sexual orientation is a relevant issue that may be avoided unless you attend to it. Take the responsibility, because you probably have less to risk than your supervisees. And if your supervisee is gay or lesbian, believe me, they are already thinking about it. [1994, p.7]

Davies and Neal (1996) discuss "cultural filters" relevant to sexual orientation that supervisors or supervisees may use. These include joking, hostility, stereotyping, denial, pity, exaggerating the significance of the client's sexual orientation, or ignoring the impact of life within a rejecting society. They describe a supervisee who has to inform his supervisor exactly what "cottaging" means, (using public toilets as meeting places for brief sexual encounters) while feeling anxious that too clear and detailed an explanation might reveal his own sexual preferences and experiences. Supervisors, as well as counsellors, need to review and monitor their assumptions, interpretations, and knowledge of sub-cultural norms.

Gender issues

Many experienced practitioners function reflectively, thinking about the work directly, and then generalizing more extensively, and, if possible, creating changes in practice from reflection. They might not call this research, but it has that commitment to testing tacit knowledge that is the basis of action research.

For example, in 1993–1994, I undertook a local and small-scale mini "action learning" research project with two counsellors, a male and a female, as they were beginning to work together in the same surgery, to look at induction into the surgery, and the impact of gender within their roles over the first year of their work. This project was a collaborative enterprise, and when our five tape-recorded reflective meetings were over, and we had analysed referral and audit patterns for the year, I wrote and we discussed a summary of the themes that had emerged. They then shared this summary with the GPs who changed their referral practice as a result.

This research project discovered interesting patterns of referral within that single GP practice. These revealed how unaware and multi-layered assumptions can affect workload and practice. The male and female counsellors worked for four male and four female GPs and were expected to work the same number of hours. However, it soon became apparent that the female counsellor was overwhelmed with work. It turned out that the female GPs referred more patients than the male GPs, 80% of the patients referred were female, they more often sought the female counsellor, and the female patients on average stayed longer than the males, even within a six session average norm.

Her first solution was a personally generous and also, to my mind, a gendered response. She booked more patients in than the hours she was contracted to do, on the assumption that some would not attend. She was flexible about her time, so if a patient did not attend, she would use that time for admin, or to liaise with colleagues, or to take a break, and then stay an extra hour. This seems like classic female care behaviour, as described by Gilligan (1982), though it was also because she had been a nurse before training as a counsellor and had a teamwork attitude in relation to the primary care service as a whole.

There are a number of thought-provoking American studies about the impact of gender on supervision, although, because they are normally about supervision of trainees and set in a different culture, care is essential before generalizing from them. Anderson, Schlossberg, and Rigazio-DiGilio (2000) asked supervisees (mainly female ones) about their best and worst experiences of supervision. While "best" supervisors were equally likely to be male or female, two thirds of the "worst" were male, who were described as having a less relational focus. This is a problem that implies a need to teach about bridging styles (see Chapter Three on emotional climates).

Nelson and Holloway (1990) deconstruct the conversational styles of a male and female supervisor to illustrate nuanced gendered differences of approach to conversation and interaction in male–female pairs of supervisor–supervisee. They draw out what is missed by the female supervisor who avoids discussion with the male supervisee about how he, as well as his client, might be avoiding his feelings. The female supervisee benefited from an exploration of how she might take more power rather than express her difficulty with her male supervisor as her problem rather than theirs.

Comparing research with same gendered pairs, Sells, Goodyear, Lichtenberg, and Polkinghorne (1997) describe male–male pairs focusing preferentially on the client, and contrast female–female pairs' focus on the client–counsellor or counsellor–supervisor relationship.

The impact of the external world

In recent years, supervisees have brought broader issues, like global warming and eco-psychology, the Iraq war, terrorism and the response of therapy to it, the credit crunch, the benefits and costs of statutory provision for counselling, and failures of funding for voluntary bodies engaged with mental health. Somehow, as the millennium passed, these seem to have intruded more into the supervisory space, and it is difficult to know how much this relates to how my own interests in these areas developed. Matters relating to spirituality are spoken of more, too, and might arise in the context of discussions about well being, or about terrorism and religious hatred. More work is reported with refugees and trauma. Many employing organizations make ever more demands, and employed counsellors are stressed by the circumstances and structures of their employment: managerial styles, workload, waiting lists, and organizational cultures that do not share counselling values.

Deciding together about when supervisees move on

I would ask in reviews, "How will you know when you have got enough from me, and it is time to move on?" A few people moved away or moved on, but some insisted on the value of staying with me. Here, the role of supervisee as "customer" can give them some role power. Annual contracts would allow for a review and recommitment, and without these, the pair may decide to end when one or the other is dissatisfied, at an impasse, moving, tired, or retiring.

Reflections

Experience is not just the name we give to our mistakes. It also develops wisdom when used as a base for reflection. It enables a more complex and subtle grasp of the tasks and the factors that influence a more or less facilitative supervisory relationship. It contributes to a "wisdom culture", where an increasingly authentic professional self can test and review training imperatives in the light of clinical practice (Page & Wosket, 2001). Bringing a wider view from a range of associated roles and tasks offers new perspectives. As the very wise Remen says (2000), "Wisdom develops when we learn not to try to fix life, but to befriend it, listen before we act, and look for the meaning of experience and connections between people".

CHAPTER FIFTEEN

Bereavement and the supervisory relationship: working in the landscape of loss

"Your joy is your sorrow unmasked.
And the selfsame well from which your laughter
Rises was oftentimes filled with your tears.
And how else can it be?
The deeper that sorrow carves into your being, the more joy
you can contain . . .
Some of you say, 'joy is greater than sorrow' and
others say, 'Nay, sorrow is the greater.'
But I say unto you, they are inseparable.
Together they come, and when one sits alone with
You at your board, remember the other is asleep
Upon your bed."

(Gibran, 1926)

Bereavement and loss play a notable part in supervision not only because it is often a factor in a client's story, but also because it is a part of life and therefore it can be relevant to any or all of the three parties involved. As soon as there is bereavement in the room, death is also there, and it reminds us that we all must die, and that all lives contain many losses. Each individual survivor finds unique solutions. I think of it like a kite in the air with a tail on which each bow is another loss. Some people's kites have long tails. Some supervisees are private about their stories and do not wish to examine them much in supervision, yet these tails will influence their reactions to both personal and professional losses. This reveals a classic boundary between supervision and therapy, where the supervisor has to find a way to acknowledge difficulties, explore necessary issues in relation to clients without prying. My experience is that some supervisees may connect with their strong feelings when treated empathically. My underlying general belief is that personal growth and gain do occur through suffering, through heightened existential awareness. Bereavement is known to act as a catalyst, and to be one way in to awareness of underlying psychological issues and attachment patterns. Sharing a narrative of loss, with its associated constructs and feelings offers opportunities to understand and make sense of grief, and of life, and also to ease the loneliness of the experience. When these issues are triggered by the work, or by a major loss for the supervisor or the supervisee, supervision should attend to it.

For instance a supervisee may have to leave a work context, retire, or move geographically. Whether the move is relatively sudden or long planned, many endings can be done at once. The supervisor and supervisee must explore how the supervisee is approaching these, considering unique client needs and differing lengths of counselling relationship. However, if s/he knows that there has been suicide, or a sudden or recent loss within the supervisee's experience, the supervisor should ensure she enquires more carefully and specifically about feelings about endings.

As we know, bereavement sometimes involves frighteningly powerful emotions, and it also may require the bereaved person to reconstruct a world of meaning that has been undermined by the loss. How we relate to this will depend on the age and stage we are at in our lives, and what lifelong experiences of loss colour our perspective on the issue. Particularly as we age and the number of people loved and lost increases, the impact of particular losses has many resonances, and these are more unpredictable to any listener who does not know the history.

Supervision can provide the space for the supervisee to fall apart, and thus, paradoxically, hold him or her together to continue to work in the safety of supervisory support (Walker & Jacobs, 2004, p. 98). When the supervisor conveys trust that the counsellor is appropriately reflective and trustworthy, this also invites the supervisee to trust himself or herself and, thus, maybe, listen more attentively to inner promptings about what work is right at this time, and create a plan for when to return to work that takes personal needs into account.

Focus on client issues

Supervision relating to bereavement commonly focuses on the experiences and needs of the client: their experience of grief; their capacity to undertake the tasks of grief; how to free chronic grieving; how to diagnose and distinguish grief from depression; or "normal" grief from "complicated" grief; how to support a client grieving a traumatic loss; and so on. Many resources and most training courses address this.

Focus on professional issues

Particular issues, challenges, and possibilities arise when the supervisor or supervisee is grieving. Normative issues here include the practitioner's resilience, self care, and "fitness to practise", whether the practitioner can work at an appropriate relational depth while grieving, and the impact on their subtle energy connection with the other person in the room (Cameron, 2004). Supervisees might mention "in passing" some family illness, and the alert supervisor might need to ask about work implications. Page and Wosket (2001, p. 100) describe this, and note that the supervisor may enquire about the implications for a bereaved client, for instance, of a sudden absence of their counsellor. Decisions need to be made about what and how much the supervisee discloses to the client. They also describe a counsellor whose client has committed suicide, who becomes more protective of other suicidal clients, and the value of discussing the impact on the counsellor of the experience. I have worked with counsellors who have experiences of suicide in their own family, so I am reminded that this is an example of how crucial it is to know enough about supervisee's history to be able to take this into account.

Gagnon's *Wounded Healer* (1994) is both an extraordinary account of courage, and shocking in its recounting continuing to work with a large caseload while in active treatment. In a readable and self-disclosing book, he describes undergoing cancer treatment while continuing practice as a therapist, without supervision, in the USA. He sees fourteen clients the day after he returns from hospital, hairless and leaning on a cane. His mother had died recently, and he is involved with winding up her affairs. It seems insane to me, yet his clients seem to do well, and he recovers. He negotiates with clients in anticipation of his surgery whether they will continue with him, and most do so. I cannot imagine a UK supervisor who would happily countenance his plan, yet there is no evidence in his account that clients suffer. I would be interested in what a UK supervisor would have invited him to consider, among manifold possibilities.

Opportunities for development, and to learn about oneself and others, include how each manages restimulations and resonances when clients or supervisees relate experiences paralleling their own, and how either practitioner might behave if they suddenly become emotionally overwhelmed.

Either person might or might not feel free to weep, or speak of personal losses, and really feel the supportive presence and understanding of the other. The supportive function of supervision is appropriately concerned with the bigger picture of the person's work in the context of their life, as well as with the "here and now" experience being revealed. "Feeling known and accepted" facilitates self-disclosure about such vulnerability. This makes exploration about the effect the bereavement is having on the work more likely to be supportive and appropriately challenging to the supervisee.

The supervisee's history of attachment and loss

An awareness of the practitioner's history of attachment and loss might emerge when initial contracts are made for supervision, or more slowly and organically as the supervisory relationship develops. Many theoretical modalities describe the process by which we make meaning: for instance, about permission to have and express dependency needs, and expectations of whether these needs will be met. Relevant to the supervisory relationship are expectations that a carer will *want* or be able to meet some needs, or that a sufferer will *want* to be seen as vulnerable, and whether or not the supervisor is to be seen as a support at this time. This is more worrying for a trainee counsellor whose supervisor is writing reports assessing their practice and development. If targets for practice hours are to be met, and the trainee is determined to graduate as planned, clients could suffer.

The fears that arise for practitioners in the face of their own overwhelming distress are often linked to old "scripts" about not being good enough, or not being able to carry on coping if the discipline and structure of work is laid aside. Indeed, since the experience of grief is, in its essence, uncontrollable, any practitioner or client with high needs for control will be challenged by this. If it is the supervisor who is preoccupied with such needs, this or her emotions could interfere with the supportive holding of the supervisee. Hence, supervision of supervision is important if it examines appropriateness of supervisory reactions and injunctions.

Grief can affect a supervisory session if a death has been recent or very overwhelming for either the supervisor or the supervisee. It is such an emotionally laden experience that a loss for either practitioner will affect emotional availability for the supervisory session or the care of a client, especially a client currently working on issues of loss.

Ethical baselines

Practitioners might resist advice to take a break or reduce caseloads when they are self-employed, because of financial pressures. They might acknowledge in supervision that they are very busy with funerary tasks, or executor roles and responsibilities, or are distressed and grieving, yet mortgage, credit, or family responsibilities, or debt is such a pressure that they feel they have no choice but to continue. I have raised the issues we must consider in supervision, and, on some occasions, my anxiety that clients might be harmed. But the supervisor is not in the counselling room and cannot know for sure how well the counsellor is able to engage with each client. In supervision, we might discuss appropriate clients, levels of workload, resilience, and self-care strategies. I have had to hold my anxiety on behalf of clients, my concerns for the resilience of the supervisee, and my uncertainties about my own judgement. Outcome measures, if used, give information about clients' "progress".

Equally complex ethical issues arise when work is the only arena of their life that is currently so absorbing that awareness and pain relating to the bereavement can usually slip into the background, and the person "feels best when working". Grappling with personal despair, alienation, and the shadow of depression *might well* enable the counsellor to go deeper with clients, and even make possible deeper connections between supervisee and supervisor. The basic position of the supervisor must be to trust the practitioner to know their own capacities, and also to express concern about what it was costing them personally to sustain counselling relationships from this state. That is, the supervisor must not choose either monitoring or support, but integrate the two with attention to each person's capacity to sustain relationship with clients.

Useful questions include the following.

- How are you coping at the end of the working day or week or term?
- Are you seeking sufficient support for your own resilience?
- Do your life scripts make you suffer in silence, or not ask for help?
- Are you ill more frequently and thus less reliable for clients?

Many authors, including Jung (1973), believe it essential to have therapy (or analysis) on the grounds that the counsellor can only go into the emotional depths as far with clients as she has gone herself. Some supervisees claim at this time that they are doing unusually sensitive and powerful work with grieving clients. However, the emotional cost to the counsellor could be very high. It is difficult to research adequately whether the "going to the depths" argument is true, but it has a ring of plausibility and is, of course, one reason why all counsellors are required to have counselling or personal development appropriate to their theoretical modality before accreditation. On this basis, the counsellor coping with a recent bereavement might argue that she is more than usually able to connect with others similarly bereaved. Yet, it is also the case that no one suffers in the same way, and there are dangers in believing one has unique empathy for a client.

A similar belief, not researched but not uncommon, is that we get the clients we currently need to help us explore and resolve our own issues, including attachment and loss, bereavement and depression. Certainly, I have had many supervisees who suddenly have a number of clients with loss issues just at the point that they are wrestling with bereavement themselves.

Theoretical and contextual elements affect the decisions to be made. A supportive employment context where the counsellor can be open to collegial support is very different from an isolated one. If the practitioner is working at less depth, one protective choice she could make is to bracket off her own experiences from her work. Many professionals do this, such as doctors who are ill themselves, or divorce lawyers who are divorcing. Most psychological practitioners, however, and especially if the work is primarily long-term and relational, will not see this as an appropriate way to be. One supervisee offering me feedback on this chapter reminded me that it is only by being fully conscious of experiences and emotions that we can prevent them from contaminating the work, and it is precisely when they are unconscious that we cannot control them. Hence, the vital role therapy and supervision play in these times. Work can offer welcome distraction and intimacy, and a hold on "normality", whereas taking time off might be pervaded by fears of "cracking up" and not recovering, whatever we might know theoretically about what is good practice. Some clients might really need the counsellor to cope and be as available as can be managed, even if this is just to be there, be still and listen, and keep breathing. Others would do better with a referral to another counsellor not currently burdened by live issues too close to the client's own. Even in rural areas, it might be possible to make reciprocal arrangements for referrals to another counsellor, though the employers need to support this. Ethical imperatives require us to consider the different needs of each client, even when in supervision it becomes clear that the counsellor might need a complete break from all the work. At least, the negotiation to have a break or end work can genuinely acknowledge that it is not a good time for some clients, in the same way as a decision to take a sabbatical, go on a long trip, stop work to care for a dependent, and other life events will disadvantage some.

Expressing a complex mix of feelings

The supervision process might focus on the needs of a grieving or needy client, the interactions and relationship the supervisee is capable of in their current state, and the impact on the counsellor of hearing the client's pain with resonances of their own. Often, however, supervision is most useful in turning the supervisee's attention to the less socially acceptable emotions: relief, ambivalence, resentment, or anger. If the supervisee works within a hospice or bereavement service, it is important to explore their own bereavement history, and how far they can "allow" these feelings in the self or in their clients. Godward (2007), from her experience of counselling patients dying of cancer, writes, "What makes counselling work difficult is not about the client and their issues, but about the therapist".

Her reactions came to affect not only her work, but also her outlook on life and her capacity for self-care. For her, supervision's role in acknowledging her personal responses and dealing with them and their historical roots in her experience saved her compassion and sanity. The restorative element of supervision became more important as time went by and she moved into "empathy overload" and towards burnout, but would not allow herself to consider doing other work. In the short term, it was "an emotional lifeline". In the longer term, it facilitated an exploration of her shadow fears of losing loved ones to cancer, which were exacerbated when she, too, had to go for tests. Exploration of parallel process in the supervision offered her insight that, when she was not listening to a client who was not listening to his partner, it was because of her history as well as the client's relationships.

Interestingly, she also comments, "My supervisor had had similar experiences to myself in terms of family illness and bereavement . . . Sharing experiences helped me feel supported and not alone with the feelings I had" (Godward, 2007, p. 20).

Jones (1999) collated four responses to a practice dilemma as follows:

> You supervise a counsellor who works in several settings: A hospice, a counselling agency for women (issues of childhood sexual abuse, poverty, domestic violence, and addiction) and in her own independent practice with five private clients, some recently new and some long-term. The counsellor's partner has recently suffered a third and fatal heart attack. How do you and the counsellor determine when she is functioning well enough to resume counselling, and how much might her theoretical approach(es), the needs of individual clients and the settings of her work influence the decision. [p. 195]

The four responses reflected differing reactions related to theoretical orientations, assumptions about what would have been discussed and arranged in advance in a supervisory relationship, focus on the supervisee or the clients, and how she is able to adjust to her loss in relation to the demands of her work as a counsellor. All commentators were aware of ethics and the impact of different work settings. Religious and cultural origins and beliefs were named, and the pressures from negative social attitudes if the relationship was a lesbian or heterosexual one. One respondent considered the boundary the supervisor needs to keep between supervision and therapy; another explored balance between the needs of the counsellor and her clients. All referred to assessing the counsellor's support needs and capacity to function at work. Some considered longer breaks in one setting than another.

The impact on the supervisory relationship

I have been very struck by the impact on supervision of *shared* experiences of loss, whether recent or long ago, particularly in long-term supervisory relationships. If *both* the supervisor and supervisee have experienced the death of a child, a parent, or a sibling, the resonances in the room when the client who has a similar loss is discussed can be considerable. Both supervisor and supervisee may be open about their own responses, curious, and yet keen to focus on the uniqueness of the client's loss. Being attentive to the emotional cost of going into this territory as a worker heightens possibilities that the welfare of the client can be enriched by this ' tender empathy. If suicide or attempted suicide is known to both personally, the understanding of shame or rage relating to it can be more subtle and developed than for those whose knowledge is based only on theory. The details of the landscapes of loss are different in every case, but the traveller who has traversed a territory can know some major features very well.

The supervisee facing predictable losses, either a relative dying slowly or a diminution of health, needs particularly careful support and detailed discussions about the current impact of the life events around her or him. Is s/he fit to see all clients or only some? What workload is manageable? What contingency arrangements need to be in place to support clients in the event of a sudden break? Are there suitable and available colleagues to whom to refer? Is it appropriate to tell the client of the counsellor's needs in order to plan the client's ongoing care together? These are complex matters when the supervisee works in an agency. They are doubly difficult if the context is private practice or when the supervisee is a trainee. Barden (2001, pp. 48–49) discusses how a supervisory group worked with a trainee with multiple sclerosis whose illness took a turn for the worse, facing the need to acknowledge the changes in her alertness that they were observing, and then having an open discussion about how best to manage it.

When the counsellor's health and survival are in question, a detailed discussion of a "therapeutic will" is important. Failure to do this (Martin, 2006) can have difficult repercussions for clients or supervisees if bereaved family members are left to give the news of a sudden death. The "therapeutic will" includes detailed arrangements made in advance and notified to a colleague who will act in case of a sudden incapacitation or death. Usually, it covers:

● contacting current clients, supervisees, and referring agencies;
● supporting clients to make decisions about their future counselling;
● appropriately secure disposal of notes and records.

For private practitioners, arrangements to wind up their counselling "business" are also essential, and this may be done separately, but need to consider issues of client confidentiality.

Accepting sensitive responses from clients

Serving others requires care of the self. As they say on aeroplanes: "If the oxygen masks fall, put yours on first and then turn to help others" (Remen, 2000).

"You–me" talk can create profound moments of meeting and mutual connection. Some clients whose sessions have to be cancelled may respond by seeking to offer comfort to their counsellor. Within the boundaries and clarity that this is a relationship in service of the client, there can be healing here. Some supervisees have been moved by the capacity of some very needy clients to "hold on and wait" while the counsellor attends to a death. It can be most healing for clients or supervisees to move out of role temporarily, and "give back" to a carer some generosity and not always be the receiver.

Exposure as a grieving supervisor

When my brother died suddenly after a period when I had been his main close relative and, therefore, carer, I continued with supervisees, believing myself to be "fit to practise" with them. Some six months later, a supervisee brought a client whose relative had had a disastrous medical experience in exactly the way that my brother had died. She did not know of the parallels, as my loss had happened suddenly just after I had seen her, and I was working by the time of our next session, so I had not mentioned it. To my great embarrassment, I suddenly experienced a "whoosh" of emotion and could not stop myself from recounting the details of my brother's medical mismanagement. I became tearful. I left the room briefly, recovered myself, returned, and insisted that I was fine to continue work to her original agenda for the session. We ended with some feeling of constraint.

Despite it being a warm supervisory relationship between experienced practitioners, I felt that as she was paying me I should not take "her" time for my distress. My behaviour was rigid, and I did not let her in as a person. My implicit rules about control, service to others, giving value for money, not being vulnerable without choosing it, and shame at exposing my own raw emotion were writ large to both of us, but unspoken at the time.

The frozen fountain: a metaphor for loss and bereavement.

I took it to my own supervision and we agreed that I had to raise the issue at the start of my supervisee's next session, which I did. She was relieved and said that she had wanted to say something to me at the time, but had not been sure whether it was all right, or how to tackle it. We then had a useful exploration about it. It was the basis of several salutary lessons. When the relationship between supervisor and supervisee is suddenly shifted like this, it can have long-term benefits if the incident can be addressed openly, or it can be the start of a negative spiral if avoided: I learnt, again, about the value of speaking the unspoken, risking being seen with less of the mask of a role, trusting that supervisees can give me what I hope to offer them, the "bi-focal" vision which sees both resilience and vulnerability and does not suffer "either/or" thinking.

Cameron's (2004) ideas about the benefits of "energetic" aware-ness for psychological contact are very pertinent to this discussion, exploring as she does the impact of our intuitive sensing, and the "subtle energy", empathy, and emotional availability to one another. She quotes Rogers' description of his "inner spirit reaching out to touch the inner spirit of the other", with a great potential for intimacy and a healing depth of relationship. Such intimacy is only possible, she says, "if the counsellor is sufficiently grounded within themselves". Both supervisor and supervisee, then, can usefully notice the ebb and flow of their psychological connection. Ideally, they will have created a safe enough relationship to comment on changes that they wish to explore as they experience them. The frozen fountain photo shows how the supervisor's capacity to reflect is impaired when her part of the supervisory pond is frozen.

Grief is a powerful emotion, and bereavement can have very intense and sometimes long-lasting effects. There can be moments in counselling and supervision when a long grieved personal loss can be recalled in all its vivid and acute sorrow. It is important for all practitioners to be able to bring the issues to supervision and monitor how they are bearing the pain, and how their responses are affecting the professional work, and ask honestly whether, and how, their work with clients is compromised or enhanced.

CHAPTER SIXTEEN

Supervision of brief counselling

"Nothing in my twelve years of supervising long-term psychodynamic work, in groups and individually, prepared me for the task of supervising counsellors doing brief and time limited work"

(Mander, 2002a)

I began supervising brief, time-limited work in the 1990s, though from a different theoretical orientation from Mander, having developed interests in solution-focused counselling and then supervision. At this time brief work was new to a majority of practitioners, and often seen as second best by those trained to do open-ended and long-term counselling, and supervise this. We had to develop ideas and practice to fit the new potential and limits of brief work. Some earlier workers (Talmon [1990], for instance) had advocated single session therapy as the only reliable way to work, since many clients only come for one session.

Brief work has become a norm for counsellors who work in settings where someone other than the client pays for the service. The dominant counselling contracts in primary care and universities, employee assistance programmes (EAPs), and some voluntary contexts are often for up to six sessions, sometimes only four. Mander (1998, 2002a) usefully reminds us of the likelihood, given funding pressures, that clients from deprived backgrounds and other cultures will find their way into counselling within brief contracts, even when their needs are complex. Multi-cultural sensitivity in supervisor and supervisee is a crucial prerequisite for this work. A shared interest in public service and organizational dynamics will create a more encouraging environment for supervision than one where the supervisor undermines counsellor confidence by over-emphasis on the negative potential of limited time.

Counsellors who have been trained primarily to do long-term work might find the limits do not suit their temperament. Others like the opportunity to offer many clients more psychological awareness and capacity to explore their own needs and ways of being, and consider the perspectives and needs of others as these impinge on them. Cummings and Sayama (1995) advocate "brief focal psychotherapy through the life cycle". They show how valuable a series of brief interventions can be for someone who is fortunate enough to meet up with the same therapist for a number of encounters when needed, spanning many years (pp. 2–6). Many clients prefer time-effective work to avoid the dependency or stigma of "illness" and referrals to secondary services. Clarity about the ending from the start may, for some, increase motivation and focus.

There is a huge range of preferred theoretical modality and professional style of supervisors of brief counselling. However, all seem to agree on the need for flexibility, clear contracts and goal setting, capacity to relate in brief encounters, and the relevance of the context for the work. The client's, counsellor's, and supervisor's assumptions about how change happens in counselling needs exploration, too. Explicit goals can build the client's capacity to notice their responses, make contact, relate more authentically or complete unfinished business.

For supervision to be useful, it is necessary for supervisor and counsellor to ensure clarity about the methods being used and consistency in the power relationship between client and counsellor across the methods.

How often to meet for the work being done

The supervisor and counsellor can set frequency for supervision weekly, fortnightly, or monthly. Because the BACP norm for accredited counsellors suggests a minimum of one and a half hours a month, many practitioners do work to that minimum irrespective of caseload. A number of authors have raised the concern that monthly supervision is not sufficient (Jeffrey, 2008), and most supervisors propose some flexibility. Certainly, for inexperienced counsellors who work to a brief contract, weekly supervision in some form is desirable.

To spell it out, the counsellor who works for two or three half-day sessions might be holding a caseload of up to fifteen clients if they work flexibly and do not see every client weekly. Many counsellors space out the frequency of meetings from a weekly beginning, in response to the preferences or needs of the clients or the availability of the counsellor. On average, this might include three new clients per month. One colleague recently told me that he had seen almost two thousand patients in seventeen years as a primary care counsellor, working ten hours a week. That *averages* almost ten new clients per month. Burton, Henderson, and Curtis Jenkins (1998) found in their sample of primary care counsellors that caseloads open at any one time were reported as being between three and sixty-five clients, with a mean of fourteen. Full-timers who spend twenty hours in direct work, but juggle the clients between weekly, fortnightly, and more extended breaks between sessions, can easily have forty to fifty people with whom they are in current psychological contracts of one sort or another. If they manage to discuss two or three in a monthly one and a half hour supervisory session, this demonstrates vividly that the majority will never be brought to supervision, and some will have come and gone between supervision sessions. Most experienced counsellors would not consider it necessary to bring every client to supervision anyway, but this is not sufficiently spacious supervision for this workload.

Commentators on the impact on counsellors of a large caseload emphasize the risks of burnout (Page & Wosket, 2001).

When most clients are seen briefly, so that turnover is also high, this risk must be significant when the necessary level of psychological contact exists between the counsellor and clients. Extreme comparisons are between the working life of a psychotherapist who sees a small number of clients four or five times a week over many years, and, thus, might see only fifty or sixty people in a working lifetime, and the primary care counsellor who might have that number of clients on a current caseload. The supervisor needs to understand the experience of those s/he is supervising and not apply standards and expectations from a different model.

The supervisory contract

With this level of turnover of clients, it is useful for the counsellor to bring a list of current clients at agreed intervals, so that the supervisor at least has an overview of the workload, and can discuss the implications. The counsellor and supervisor can identify those who have never been discussed in supervision, and occasionally talk briefly about how that work is going. In my experience, this encourages the counsellor to do her own internal audit, reflection, and preparation for supervision, and thus to identify which clients or issues s/he brings and which s/he does not—and why. Many primary care settings at least expect an annual audit of the work, so the counsellor has to keep statistics anyway.

I have found the log required for accreditation makes supervisees specify and acknowledge their workload, and is sometimes a useful trigger to discuss it. If people are working in frenetic and pressured environments, so many hellos and goodbyes, working at relational depth so briefly and letting the relationships go, is emotionally very demanding, particularly when the needs are too complex for the time allocated by more rigid systems.

Where counsellors have more than one supervisory arrangement, it is important to be explicit about which supervisor will undertake the normative functions. Consideration of the overall service the counsellor gives, any outcome records or audit, and consideration of the counsellor's developmental needs can usefully be reviewed with one supervisor. Discussion of how responsibility is to be allocated between the supervisors is crucial if a supervisee attends a group in addition to individual supervision, or has peer supervision as well as the paid one. One bonus of more than one supervisor is that it can be very convenient where the client's confidentiality needs to be preserved and the supervisor knows the client or others connected to her, for those clients to be taken to the other supervisor or the group.

Focus on the brief encounter

Supervision may explore the counselling relationship of the counsellor and client. Whatever the theoretical approach to brief counselling, the counsellor must be capable of creating rapport and a working alliance within the first session or two. S/he has to develop a capacity to work deeply while making choices in interventions that reduce or avoid the creation of dependency. Daniel Stern, an American psychiatrist, talked at a conference of "moments of meeting", unplanned resolutions that support a leap in therapy, those occasions when genuineness and immediacy (my terms for his ideas) pervade the exchange, and something transformative happens to create a new intimacy and sense of connection for both client and therapist, and enable the client to move on. He later wrote about "now" moments (Stern, 2007, p. 4), moments of crisis and opportunity demanding an authentic response that alters the intersubjective field between the two. "It is a two-person event involving a perturbing change in the inter-subjective field of the total relationship, transferential and real" (*ibid.*). It is my experience that these can happen in brief as well as long term therapy.

Counsellors may discuss motivation and readiness to change, and willingness to engage in brief therapy, with the client. The aim is usually to "make a difference", look for leverage for change, and give the client courage and, if possible, some self-belief that they can go forward with their life and face difficult life events.

Assessment is a major challenge. It is not uncommon for assessment to take two or even three sessions when the situation or the person is complex. Arrangements for the counsellor to contact the supervisor between supervisions, by phone or e-mail, to talk through uncertainties about appropriateness of counselling for a client, or possibilities of referral are necessary, and might run the risk of becoming frequent if the supervisions are on a monthly basis. In many EAPs and some managed services for primary care or voluntary agencies, someone other than the counsellor does the initial assessment and then allocates clients to the counsellor.

Counsellors need to develop a more active style in brief therapy than in long-term work within many theoretical orientations, both psychodynamic and humanistic. Here, Mander's (2002a) encouragement to tackle issues of motivation, and the implications of diversity of cultural background between counsellor and client (or counsellor and supervisor) explicitly seems wise (p. 103).

When more than one client is discussed in a supervisory session, a choice might be to bring several clients with similar issues, e.g., contracting at the start of a session might begin with, "I seem to have a lot of clients with relationship crises and I'd like to talk about two of them while thinking: 'How can trust be regained after an affair?'"

Brief work in voluntary and statutory organizations

> The soft end of pathological defence is stoicism; the hard end is manic denial, a psychotic process that attempts to obliterate despair by manufacturing excitement. In manic states of mind people are oblivious to both pain and danger. [Dartington, 1994, p. 108]

Primary care is a particularly complex working context, and the pace there is often re-created in supervision through parallel process as supervisees follow the impulse to bring many clients in very little depth. This mirrors the counsellor's struggles to manage large numbers of patients in a busy environment, within a culture of scarcity. Supervisees respond differently to the "bottomless pit of suffering" they meet in many disadvantaged areas and statutory settings. It is easy for the supervision also to get so busy that there is a sense of there being too much to attend to reflectively. It is a discipline, then, to create a sense of space for whatever is most useful, which parallels the focus required in brief therapy. The supervisor is required to hold the "helicopter vision" (Carroll, 1996) and keep a weather eye on the perennial issues about boundaries, responsibilities, and the relationships and structures of the context. Acknowledgement and management of fear and powerful feelings parallels the GP's pressures as they deal with issues of life and death, and the projections on them of omniscience or expertise, or rage at an ineffectual or inefficient service.

In my years as a primary care supervisor, it was a norm that we contracted for supervisees to contact me if urgent supervisory needs arose. People usually phoned to arrange a mutually convenient time to talk in the next few hours. Sometimes, in complex cases (e.g., being asked to provide court reports, or support for housing applications, or criminal injuries compensation), e-mailing was more suitable, with careful anonymity preserved. My position was that, in the teeth of any serious ethical dilemma, I would much rather, as a supervisor, have the chance to create a brief space to reflect, or influence action, or encourage a waiting position, than for us to have to pick up the pieces of a distressed supervisee arising from a reactive and unsupervised response. Even experienced colleagues can feel put on the spot when first engaging with such requests and without a chance to air their thoughts can do something impulsive around breaching confidentiality, for instance, that can have repercussions they had not considered. I never ever felt a supervisee abused this facility for immediate consultation.

Experienced counsellors seem to vary enormously in their felt need for casework supervision. Often the counselling work appears normally to be well within their confidence and competence, and they may be more inclined to discuss matters about the organizational context of the work (Henderson, 1999). Issues might include appropriateness of referrals, coping with the current structures for managing psychological services (in 2009 that is increasingly a "stepped care approach" with many providers within primary care), a lack of alternative services for complex cases, funding for counsellor work, colleague relationships and how they interact with the work, and so on.

Typical issues for supervision that have particular complexities can include caseload management and coping with the waiting list, assessment and referral, and ethical dilemmas. Within primary care, where the counsellor works on site with other members of the multi-disciplinary team, the impact of surgery dynamics between receptionists and doctors, the GP partners, a covert sexual liaison between a GP and a practice nurse, and similar disruptions of colleague relationships outside of the counselling room and day-to-day practical management might sometimes dominate supervision time. I have known a number of practices where the religious affiliation of a GP affected patients who were required to pray with the doctor, and who then complained to the counsellor. Sometimes contact between a doctor and a patient that the patient perceives as inappropriately sexual is reported to a counsellor, who brings the issue of what to do with this confidence to supervision.

Tudor (2007, p. 199) dismisses this emphasis on a service-centred approach, encouraging supervisors and counsellors not to take responsibility for the waiting list, as this belongs to the management of the service. I do agree with him and with Wakefield (2005) that limits may be imposed unnecessarily. *An annual average of six sessions per patient in such settings allows sufficient flexibility for most circumstances.* However, the stress on the supervisee arises because of a small percentage of clients who need much more time or more skill, and for whom there may be no appropriate service. Supervision provides a space for some thinking about the wider view, about mental health services in an area, and about other providers. When a service or jobs are at stake through reorganizations or cut-backs, supervision might be the place to discuss how to influence political decisions about funding within large statutory organizations or voluntary providers.

Different theoretical approaches to brief work

The match of supervisor–supervisee frames of thought and language is important, and lack of it can sometimes be very difficult if a counsellor is allocated to a supervisor s/he would not freely choose. In Burton, Henderson, and Curtis Jenkins (1998) study of primary care counsellors, most of whom worked in brief contracts, 89% noted a good match between their theoretical frame and their supervisor's, and 96% noted there was a good match of personal style with their supervisor. Comments they made in reply to the question (not included in the 1998 article) signal some of the ease and the difficulty that can occur in difference:

> I'm moving away from psychodynamic work, utilizing systems and brief therapy models more. Often we are learning together about these models. She is still very helpful, but it's often more of a peer relationship.

My clinical supervisor has recently done further training in brief therapy as she is aware her training is in long-term therapy. I feel she understands the problems of transference in brief therapy and has helped me with this.

I sometimes feel I cannot follow any direct advice that is given because it does not fit my training. Also we have different attitudes to clients and therapy generally at times.

Ten years later, the political and organizational pressures are to incorporate CBT, CAT, IPT, and related methods and ideas into short-term work with similar tensions between practitioners trained differently (Jeffrey, 2008).

Flexibility

Supervisors may discuss the use of time with clients by the counsellor, who might vary session lengths, offering shorter or longer than standard sessions for initial assessment, according to a theoretical base, or might alter the frequency of meetings with clients from weekly to fortnightly to monthly. As Tudor comments (2007), "Time is deeply cultural and highly political". Tudor notes that assumptions include:

Does change and therapy take a long time?
Are complex client problems resolvable in a short time?
How do the client, counsellor and supervisor feel about limits?

Working assumptions

Thomas (1996, pp. 131–134) names eight assumptions held by solution-focused supervisors:

1. It is not necessary to know the cause or function for a complaint in order to resolve it. Instead, focus on what prevents the problem being resolved.
2. Therapists know what is best for them. If the supervisor establishes a "contextual reality of competence", the therapist will

feel encouraged to access resources to resolve their therapeutic dilemmas.

3. There is no such thing as resistance. The supervisors' task is to find ways to cooperate with the learning experience and style of the therapist.
4   The supervisor's job is to identify and amplify change, through solution talk.
5. A small change is all that is necessary. Snowball or ripple effects will lead to additional change.
6. Change is constant, and rapid change is possible. The responsibility of the supervisor, then, is to locate differences that are inevitable and signify them.
7. Supervision should focus on what is possible and changeable. Recognizing capabilities and identifying what can be done next, rather than raking over past errors makes good use of supervisory time.
8. There is no one way to view things, therefore entertain additional views, be curious, and respectfully question rigid thinking.

I find this approach encouraging and pragmatic. Solution-focused ideas have become popular in educational and primary care settings in the UK, largely because they are client-centred, very focused, and encouraging. They are distinctive for their emphasis on conveying optimism and hope of making life changes. They emphasize co-operation with the client, using client-preferred solutions rather than a focus on the problems. Through exploring desired solutions, exceptions when the problem does not occur, and scaling questions, the therapy work can seem formulaic and simple. Simplicity requires skill, however, and it takes a lot of practice and careful observation to achieve it, and a change of focus for thought from problems to solutions. "Pre-suppositional language", which embeds part of the solution in a question, is part of the approach: "What will be happening when (not if) a change has occurred".

McCurdy (2006) demonstrates how solution-focused ideas can influence Adlerian supervision. Solution-focused supervision looks for strengths in the counsellor, noticing what is working, and identifies the next small steps, and thus building counsellor awareness of what is going right, even when they feel stuck because it is difficult or it is not yet right enough. These ideas share roots in the narrative methods popularized by White and Epston (1990): making meaning through creating coherent narratives, less problem saturated narratives, and exploring symptoms and addictions by "externalising the problem". O'Connell and Jones (1997) offer useful brief transcripts that exemplify the method, and the creative methods discussed in Chapter Nine, which externalize a problem through use of objects, show some ways to approach it.

Thomas calls this "using isomorphic structures to coax expertise from the counsellor". He quotes a woodcarver making a flute who said: "The branch will tell me how to carve it . . . each piece of wood has its own shape which you must respect . . . In each . . . branch lies a flute; [my] job is to find it" (1996, p. 128).

There is now a body of ideas about how to work briefly with clients, and how to supervise this work. Most supervisors who are experienced work within more than one theoretical frame, and now can work on short-term therapy. Supervisors use methods derived from humanistic approaches (exploring and using metaphors, working in the here and now, and so on) and psychodynamic approaches, and it is important to note how new these developments are.

Lees (1997) emphasized hope and clients' strengths. He described his own development of primary care counselling work in a very economically deprived area from a psychodynamic base. Without abandoning psychodynamic ideas about the importance of the counselling frame, he reframed a client's "acting out" and slowly committing to the therapy as "giving her the power to determine the rules of the encounter". Lees created a variety of ways for the clients to be in relationship to him. He developed a one-hour drop-in with four fifteen-minute sessions; he experimented with seeing some long term clients every four to six weeks. Others were doing the same, discovering what worked through attentive and reflective experiment.

Mander, from the psychodynamic base (2002a), describes how she had to "invent a method that allowed me to cope with assessment, focusing, ending, loss and, moreover, with a fast turnover of clients" (p. 97, see also Mander [2002b]). She had to overcome her own prejudice against short-term work, accept more limited goals for the brief counselling work, and work with the ending from the beginning in the manner of the brief focal psychotherapy model of Balint (1972) and Malan (1963).

She describes this kind of supervision as watching people travel up an escalator: they are on and off in a flash and you catch no more than a glimpse of them. She notes that this urgency also makes one inventive, and emphasizes the crucial role of assessment after the first session, which her working context initially allowed.

Ethical dilemmas in brief work

Some ethical issues give a flavour to difficulties of supervision of brief work. In primary care or EAPs, there can be pressure for changes of contract with a client as a result of rigid limits. Many EAPs and surgeries make a firm rule that the client may not continue with the counsellor privately. Some also insist that there be no flexibility about extra sessions. In my view, such rigidity can sometimes be unhelpful to clients and put the counsellor in a serious professional dilemma. The supervisor must be clear about her responsibility for any advice s/he gives in these circumstances. Many clients might be willing to become self-funding, for a few sessions, and it is necessary to decide how this is to be monitored, and where the counselling will be located. One solution is to insist that any changes in the contract may take place *only* with the consent of the GP or EAP liaison person, and after discussion in supervision. This then can raise further ethical dilemmas about the degree to which confidentiality might be impaired or breached in order to achieve this negotiation. A similar problem occurs within university counselling services about requests for extensions of the normal limit if requests are discussed with others beyond the counselling service. It is useful to refer to the Caldicott principles (see Glossary) or check with a resource like Bond and Mitchels (2008, pp. 92–102) about sharing information between professionals .

A six-session fixed limit per client may be very unhelpful. Counsellors can bend the rules in order to provide the appropriate service, but it is useful to discuss the impulse to make the particular client special in this way. If most clients get two to four sessions, what is the rationale for one to get forty-four? The point is that there often is a rationale that can be defended, but it is useful if a supervisor and supervisee explore it.

Similar issues arise in EAP work when creating a feedback loop to the organization about clients who are off sick, or on disciplinary charges, or taking out a grievance. An individual client who has come for counselling in response to stress created by work intensification, for example, or bullying, might be treated by the organization as if s/he is the problem rather than that the system is at fault. Once the counsellor has seen a number of people from the same department with similar issues, s/he has a moral dilemma. S/he may form a view that there are organizational pressures that need to be addressed. The counsellor and the supervisor need to be clear about their contracts with the organization, and how to manage the confidentiality difficulties that can arise from annual reports or other feedback systems. There are some organizations that are inclined to use counselling to discharge their duty of care to their employees, but do not wish to be invited to consider the pathology of their system.

Reflections

This chapter has been included because brief therapy has become common in my working lifetime, and the supervisor needs clarity about focus in order to be of service. It is too easy to let frustration at the real limits undermine what can be done in a brief encounter. The supervisor has to notice what is effective in brief work and support the counsellor to manage the tensions of it.

CHAPTER SEVENTEEN

Endings and retirement

I n private practice supervision, external pressures to end with a particular supervisee are absent unless one party or the other is completing a course or placement, or changing work or moving, or is dissatisfied. Long-term supervisory relationships can become significant emotional attachments for both parties. A change of supervisor may be a time to acknowledge the relationship, and also has to include thought about any potential impact on clients, some feedback or review of the development of the supervisee, and attention to any necessary administrative tasks associated with training, or membership of or accreditation by a professional body.

Any professional ending may be usefully viewed through ideas about attachment and loss, and Worden's "tasks of mourning" can be adapted to professional endings (Worden, 1983). Thus, the supervisor and supervisee can expect to acknowledge the specific reality of the ending of their unique relationship, articulate feelings and work through them, come to terms with the responsibilities, roles, or tasks in moving to a new supervisor, and the supervisee can then invest emotionally in the new relationship.

Chambers and Cutliffe (2001) argue that a good ending with a supervisee will have a number of specific features. It will be negotiated, gradual, all parties will hold the ending process in mind and articulate preferences about it, the supervisee will retain some control over the timing and process, and both will aim to achieve some sense of closure.

Despite all this good practice, however, when the supervisor decides to end work with an individual, the supervisee is powerless to change that decision, even if many months of warning are given so a sudden wrench is avoided. Early attachment experiences can be revived. So, too, can anxieties that contribute to self-esteem or the lack of it in a time of change.

The supervisee's perspective

Self-discovery in supervision requires emotional investment for all parties and for individuals to give of themselves. A supervisor might find it difficult to accept that she is no longer needed or wanted when a *supervisee* wants to leave. Mander (2002c) describes the "yoke" of supervision, and negative experiences for supervisees, like this: "Anxiety and irksome responsibilities of preparation, coming and going on time, breaks and fees . . . and experiences of exposure, self doubt, confusion, and depressing inadequacy" (p. 141).

When it becomes stale, monotonous, boring and repetitive it is time to leave.

Conversely, if the supervisee wants to stay but the supervisor insists on ending, the supervisee might feel powerless or abandoned. A supervisee might fear they have somehow transgressed, or disappointed or wearied the supervisor. S/he might feel daunted by the inevitable discomforts of finding and beginning with a new supervisor, and some personal sadness at ending with the familiar one.

The aging or failing supervisor

Mander (2002c) continues:

> Levels of professional ability are always changing, and probably more rapidly, though not inevitably in the supervisee. The super-

visor may simply have reached the limit of her capacity to absorb, digest and expand knowledge and understanding with age, overload or increasing routine. [*ibid.*]

Or, I would add, s/he is entitled to want to turn energy and attention to other matters.

For the supervisor who is anticipating retirement, there are also many issues relating to personal and professional identity to deal with at the same time. I "retired" in 2005, ending with all current supervisees (and clients) within a six-month period. It provoked a variety of thoughts and feelings and I was glad of guidance through my own supervision. I had worked as a supervisor for more than sixteen years. Many supervisees worked in primary health care. At the end, only one was a man. Most were very experienced practitioners, aged in their fifties and sixties. Many of them had been with me for very long periods. I had not insisted on ending with individual long-term supervisees whom I liked, and who had good professional reasons for wanting to stay.

Only one supervisee had ever left entirely on her own initiative, and she came back after a year for another period before moving on a second time. None would leave in the previous two years when I suggested it, despite my obviously reduced functioning. In the past, supervisees from a voluntary organization had changed to a new supervisor when I said it was time, sometimes to meet my needs to turn to new work, at others because I insisted it was in their interest and it was a norm in the agency in which they volunteered. Most left when they moved away.

Feltham (2000, p. 15) has asserted that long-term practitioners are "prone to countertransference errors, cognitive distortions, skills deficits, and have to cope with waning enthusiasm". I was certainly struggling with waning enthusiasm, and making some countertransference errors. It is very flattering to be so wanted and held on to, and it did feed my narcissistic needs, but it is, of course, also limiting in some ways. It was satisfying because the relationships were enjoyable and stimulating. We were both, usually, learning new things from each other. We reaped the benefits of a long-term supervisory relationship in robust explorations, but, because of their wish to stay, I postponed or avoided articulating my changing needs.

Yet, I needed to work less, and in fact to take a complete break. I ended with the two who had been coming for the longest time four months before the rest. Both were initially furious when I clarified that *their* ending was to happen thus. Indeed, I had implied that all were to go at once, and then had to "own up" nearer their end that this was not exactly the truth. I was embarrassed to be caught out in not being transparent. We had done regular reviews and careful contracting. Now my need to "be nice" was revealed again, as well as my lack of permission to meet my needs when they did not coincide with those of others. The first issues arising for both in response to this were to explore whether they were in some way at fault. Had I been holding back negative feelings about them? Well, yes, in so far as they would not all go away and I was tired. Supervision of supervision had finally helped me to face my lack of transparency, and the reality of my own wishes.

Resonances from early attachment patterns

I became interested by the degree to which some of the supervisees' response to ending also had taproots in their earlier life experiences. As Page and Wosket (2001) say of work with experienced practitioners in general:

> In our view the difference mainly comes down to Supervisor and Supervisee needing to work more closely at the interface between supervision and therapy in the service of enhancing the personal and professional development of the therapist. We would suggest that the supervision issues of mature experienced practitioners are also their life issues. . . . They need to bring to supervision those parts of the self that are touched and affected by their clients. [p. 229]

Two of my long-term supervisees had come after very bruising experiences that they had felt as abusive with a therapist or supervisor. This influenced and affected their initial engagement in supervision, and willingness to make an open supervisory relationship with me. Safety developed slowly.

For one, the relationship was significantly reparative not only of that difficulty, but also of an early life experience of abandonment.

Over a long period, she came into a sense of her own power and resourcefulness. All this then wobbled at the news of my requirement for her to end. Her initial grief was substantial. However, she had developed enough of an inner sense of her own worth and ability as a counsellor and supervisee that she could articulate her emotional experience vociferously at the news of the ending. She then protected me and worked through her feelings elsewhere, though I knew of the resonances with the recent death of her adoptive mother. Thus freed, she then chose a supervisor who was unknown to me (not easy in a town where my networks were good), initiated careful contracting with him, and settled into a new and different relationship.

The bonds of reparative relationships

A more recent supervisee, who had come after serious malpractice by her current therapist and many personal losses, could not connect consistently with me in any way that displayed feelings of dependency, and we were both carefully aware of that. I aimed to be available without being unduly intrusive, she to bring herself and her work with appropriate self-disclosure while retaining enough privacy. An interesting, and, I think, respectful balancing process was achieved on both sides. We had a very task-focused relationship in which my concerned enquiries about her self-care were batted back with well-supported arguments about the role of the counsellor when a wounded healer. We were both interested in this: when does bereavement and loss provide unique insight and a basis for profound understanding of the plight of the client, and when does the vulnerability and emotionally labile state of the bereaved practitioner lead to unsafe practice? She was self-controlled about the emotional impact on her of the supervisory ending, continuing almost to the end of the last supervision to focus on casework and workload issues, which I commented on and respected. At our last session, she had not quite got round to making a new regular relationship, but had a continuing peer relationship and a back-up arrangement in place. We met at a conference after some time, and she commented on her own pace in terms of feeling the loss.

One woman was understanding and warm when I told her of the proposed ending. She felt emotional, yet still connected, and worked openly until we ended. At the end, we discovered she had underestimated by two years the period for which we had met. The work we had done was also shot through with issues about bereavement, both personal and professional. Some months later, she rang to say she was not happy with her current supervisor, whose style was too "cool" for her, as well as having a different theoretical orientation. It became clear that the new supervisor's focus entirely on the casework had not suited her theoretical base or her personal needs, to the extent that it affected her sense of safety as a practitioner. She simply did not feel sufficiently held as a practising professional. Yet, I barely remember an occasion when we spent more than a short while on personal issues, unless they abutted right up to the counselling work. The temperature of our relationship had suited her, as well as the space to explore her work with a shared theoretical frame. Our conversation led me to reflect about relationship climates and to Chapter Three of this book.

The personal–professional overlap

Skovholt and Ronnstad (1992) assert that personal life is a central component of professional functioning. They also assert that therapists come to integrate themes of personal life into professional practice in a way that is most beneficial to clients and authentic to the individual, and that these themes often relate to pain involving family of origin, definition of self, and other fundamental issues.

Another supervisee had a lifetime of experiences with an inattentive and hurtful mother that meant she had very sensitive feelings about being attended to, and connected with. She was "the good girl" who hung in there personally and professionally, and, indeed, never ended with her clients in primary care without letting them know they could seek further counselling from her if required. She would not ever accept, over many years, that it would be a good thing to change supervisors, and always felt rejected by the suggestion while also thinking it was beneficial to her practice to stay in a supervisory relationship she found satisfactory. She trusted me, and therefore said she would tell me anything, wanting to be well known and thus kept safe. Our ending became a topic only to be discussed in a ritualized way. She would not, could not, choose to end. She chose a peer for her next supervision, partly for the real difficulty that there are few people locally with a similar level of expertise.

Unnecessary protectiveness

I had one very experienced supervisee who was herself on the cusp of slow moves towards retirement, not accepting new supervisees, winding down very slowly. I was anxious that my going might precipitate too hasty a finish for her. This was completely wasted anxiety, and when I checked it out I discovered that she accepted it and made other arrangements very pragmatically. As two women sharing a life stage, our final sessions ranged widely, exploring thoughts about how to tell if our work has been successful, whether it is worth spending our lives doing it, and whether and for whom we thought we had made a difference. This reminded me how seldom I had had a conversation about core values and assessment of the purpose and achievements of our work within the pressures of regular monthly meetings.

For others, there were matter-of-fact elements to ending this supervision relationship, such as completion of an accreditation process. This was a very satisfying conclusion, assisting us both to note and affirm the supervisee's development and experience.

Impact on the supervisor

I did not really notice the losses for myself very much beforehand, except in brief pangs, because I was focused on my longing to lay down the responsibilities of being reliable and the anticipated relief of doing so. I put my energy into thinking carefully about each and how to mark the ending. I took enormous delight in finding good cards and small gifts. This, too, is my lifelong pattern. Faced with loss, I make the realities of the uniqueness of each relationship vivid to myself with gifts. I tried to find a card that would speak individually to each one. My most satisfying one had a dog begging, holding a stick between his teeth, and with two budgies balanced on either side of the stick. I entitled it: "Managing the waiting list"! The supervisee worked in primary care, and careful thought about the waiting list had been a regular feature of our discussions. We were both so amused. Another had a Bill Brandt photograph of a seagull flying through a misty night, very dream-like, and, I hoped, suitable for the individual.

One unexpected effect on me was that I felt some uncertainty about my own reputation. I was interested to know to whom they would go next, wanting protectively to make sure they found good people, and yet be disciplined not to interfere. I imagined another supervisor, especially from a different theoretical base, might think less well of me for tolerating supervisory "bad habits", such as sometimes and for some people using too much time on personal issues. Yet, these very habits were the ones that those supervisees celebrated as having been important for their professional survival in difficult times. I think the realities of difficulties at work for many years as a therapist are seldom written about. These can include staying at work for the sake of the client or the income when under strain, sustaining a long term counselling relationship through a period of the counsellor's family distress or difficult life events. The balance of supervision for experienced practitioners does change, shifting between the restorative tasks of supervision and the forma-tive and normative. Like therapy, supervision is a very private affair, and thus it can be possible for practice to change from the norms presented while training. This can be positive in increasing flexibility and creativity, or negative in sloppiness and practice that would not survive peer review. I have not, of course, had feedback from their new supervisors, so my fantasies remain.

Multiple losses

There were many losses involved in the process, for me and for them. Some were articulated at the point when I said we would end. Others arose and were expressed in considering how to approach the search for a new supervisor. Many were expressed in the context of appreciations at the last session. In the final sessions,

I received a lot of appreciation and validation, and was sometimes very awkward in so doing, despite my planning to offer it in my turn to the supervisee. I wanted to be a model of graciousness, but my Puritan ethics upbringing intervened in the experience of much positive feedback. I tended to want to turn it aside, make a joke, or change the subject, while simultaneously feeling pleased. Sometimes, my confusion made me quite crass, and I had to discipline myself to stay with the pleasure and accept their affirmations, as I did want them to accept mine.

I was also still eagerly interested in feedback about what we might have done differently together. I am always keen to learn and reflect. However, that learning had been articulated through annual reviews. There was too much else to do at the point of saying our professional goodbyes.

I had my own issues and fears about retirement, and after the last one had left, after a week of many endings, when the house was full of flowers, I was vividly reminded of other times in my life, after a funeral, or a birth, when I was inundated with them. Then I had to face it that this was a major point of transition for me. I continued my own peer supervision for another three months to explore the impact, and shared the germs of this chapter with my peer. I felt the wrench when I had to let go of that relationship in my turn, and she had to help me fight my denial, and the impulse to extend it.

I realized that I missed these experienced colleagues, these intimately known practitioners. I missed the privilege of hearing about their practice. I was glad and sad to miss the effort to be with them as we tackled complex and anxiety-laden narratives. We had negotiated the date for each ending, how we would finish, and did review in more or less detail our professional journey together. We celebrated their development. We talked of our meaning for each other. Thus, we achieved some sense of closure. Most have continued to be in contact since in one way or another in differing degrees of intimacy and mutuality. These have included doing my part for the next re-accreditation report, doing some joint local committee work, meeting at a conference, offering a lift to a conference or a mutual friend's birthday celebration, attending a course I have run, being at the same book club, meeting for tea, in the swimming pool changing room, or in the street. One difference between supervision and counselling is that after some space we can decide if and how we want to meet in a variety of friendly ways as ex-colleagues.

Contrasting ending as a counsellor or a supervisor

"I shall not stop being the person I have become during these years of being a counsellor." This is how Jean Clark (2005) closed her article about ending her long career as a counsellor. Her age and the stamina to take on new clients were her prompts to close her practice, and she noted her sadness, and satisfaction at choosing to end while still able to do good work. She quoted contrasting styles of stressful endings: "running through the thistle patch" as fast as possible, giving short shrift to the most painful parts of the experience, *vs.* "the sponge approach", absorbing other's pain about it in a passive and life-draining way. The better alternative was to stay congruent, authentic, and genuine, leaving space to articulate the mix of feelings, while also remaining conscientious about the work to the end. "Unfinished business" is, by its nature, unpredictable, and a review of each relationship, taking risks to share delights and disappointments, offered the opportunity for more meaningful closure. She noted the impact on her identity and how it was expressed practically, in terms of decisions about what to do with the room in which she used to see clients, and even less restraints about cooking food which might leave lingering aromas.

Like Jean Clark, I have retained my membership of BACP, and, unlike her, I also kept up my accreditation, to keep options open as regulation looms. Being eighteen years younger, I knew I would want to do some professional work. We each had a pang about the losing of connection to the professional body whose early development we had made some contributions towards. I was among the first 2,000 members of BAC, when the AGM was exciting, alive, and stormy, and practitioners determined policy. Newcomers to BACP join an organization of 32,000, where few members take on active initiation of policy, or contribute to representing BACP on government bodies. It is simply too time-consuming and specialist for many people, whose primary role is to work as a private practitioner, but the result is a less personal sense of felt connection with it.

I also shredded many client notes, burning them to ensure no leaks of confidential material. Seeing the shared stories go up in smoke was both a huge relief and a sad evening as I reflected on the privileges of being a companion to many personal journeys. As this book demonstrates, I kept supervisory records, knowing I wanted to write about these experiences.

Reflections

The professional issues entailed in retirement require careful preparation for personal and professional endings with sufficient forward planning, where possible, to create a sense of a rite of passage and space to explore whatever loss is involved. Other elements include appropriate disposal or retention of notes and records, attention to related administrative tasks, and letting go.

I have latterly returned to do some supervision, training, and research work. Like Frank Sinatra, though, I learnt a lot from retiring my way.

CHAPTER EIGHTEEN

Consultative supervision for supervisors

> "Experienced practitioners never lose their doubts, but learn to work with them and despite them"

> (Jacobs, 2000, p. 202)

Supervision of supervision is a consultancy process. It supports an experienced colleague or group of colleagues to develop and reflect on supervisory styles, and monitor work, especially any parts that create anxiety. For simplicity, and to clarify that no responsibility is taken for direct work with clients, I will call it consultative supervision. Clinical governance and a baseline legal knowledge form an essential foundation, and facilitative skills and expert knowledge both play a part.

Group consultative supervision is particularly useful because it provides multiple perspectives for problem solving and for feedback. Often the focus is about themes and general principles or professional or ethical issues. Because group members are all experienced practitioners, any variety in their responses can be particularly useful to identify parallel process or to debate complicated and multi-faceted dilemmas.

Consultative supervision adds one layer more of complexity beyond supervision of counselling. To hold in mind the client–counsellor system and the supervisee–supervisor one requires a wider angled lens, and willingness to wait until a complex story reveals a potential focus. It is further away from the client, yet the client's welfare still forms the major underlying rationale.

Mander (2002d, p. 132) develops a camera analogue and notes that flashbacks, close-ups, stills, and observation of processes and patterns may enable the process: that is, methodological variety and creativity come into useful play. To add to it further, this picture imagery prompts further thoughts about the value of reframing what is presented to bring attention to new elements, perhaps particularly in the organizational or professional systems that also frame the work. Mander (2002d) makes play of the Breughel painting featuring the fall of Icarus to remind us to turn attention to those elements not apparently central to the picture that might be highly significant about the suffering of the client, or their own contribution to their disaster. As Auden's poem on the same painting says:

About suffering they were never wrong,
The Old Masters: how well they understood
Its human position; how it takes place
While someone else is eating or opening a window or just walking
    dully along;
. . .
In Breughel's Icarus, for instance: how everything turns away
Quite leisurely from the disaster; the ploughman may
Have heard the splash, the forsaken cry,
But for him it was not an important failure . . .

(Auden, 1958)

Staying sensitive to honour the feelings about "important failures" that clients and professionals experience can help a supervisee put a finger on some issue not being addressed. Because our blind spots are less accessible to reflection via "internal supervision", some external consultation plays an important part in sustaining openness to insight. Other chapters have already explored blind spots in relation to difference and diversity, and development of multi-cultural sensitivity.

Rapp (2001, p. 140) offers a vivid example of a sudden difficulty and reveals the complexity that might be a part of a disruption even of a long supervisory relationship, and the value of consultation about it. The supervisor was responsive to the professional resonances and distress of a supervisee who counselled adult clients abused as children. The supervisee had had a troubled childhood herself, and the supervision generally identified parallel process in a useful way. In one session, the supervisor impulsively put her hand on her supervisee's arm when she was weeping, intending to offer support. The supervisee's response was frozen horror. It took several supervision sessions to unpack a complex mix pertaining to her response. The catapulting back to personal pain that this impulsive gesture had created connected to resonances of the supervisee's abuse. She disclosed as a part of the repair process that she was lesbian.

The consultant supervisor helped the supervisor disentangle four strands of the issue, as follows.

1. The ethical use of touch. This is permitted, or is part of some forms of therapy, and forbidden or distrusted in others. It is seldom appropriate in supervision, and especially when the topic is sexual abuse. Touch might conjure up sexual meanings: some think it always does.
2. The complexities of working with abuse.
3. Sexual orientation, and the potential for sexual feelings that might be revealed or held private in supervision, but are relevant.
4. What can and should be worked with in therapy that is different in purpose and process from supervision.

Is consultative supervision distinct?

Collegiality is more likely to characterize this relationship. Ideally, congruence will, too. Some writers comment that it gets harder to expose practice as experience increases because of internal injunctions to be able to manage issues independently. My experience has been that shame plays less of a part as experience increases, but that might be different with a new supervisor, or in a more rivalrous new group until the pecking orders have settled down.

Supervision at this stage balances authoritative and facilitative aspects of the role between the containing, enabling, educational and therapeutic tasks of it. Page and Wosket (2001) suggest the internal supervisor of the *consultative supervisor* may be more aware of, and willing to reveal, his or her processes, thoughts, and emotions. Clearly, then, risk and self-disclosure may be hallmarks of good consultative supervision, especially if the consultant supervisor has done a lot of therapy or personal development.

Ageing and its impact

However, with collegiality might come a sense of comfort and deep and affectionate connection that increases the difficulty of making or hearing an unwelcome challenge. A combination of compassion and accurate listening is necessary to name signs of failing hearing, memory, or concentration, or loss of touch with current norms of professional practice. It is particularly important if the need arises to explore with a much loved and ageing colleague whether or not it might be time to reduce or stop work. The colleague might still be functioning well enough not to do harm. S/he might still have all the benefits of long experience to call on. Yet, s/he might also be allowing boundaries to slip, dual relationships to flourish, or personal needs to take precedence. Needs to sustain a familiar identity and time structure in therapeutic hours (Clark, 2005) might keep the practitioner at work beyond the time to stop. A group member who risks saying the unsayable, possibly the unthinkable, might provoke other members to respond protectively to what is likely to be felt as unkindness, judgement, or attack. In principle, the base position must still be "trust practitioners so they will trust themselves". Raising the issue and then trusting the other is very different from protectively not raising the issue. It is important to create the possibility of some shared reflective enquiry. Could s/he be doing harm? What is the evidence either way? Asking the individual, "When will you know it is time to stop?" can also put the issue on the agenda. Clark (2005) knew she wanted to stop while she was still able to do good work. If the person's internal supervisor is not a guide, colleagues are an important resource, and "therapeutic will" arrangements are essential.

At one point, a dear friend and colleague some years older than me moved back to my town, and began some unpaid work with an ex-client, a recently qualified counsellor seeking clients towards her accreditation, who had financial pressures. The ex-client wanted my friend to offer her both supervision and counselling, varying the use of their shared time depending on whether or not she currently had clients. My colleague had been trained but not accredited by an unorthodox psychotherapist, and she was no longer a member of a professional body or carrying professional insurance. She was keen for me to supervise her arrangement, aware that there might be pitfalls in the varying focus. Yet, she felt blithely content with it, glad to be "feeling useful in a familiar way" again. When I explained that I could not do so, and the multiplicity of issues I saw that were difficult, she unravelled her arrangement very regretfully, and ceased the work. I was left to review in my consultative supervision my sense of sadness at raising the many boundary issues I had seen that then stopped her from doing what she wished for so poignantly. I wondered what my preoccupation with professionalism was doing to my human connections. The unorthodox set-up was all unpaid, and in many cultures might have been entirely acceptable. The castle of arrangements had to tumble down for me because without professional membership or insurance, the client was unprotected. She would have had nowhere to go with any complaint. My friend's lack of awareness of this in self-supervision indicated that she was out of touch with the risks and current ethical imperatives. We still met as friends.

Supervision of novice supervisors

Consultative supervision is very valuable when first undertaking the role of supervisor. When a practitioner is training to supervise, group consultative supervision provides opportunities to reflect on practice. Developmental feedback connected to personal learning goals is particularly useful at this point. Specifically, it provides a space for encouragement, for support as the novice supervisor takes authority, for discussion to develop confidence in ethical problem solving, and for discovery that ethical dilemmas usually also have personal resonances. As the group confidence increases, excitement about the multiplicity of perspectives and contributions can be enjoyable and build confidence. With sufficient safety and challenge in the culture of the group, there is a sense of rapid development into the role. With trust, echoes of "sibling rivalry" can emerge in a raw way, and be understood. The group really can become an environment where different ways of working can be examined curiously and acknowledged, while each can ask internally, "Would this work for me?"

Supervision of novice counsellors by novice supervisors

Inexperienced supervisors who work with trainee counsellors have parallel and steep learning curves to climb: to undertake the negotiation process and contract for supervision; to practise giving and getting feedback about development, and support and encouragement to tackle uncomfortable issues; to note when and how much they have to exercise some power or authority with a trainee. Each has personal expectations and attitudes to these developmental steps.

Consultative supervision can assist preparation of any particularly difficult assessment report about a trainee counsellor. When the assessing supervisor lacks formal or informal contacts with the course, or is struggling with how to express reservations or concerns to the supervisee verbally or in writing, other perspectives can be highly enabling. The new supervisor needs clarity about expected standards, and coaching to convey this without losing the base of the established relationship while offering genuine encouragement about development.

Problems typically arise when the initial contract for the supervision of the trainee has not been negotiated clearly enough. When the supervisor has avoided giving some essential critical feedback about the trainee's work or professional development at the time, the chickens of avoidance come home to roost when reservations later have to be articulated for a report. Although the supervisor of supervision might well be feeling "we shouldn't be starting from here", as she helps the supervisor to pick up the pieces of the relationship or the normative task, she can be congruent about her thoughts and feelings, thus modelling how to engage in such exchanges.

Supervision of trainees

A supervisor working with trainee counsellors can benefit from consultation. S/he has to support inexperienced practitioners, assess their competence, and work with implicit or explicit three- or four-way contracts with a training course and trainee placement manager. The supervisor has a chance to air concerns with another perspective on the routine and the extreme challenges that arise during supervision of counsellor training. For example, one supervisor realized that two of her supervisees, one a trainee, another experienced but working in a different voluntary organization, were seeing the same client, who had not revealed to either of them that she was attending two agencies. It was complex to unravel this within limits of client confidentiality, and very useful to be able to talk it through with a consultant not caught up with the details of the relationships and organizations.

Keeping an eye on the whole workload

In general, consultative supervision seems to me to make a major contribution by inviting the supervisee to *stay alert to* monitoring the competence, efficacy, and impact of their own supervision practice. The habit of thinking about *all* supervision work, in order to decide what needs to come to any specific supervision keeps the system healthy and the "internal supervisor" vigilant. One may not actually bring all the supervisees, but thinking about them all in order to decide whom or what to bring is useful in its own right, just as it is for supervision of clients. For those with many supervisees, this is demanding. Habitually, every two or three months, I took a list to supervision of everyone I was seeing with a brief summary of current issues. This built, over the years, into a helpful record that I could review annually or as required, and since most of my counselling work was short term, it was of most value for reviewing supervision.

Role as shock-absorber and buffer

Page and Wosket (2001) use these metaphors to describe the role of the consultant supervisor, no matter how experienced the counsellor and supervisor may be, in the context of work with trauma. They assert (p. 245) that there is a need for several layers of containment to help absorb the aftershocks and brace the system, to buffer the impact that the client's experience has had on the counsellor and then the supervisor. Etherington (2000) describes vicarious traumatization very vividly in relation to supervision of sexual abuse counselling, and makes clear that this is a serious issue that needs to be addressed, and that researchers in this sphere also need supervision.

Sometimes, however, even consultative supervision can be traumatizing, because workers in specialist agencies can carry heavy loads, and bring many disturbing issues to a session.

Counsellors can also feel very battered by the institutions in which they work. I like a description by psychiatrist Rachel Freeth, contrasting person-centred and NHS supervision for her role (2004, p. 262). In a useful and complex reflection about power, she describes working in the mental health profession as sometimes feeling like attempting twelve rounds in a boxing ring. Continuing the analogue, her supervisor acted as her "second" in the corner of the ring, who "provides refreshment, dries me down with a towel, provides me with a bucket to spit into and gives me vital words of support and encouragement". For her, person-centred supervision was of value because, counter-culturally in the NHS, it allowed her to appreciate that not only did the patients matter, but so did *her own* feelings and thinking, and the collegial supervisory relationship, too. Hamilton (2006) echoes this story of enabling connection to feelings in the work, in her article on supervision of community psychiatric nurses.

The hall of mirrors

The emotional distance from the client of the consultant supervisor can be a benefit (Walker & Jacobs, 2004), but the distance might also create a less sharp focus on key elements of the client–counsellor relationship. Intellectually, it may be a stimulating process; the client's, the supervisee's, or the supervisor's patterns of assumptions, thought, relationship, or behaviour might be writ larger as the complex detail of individual sessions is summarized into an ethical issue or developmental challenge. However, the potential for distortion through self-presentation and holding back is also great. Lago and Thompson's work on the proxy self (1997) draws attention to this and the complexities that arise, particularly when there are triangles of difference to which any member of the triangle chooses only to bring what they consider the acceptable part of their self. Of course, any experienced practitioner should be aware of varying learning styles, religious and cultural beliefs, thoughts about what helps clients to change, and sensitivity to organizational or internalized oppression. But the internal supervisor may have been formed in highly Western frames of thought and assumptions. Does attachment theory apply across all cultures, for instance, or are collegial supervisory relationships culturally comfortable to supervisees brought up within Asian cultures of respect for elders?

Group consultative supervision

In my experience, group consultative supervision is much to be desired for both novice and experienced supervisors. Members deepen their experience by hearing of others' work as supervisors. They learn by receiving supervision in differing styles. Non-local groups are preferable to reduce the exposure of supervisees who are being discussed if there are shared networks with dual or multiple relationships. However, there are also benefits to the group members if groups are local. Members can share information about events and developments in their locality, they might hear about work opportunities, develop a view about good contexts for practice, and begin to be aware of poor practice in a particular agency. Clarity about what constitutes responsible reporting and what is gossip requires explicit contracting and review. I like to have a Russian doll or toy in a prominent place, to represent the supervisee being discussed as if the person is a fly on the wall listening to the session. Explicit agreements about confidentiality and notes are essential.

Ethical thinking is promoted by looking at competing ethical principles, and when or whether it is legitimate to break the rules, and how to confront each other when they have. Proctor (2008) makes a good case for all supervisors to have some time in groups for developing supervision, encouraging us to think in peer groups about the developmental exigencies of our emerging profession.

Any group of experienced practitioners is likely to have established strategies for tolerating uncertainty and can allow for different thinking and responding styles. Understanding the different ways members of a group express anxiety is also important. Someone needs to notice who becomes cooler and more intellectual when anxious, or more heated and verbose; who slides into silence, and who revs up into conflict.

Learning to reflect on supervision

Training of supervisors to reflect on supervision process and outcomes includes more focus on observation and meaning making. Hawkins and Shohet (2006) describe a course they offer for experienced supervisors who may take on consultative supervision, and offer the following questions to assist review of a session.

What do you notice the supervisor focusing on?
Why do you think they are doing this?
What do you think the session achieved?
Did you notice any resistance in the client, the therapist or the supervisor?
What strategies did you notice being used by the supervisor?
What did the supervisor ignore that you might have worked with?
What did the supervisor work with that you might have ignored?
Find a symbol for the therapy or the supervisory relationship.
What makes them switch from focus on one process to another?
How effective is the switch?
What aspects of the following are present but not explored: Paralleling? Supervisee's countertransference? Supervisor's countertransference? (Table 9.8, p. 145.)

Worthen and Lambert's (2007) research indicates that use of a client monitoring system can enrich supervision as well as enhance client outcomes.

Separation of supervision of counselling and of supervision

Wheeler and King (2001, pp. 168–178) did some survey research by questionnaire about supervision of supervision. Their seventy respondents had considerable experience. Almost all had consultative supervision, and three quarters said they would have it, whether it is professionally required or not. Of those with separate arrangements, the range of time spent on this consultative supervision lay between six and twenty-four hours per year. Of the thirty respondents who had the same person as supervisor of supervision and counselling, and who regularly discuss supervision, on average used about one third of the time for consultative supervision.

They identified the issues most commonly discussed in consultative supervision. They were ethics, boundaries, competence of supervisees, and training. Contracts and the supervisee–client relationship arose, but less frequently.

In my current research project with experienced practitioners, I have begun to build on the Wheeler and King research and invited a different mix of experienced supervisors to be explicit about how much supervision they have, for how long, and whether one-to-one, in a group, or with a peer or peer group, separately or jointly for their counselling, supervision and training work. What is becoming clear is that, in 2008, many still combine their supervision of counselling and supervision, and generally have informal arrangements, if any, about the proportion of time spent reviewing their supervisory work. Most are happy about this, trusting to their own internal supervisor to identify when to bring issues for another's perspective.

Taking responsibility for personal development as a supervisor

When I sought consultative supervision about both counselling and supervision, the topics I raised were largely problem-focused, and all came within Wheeler and King's categories. They were often focused on the *supervisee's* behaviour, attitude, or approach. I became aware that my impulses to discuss supervision arose reactively and in complex situations, fire-fighting *after* a problem had arisen, or when I had waited too long to address difficulties in the relationship. My supervisor commented at the time, "People rarely bring supervisees to supervision, so they don't discuss them except in a crisis."

When I took separate and regular time for consultation, I began to reflect on wider professional issues, think beyond casework dilemmas, and seek more awareness of how my style and personality was affecting the supervision I offered. My own contribution to issues was explored. In one instance, I engaged with my own shame about an issue I had been avoiding with a supervisee, and—eventually—took the risk to share it with her. In another session, I became more aware of the impact of her wish to continue in supervision with me indefinitely on the basis of "only you will do". In consultative supervision, we asked ourselves useful questions, such as, "What am I not doing with her that I should as a supervisor?" and "What would be more satisfying for me?" The former indicated that I was not challenging her about aspects of her work where development could be useful; the latter was an eye-opener. It led to a palpable shift in my self-care when I could consider as legitimate my own needs in these relationships. I came to accept that my preferences and needs as a supervisor could be weighed in the equation, and set up reviews to make this more explicit. With my self-sufficient supervisees, consultative supervision provoked me to ask myself where they were taking uncertainty, if not bringing it overtly to me.

I initiated discussion of issues with my supervisees more often as a result, because I had taken the time to reflect generally on their developmental needs as I knew them, and on where our supervisory relationship was going. I then became clearer about the value of, and necessity for, an annual review. I had normally intended to do these, but it sometimes slipped. Our focus moved to discussion of our learning edge as a supervisory pair.

Discussing the supervisory relationship

Burton, Henderson, and Curtis Jenkins' research (1998) confirmed patterns others have identified of idealization of the supervisor, and unwillingness to raise issues about the relationship from the perspective of the supervisee. Bernard and Goodyear (2004, p. 153) show how few American trainees raise issues about their supervisor's shortcomings.

Having had space to talk more fully and calmly about my experience of each supervisory relationship in my consultative supervision, I was more open to expressing curiosity in my discussions with supervisees about the patterns of our interaction. "What do you want more or less of?" I would ask. It was surprisingly difficult to get an answer about change. "I like it as it is", many would say, and my narcissistic needs would apparently be stroked, but my wish to offer more focused developmental opportunities was not fulfilled.

Power and evaluation

Even between equally experienced practitioners, issues of power may be salient. Status and role require supervisors to write references and reports. The supervisor must still exercise authority if it becomes essential for a reluctant supervisee to take a break. If the relationship is unsatisfactory, the supervisor has the responsibility to take the courage to explore it. Avoidance of discomfort could lead to avoidance of challenge or of exploration of what is unsatisfying in the supervision, or to failure to explore concerns about competence.

Supervision development groups

Another group I attend, which focuses on developing our ideas and practice of and about supervision, stimulates and energizes me. It is influenced by Proctor's ideas (2008) on using groups to develop supervisors. In this group, we explore a range of matters of interest: feelings of vulnerability and limitations; the impact of ageing on our practice and our thinking; issues for the development of supervision more broadly; reflections on how supervision changes through the professional lifespan. We recommend books and resources to each other, review what we are writing, share puzzles or dilemmas, raise issues which may have broader or thought-provoking implications, or brainstorm ideas for training events. We do have fun, and I always come away energized, and with my internal supervisor feeling well fed and exercised. That's my criterion for good consultative supervision.

Concluding comments

My intention has been to engage the reader in the pragmatic and juicy realities of supervision, keeping one eye on the writing and research that offers us theoretical and reflective professional frames for thought, and the other firmly fixed on reflection on experience of the relationship at the core of the working alliance.

I have been grateful for conversations and e-mail exchanges with ex-supervisees as I sought their consent for including material relating to them. Often, their memories differed from mine, and some accounts have been adjusted accordingly. What stands out for each has been not necessarily what I had highlighted as important. Thus, the man who taught me to pay more attention to subtle signals and developing sensing (Chapter Six) said,

> I do not remember the incidents and am happy for you to include them as they are. I do remember you as a supportive and encouraging supervisor at a time when I was very unsure of my suitability to be a counsellor and also coming to terms with the loss of my mother.

The woman whose bereavements had led me to worry about her wrote many helpful comments and prompts for me to continue my reflection:

> Re endings and retirement—I wonder if there was a difference with supervisees who had mainly short-term contracts? This renewed contact with you has made me rethink my work at the medical centre, which is often about endings. (As regulations tighten, the opportunity for extending contracts is ever more limited.) One spin off (from my research actually) is that this time limit or knowledge of an end helps to focus the mind and ensure that all important issues (at the time) are at least aired. Did you notice any positive effects? Did the supervisory work that you were doing become more focused (not on the ending but on the clients)?

Another whom I had noted as understanding about my retirement noted:

> Good to hear from you. I chuckled when I read the paragraph about me! Not sure if I really was that understanding! Congruence? I'm fine about you including it in your book. In fact feel quite honoured as I've never been mentioned in a book before! Albeit anonymously!

The experienced colleague with whom I became more aware of the negativity of my own inner critic early on (Chapter Two) wrote,

> As you say, it all feels a life time ago, perhaps even more so as I retired last year! I was interested to read your thoughts, (and impressed by your memory) concerning our supervisor–supervisee relationship.

> I'm not sure that "my self-esteem lay so greatly in my role as a counsellor"—it's a long time ago so perhaps it was the only aspect of my life at that time that had continuity.

> I don't have any issue about the content of what you have written, but feel that perhaps the second paragraph lacks clarity because it contains so many issues.

> To add yet another issue which I have found to be of enormous significance as a supervisor, and I think with hindsight, contributed to our difficulty, is the unacknowledged loss of the previous

supervisor. In my case X (who recommended you to me) was a very experienced, laid back, accepting Irish man (probably with hindsight a good father figure!).

Having re-activated old memories, I'd be very happy to meet up face to face for a cuppa sometime.

In spite of our difficulties I think we both learnt from them. I certainly valued your experience of working in more focussed [sic], short-term work with students and have recommended you as a supervisor many times over the years.

Another commented:

Having done a second reading in the luxury of a bath this morning, I am responding promptly for a change. My first response was delight at the open willingness in exploration that you portray throughout the work in your writing style, a solid and warm reminder of your congruence that I experienced when I worked with you. I experienced a real invitation to explore further some of the references as will your future readers. It isn't dry, just real and I like it and look forward to buying the book.

It was useful and interesting to me to reflect on the memories of the incidents about which you wrote and review my feelings/thoughts in retrospect.

She then added many useful comments that I incorporated into the text, and once more, we decided to meet up again.
One of my peer group responded to several chapters, saying,

Well! That was a very good read. Such humanity, compassion, honesty, tough "fair witnessing" PLUS lots of useful pointers clearly laid out. I liked the fact it drew on so many other writers. I can imagine it being a most helpful book for anyone starting out on supervision and a great comfort to those who have been doing it for a few years!

I was reading it avidly for help with discerning in what ways my current mentoring role could be called supervision—what ways of working and attitudes I could take with me into that process and where it differs.

It did help me get clearer about the discussions about a contract that I want to have. And, like the conversations I have had with you about it on the phone, it brought my professional identity back to life and reminded me of what I DO know.

Another was protectively a bit worried that my focus on learning from mistakes might make people misconstrue my general competence. What these comments convey to me is the power of a supervisory relationship to sustain a sense of connection or affection many years on; that there was—or now is—sufficient equality in the relationship that they could set me straight, in an egalitarian and warm way. Each also shows habits of continuing to reflect about incidents that is the mark of a reflective practitioner.

I salute them, and note how grateful I am for all I have gained from being in relationship with them. My own supervisors and colleagues have hugely stimulated my thought and ideas and I feel delighted to have shared our developmental journeys.

GLOSSARY

Caldicott principles and guidance: These are six principles of data protection, and guidance for security controls and confidentiality, originating in the National Health Service (NHS) and between the NHS and other organizations. See *Report on the Review of Patient-identifiable Information* (DoH, 2006) They are: justify the purpose for using confidential information, only use it when necessary, use the minimum required, permit access only on a strict need-to-know basis, all must understand responsibilities, and understand and comply with the law.

CORBS: Hawkins and Shohet's (2006) feedback model stands for CLEAR, OWNED, REGULAR, BALANCED, AND SPECIFIC.

DSM-IV: This is a diagnostic handbook published by the American Psychiatric Association and used by mental health professionals. It lists categories of mental disorders, and the criteria for diagnosing them.

Formative supervision: This is a broadly educational task that focuses on the supervisee's development, and some teaching if appropriate (Inskipp and Proctor, 2001, p. 6).

Heron's six-category model: Heron (1975) lists six categories of intervention useful for a counsellor (or supervisor, or other professional). These are prescriptive, informative, confronting, and cathartic, catalytic, and supportive. His model has been widely used in training to identify those a practitioner habitually uses or avoids.

Internal supervisor: Patrick Casement's phrase (1985) points out the process of following cues internal to the therapist (or supervisor) during a session and being reflective enough in the moment to seek insight about what the patient (or supervisee) might be conveying indirectly about the relationship. This combines with foresight and hindsight co-created with an external supervisor.

Interpersonal process recall (IPR): A process created by Kagan and Kagan (1991) to use video and a process of inquiry to identify thoughts, feelings, fantasies, and reflections to promote self-awareness in communications work.

"Life style": This is an Adlerian term that encompasses what is typically meant by "personality". It refers to the social and psychological implications of assumptions or internal working models.

Mirror neurons: The brain fires when watching an activity or hearing about it, in the same place as when doing it. First observed in monkeys by Rizzolatti, Fadiga, Gallese, and Fogassi (1996).

Neuro-linguistic programming (NLP): This is an interpersonal communication model and approach to therapy that pays great attention to the ways people process information. It began with focus on language, communication, and the ways people learn to change through observation and modelling.

Normative supervision: This task attends to the effectiveness of work and ethical practice of the worker through self-monitoring and supervisor monitoring (Inskipp & Proctor, 2001, p. 6).

Parallel process: The possibility of unconscious re-enactments by the supervisee within the supervision session or relationship of what has not been spoken by the client, or by the supervisee with the client of the supervisor-supervisee relationship.

Restorative supervision: This task supports supervisee resilience and creativity through attention to the personal /professional needs of the practitioner (Inskipp & Proctor, 2001, p. 6).

Superiority–inferiority dynamic: This is an Adlerian concept relating to Adler's ideas of the inferiority complex, and to striving to compensate for subjectively felt inferiority. Striving for superiority entails attempts to achieve mastery in a given domain of interest or activity. There is a differentiation between two levels of superiority striving, one of which involves competition with *oneself* to achieve personal bests in some area of endeavour. The more unhealthy orientation involves striving for personal superiority over others; to achieve a sense of mastery and power over others by defeating them or relishing their losses or shortcomings. Superiority striving in this sense precludes the kind of co-operation and caring for others that underlies emotional health and social interest. If caught in this dynamic, people are preoccupied with judgement and failure or success, rather than a calm examination of what has happened and how they are behaving.

REFERENCES

Acker, S., & Feuerverger, G. (1996). Doing good and feeling bad: the work of women university teachers. *Cambridge Journal of Education*, 26(3): 401–402.

Addison, J. (1704). A letter from Italy, to the Right Honourable Charles Lord Halifax.

Allen, P. (2004). The use of Interpersonal Process Recall (IPR) in person-centred supervision. In: K. Tudor & M. Worrall (Eds.), *Freedom to Practise: Person-Centred Approaches to Supervision* (pp. 153–170). Ross-on-Wye: PCCS Books.

Anderson, S. A., Schlossberg, M., & Rigazio-DiGilio, S. (2000). Family therapy trainees' evaluations of their best and worst supervision experiences. *Journal of Marital and Family Therapy*, 26(1): 79–91.

Auden, W. H. (1958). Musée des Beaux Arts. In: *W. H. Auden: Selected by the Author*. Harmondsworth: Penguin.

Balint, M. (1972). *Focal Psychotherapy, An Example of Applied Psychoanalysis*. London: Tavistock Publications.

Barden, N. (2001). The responsibility of the supervisor in the British Association for Counselling and Psychotherapy's Codes of Ethics and Practice. In: S. Wheeler & D. King (Eds.), *Supervising Counsellors: Issues of Responsibility*. London: Sage.

Beattie, M. (2001). *Codependent No More: How to Stop Controlling Others and Start Caring for Yourself.* Center City, MN: Hazelden.

Belbin, R. M. (1981). *Management Teams* (2nd edn). Butterworth Heinemann, 2003.

Bell, J. (2007). Person-centred expressive supervision. In: K. Tudor & M. Worrall (Eds.), *Freedom to Practise, Volume II* (pp. 59–71). Ross-on-Wye: PCCS Books.

Bennet, G. (1979) *Patients and Their Doctors: The Journey Through Medical Care.* London: Ballière Tindall.

Bernard, J. M., & Goodyear, R. K. (2004). *Fundamentals of Clinical Supervision* (3rd edn). Boston, MA: Pearson Education.

Bloom, W. (2001). *The Endorphin Effect.* London: Piatkus.

Bolen, J. S. (1994). *Crossing to Avalon—A Woman's Midlife Pilgrimage.* San Francisco, CA: HarperCollins.

Bollas, C. (1987). *The Shadow of the Object: Psychoanalysis of the Unthought Known.* London: Free Association.

Bolton, G. (2001). *Reflective Practice: Writing and Professional Development* (2nd edn). London: Sage, 2005.

Bond, T., & Mitchels, B. (2008). *Confidentiality and Record Keeping in Counselling and Psychotherapy.* London: Sage.

Bradley, L. J., & Ladany, N. (2001). *Counselor Supervision: Principles, Process and Practice.* Philadelphia, PA: Brunner-Routledge.

British Association for Counselling and Psychotherapy (2004a). *Guidance for Ethical Decision Making: A Suggested Model for Practitioners. Information Sheet P4.*

British Association for Counselling and Psychotherapy (2004b). *Am I Fit to Practise as a Counsellor? Information Sheet P9.*

British Association for Counselling and Psychotherapy (2005). *The Ethical Framework for Good Practice in Counselling and Psychotherapy within the NHS. DG10.*

British Association for Counselling and Psychotherapy (2008a). *Confidential Guidelines for Reporting Child Abuse. Information Sheet E6.*

British Association for Counselling and Psychotherapy (2008b). *Access to Counsellor Records. Information Sheet G1.*

British Association for Counselling and Psychotherapy (2008c). *Confidentiality, Counselling and the Law. Information Sheet G2.*

British Association for Counselling and Psychotherapy (2008d). *Making a Contract for Counselling and Psychotherapy. Information Sheet P11.*

British Association for Counselling and Psychotherapy (2008e). *Making Notes of Counselling and Psychotherapy Sessions. Information Sheet P12.*

British Association for Counselling and Psychotherapy. (2008f) *Contingency Plans if Personal Crises Impact on Independent Practice. Information Sheet P14.*

Broughton, V. (2006). Constellations work in supervision. *Therapy Today, 17*(9): 27–30.

Burton, M., Henderson, P., & Curtis Jenkins, G. (1998). Primary care counsellors' experience of supervision. *Counselling, 9*(2): 122–133.

Cameron, R. (2004). Shaking the spirit: subtle energy awareness in supervision. In: K. Tudor & M. Worrall (Eds.), *Freedom to Practise: Person-Centred Approaches to Supervision* (pp. 171–188). Ross-on-Wye: PCCS Books.

Carroll, L. (1871). *Through the Looking Glass.* Digital Scanning, 2007.

Carroll, M. (1996). *Counselling Supervision: Theory, Skills and Practice.* London: Cassells.

Carroll, M. (2001a). The spirituality of supervision. In: M. Carroll & M. Tholstrup (Eds.), *Integrative Approaches to Supervision* (pp. 76–89). London: Jessica Kingsley.

Carroll, M. (2001b). Supervision in and for organisations. In: M. Carroll & M. Tholstrup (Eds.), *Integrative Approaches to Supervision* (pp. 50–64). London: Jessica Kingsley.

Carroll, M., & Gilbert, M. (2005). *On Being a Supervisee: Creating Learning Partnerships.* London: Vukani.

Casement, P. (1985). *On Learning from the Patient.* London: Tavistock.

Casemore, R. (1999). Why can't we own our mistakes? *Counselling, 10*(2): 94–95.

Casemore, R. (Ed.) (2001). *Surviving Complaints Against Counsellors and Psychotherapists.* Ross-on-Wye: PCCS Books.

Chambers, C., & Cutliffe, J. Jr. (2001). The dynamics and processes of ending in clinical supervision. *British Journal of Nursing, 10*(2): 1403–1411.

Clark, J. (2005). Coming to an end. *Association for University & College Counselling Journal,* Summer: 6-7.

Clarkson, P., & Gilbert, M. (1991). The training of counsellor trainers and supervisors. In: W. Dryden & B. Thorne (Eds.), *Training and Supervision for Counselling in Action* (pp. 143–169). London: Sage.

Claxton, G. (1984). *Live and Learn: An Introduction to The Psychology of Growth and Change in Everyday Life.* London: Harper & Row.

Coe, J. (2008). Being clear about boundaries. *Health Counselling and Psychotherapy Journal, 8*(1): pp. 11–15, January.

Coleman, H. K. L. (1999) Training for multi-cultural supervision. In: E. Holloway & M. Carroll (Eds.), *Training Counsellor Supervisors*. London: Sage.

Crawford, J., Kippax, S., Onyx, J., Gault, U., & Benton, P. (1992). *Emotion and Gender: Constructing Meaning from Memory*. London: Sage.

Crick, P. (1991). Good supervision: on the experience of being supervised. *Psychoanalytic Psychotherapy, 5*(3): 235–245.

Cummings, N., & Sayama, M. (1995). *Focused Psychotherapy: A Casebook of Brief, Intermittent Psychotherapy Throughout the Life Cycle*. New York: Brunner-Mazel.

Curtis Jenkins, G. (2001). Counselling supervision in primary health care. In: M. Carroll & M. Tholstrup (Eds.), *Integrative Approaches to Supervision* (pp. 108–121). London: Jessica Kingsley.

Curtis Jenkins, G., & Henderson, G. (1997). *Counselling in Primary Care Trust. Supervision* (Suppl. No. 3), August [out of print].

Daines, B., Gask, G., & Usherwood, T. (1997). *Medical and Psychiatric Issues for Counsellors*. London: Sage.

Daniels, J. (2000). Whispers in the corridor and kangaroo courts: the supervisory role in mistakes and complaints. In: B. Lawton & C. Feltham (Eds.), *Taking Supervision Forward: Enquiries and Trends in Counselling and Psychotherapy* (pp. 74–92). London: Sage.

Dartington, R. (1994). Where angels fear to tread: idealism, despondency and inhibition of thought in hospital nursing. In: A. Obholzer & V. Z. Roberts (Eds.), *The Unconscious at Work* (pp. 101–109). London: Routledge.

Dass, R., & Gorman, P. (1981). *How Can I Help?* London: Rider.

Davies, D., & Neal, C. (Eds.) (1996). *Pink Therapy*. Buckingham: Open University Press.

de Shazer, S. (1989). Resistance revisited. *Contemporary Family Therapy, 11*(44): 227–233.

DoH (2006) *Report on the review of patient identifiable information* (access on http://www.doh.gov.uk/confiden/crep.htm).

Dowrick, S. (1992). *Intimacy and Solitude*. London: Women's Press.

Driver, C., & Martin, E. (2002). *Supervising Psychotherapy—Psychoanalytic and Psychodynamic Psychotherapy Perspectives*. London: Sage.

Dunkley, C. (2003). Supervising trainee counsellors in basic risk awareness. *Counselling and Psychotherapy Journal, 14*(10): 50–51, December.

Dunkley, C. (2006). Supervising in cases of suicide risk. *Therapy Today, 17*(1): 31–32.

Dunkley, C. (2007). Pacing the learning. *Therapy Today, 18*(9): 41–42.

Egan, G. (1990). *The Skilled Helper* (4th edn). Pacific Grove, CA: Brooks/Cole.

Eichenbaum, L., & Orbach, S. (1983). *What Do Women Want? Exploding the Myth of Dependency*. London: Michael Joseph.

Epstein, R. M. (1999). Mindful practice. *Journal of the American Medical Association*, 292(9): 833–839.

Estes, C. P. (1992). *Women Who Run With the Wolves: Myths and Stories of the Wild Woman Archetype*. London: Random House.

Etherington, K. (2000). Supervising counsellors who work with survivors of childhood sexual abuse. *Counselling Psychology Quarterly*, 13(4): 377–389.

Feltham, C. (2000). Counselling supervision: baselines, problems and possibilities. In: B. Lawton & C. Feltham (Eds.), *Taking Supervision Forward: Enquiries and Trends in Counselling and Psychotherapy* (pp. 5–24). London: Sage.

Freeth, R. (2004). A psychiatrist's experience of person-centred supervision. In: K. Tudor & M. Worrall (Eds.), *Freedom to Practise; Person-Centred Approaches to Supervision* (pp. 247–266). Ross-on-Wye: PCCS Books.

Gagnon, J. H. (1994). *Wounded Healer*. New York: Ablex.

Gautney, K. (1994). What if they ask me if I am married? *Supervisor Bulletin*, 7(1): 7.

Gibran, K. (1926). *The Prophet*. London: Heinemann.

Gilbert, M. C., & Evans, K. (2000). *Psychotherapy Supervision; an Integrative Relational Approach to Psychotherapy Supervision*. Buckingham: Open University Press.

Gilligan, C. (1982). *In a Different Voice*. Cambridge, MA: Harvard University Press.

Gilmore, S., & Fraleigh, P. (1983). *Style Profile for Communication at Work*. Eugene, OR: Friendly Press.

Glouberman, D. (2003). *The Joy of Burnout*. London: Hodder and Stoughton.

Godward, J. (2007). Cancerland. *Therapy Today*, 8(4): 18-20.

Granello, D. H. (1996). Gender and power in the supervisory dyad. *Clinical Supervisor*, 14(2): 53–67.

Grosch, W. N., & Olsen, D. C. (1994). *When Helping Starts to Hurt*. New York: Norton.

Guggenbuhl-Craig, A. (1971). *Power in the Helping Professions*. Dallas, TX: Spring.

Hamilton, A. (2006). Supervising CPNs. *Healthcare Counselling and Psychotherapy Journal*, 6(1): 14–17.

Hawkins, P., & Shohet, R. (2006). *Supervision in the Helping Professions* (3rd edn). Buckingham: Open University Press.

Hellinger, B., Weber, G., & Beaumont, H. (1999). *Love's Hidden Symmetry, What Makes Love Work in Relationships*. Redding, CT: Zeig Tucker and Theisen.

Henderson, P. (1999). Supervision in medical settings. In: M. Carroll & E. Holloway (Eds.), *Counselling Supervision in Context* (pp. 85–103). London: Sage.

Henderson, P. (2001) Supervision and the mental health of the counsellor. In: M.Carroll & M. Tholstrup (Eds.), *Integrative Approaches to Supervision* (pp. 93–107). London: Jessica Kingsley.

Henderson, P. (2002). Mistakes in supervision. *Counselling and Psychotherapy Journal*, 13(8): 26–27, BACP.

Henderson, P. (2003). How long is too long? *Counselling and Psychotherapy Journal*, 14(2): 38–39.

Henderson, P. (2005). Bereavement and the supervisory relationship. *Therapy Today*, 16(7): 30–32.

Henderson, P. (2006). Training counsellors to work in primary care. In: D. Hooper & P. Weitz, (Eds.), *Psychological Therapies in Primary Care: Training and Training Standards* (pp. 77–96). London: Karnac.

Henderson, P. (2008). Diversity and supervision: how two middle class middle aged white women taught about diversity and equality. In: P. Prina, A. Millar, C. Shelley & K. John (Eds.), *UK Adlerian Year Book 2007*. London: Adlerian Society and the Institute for Individual Psychology.

Heron, J. (1975) *Six-category Intervention Analysis*. Guildford: University of Surrey.

Herrick, J. (2007). Placements: support or confusion? *Therapy Today*, 18(1): 42–44.

Hewson, J. (1999). Training supervisors to contract in supervision. In: E. Holloway and M. Carroll (Eds.), *Training Counsellor Supervisors* (pp. 67–91). London: Sage.

Hewson, J. (2008). Passionate supervision: a wider landscape. In: R. Shohet (Ed.), *Passionate Supervision* (pp. 34–48). London: Jessica Kingsley.

Honey, P., & Mumford, A. (1992). *The Manual of Learning Styles*. Maidenhead: Peter Honey.

Houston, G. (1995). *Supervision and Counselling*. London: Rochester Foundation.

Inskipp, F. (1999). Training supervisees to use supervision. In: E. Holloway & M. Carroll (Eds.), *Training Counselling Supervisors* (pp. 184–210). London: Sage.

Inskipp, F., & Proctor, B. (1993 [2001]). *The Art, Craft and Tasks of Counselling Supervision, Part 1: Making the Most of Supervision.* Twickenham: Cascade.

Inskipp, F., & Proctor, B. (1995 [2003]). *The Art, Craft and Tasks of Counselling Supervision, Part 2 Becoming a Supervisor.* Twickenham: Cascade.

Jacobs, M. (2002). Supervision of supervision? In: B. Lawton & C. Feltham (Eds.), *Taking Supervision Forward* (pp. 201–202). London: Sage.

Jeffries, R. (2000a). Self disclosure. *Counselling, 11*(7): 407–411.

Jeffries, R. (2000b). The disappearing counsellor. *Counselling, 11*(8): 478–481.

Jeffrey, B. (2008). All at sea. *Therapy Today, 19*(2): 37–38.

Jenkins, P. (2006). Supervisor accountability and risk management. *Healthcare Counselling and Psychotherapy Journal, 6*(1): 6–8.

Jenkins, P., Keter, V., & Stone, S. (2004). *Psychotherapy and the Law: Questions and Answers.* London: Whurr.

Johns, H. (1996). *Personal Development in Counsellor Training.* London: Cassell.

Jones, C. (1999). Practice dilemmas. *Counselling, 10*(3): 195–197.

Jung, C. G. (1973). *Collected Works.* Princeton, NJ: Princeton University Press.

Kagan, N., & Kagan, H. (1991). Teaching counselling skills. In: K. R. Cox & C. E. Ewan (Eds.), *The Medical Teacher.* Edinburgh: Churchill Livingstone.

Keirsey, D. (1998). *Please Understand Me II—Temperament, Character Intelligence.* Del Mar, CA: Prometheus Nemesis.

Khele, S., Symons, C., & Wheeler, S. (2008). An analysis of complaints to the British Association for Counselling and Psychotherapy, 1996–2006. *Counselling and Psychotherapy Research, 8*(2): 124–132.

King, D., & Wheeler, S. (1999). The responsibilities of counsellor supervisors: a qualitative study. *British Journal of Guidance and Counselling, 27*(2): 215–229.

Kitzrow, M. A. (2001). Application of psychological type in clinical supervision. *Clinical Supervisor, 20*(2): 133–146.

Knowles, M. (1975). *Self Directed Learning: A Guide for Learners and Teachers.* London: Associated Press.

Kolb, D. (1984). *Experiential Learning: Experience as the Source of Learning and Development.* London: Prentice Hall.

Kopp, R. R., & Robles, L. (1989). A model of supervision of resistance based on Adlerian psychology. *Individual Psychology*, 45(1&2): 213–219.

Kottler, J. A., & Carlson, J. (2003). *Bad Therapy: Master Therapists Share Their Worst Failures*. New York: Brunner-Routledge.

Ladany, N., Lehrman-Waterman, D., Molinaro, M., & Wolgast, B. (1999). Psychotherapy supervisor ethical practices: adherence to guidelines, the supervisory working alliance and supervisee satisfaction. *Counseling Psychologist*, 27: 443–475.

Lago, C., & Thompson, J. (1997). The triangle with curved sides: sensitivity to issues of race and culture in supervision. In: G. Shipton (Ed.), *Supervision of Psychotherapy and Counselling*. Buckingham: Open University Press.

Lahad, M. (2000). *Creative Supervision: The Use of Expressive Arts Methods in Supervision and Self-Supervision*. London: Jessica Kingsley.

Lambert, M. (2005). Comments from a Conference Presentation. University of Leicester, April.

Lees, J. (1997). An approach to counselling in GP surgeries. *Psychodynamic Counselling*, 3(1): 33–48.

Lemma, A. (1996). *Introduction to Psychopathology*. London: Sage.

Lochner, B. T., & Melchert, T. P. (1997). Relationship of cognitive style and theoretical orientation to psychology intern's preferences for supervision. *Journal of Counseling Psychology*, 44(2): 256–260.

Luft, J., & Ingham, H. (1955). The Johari window. See http://en.wikipedia.org/wiki/Johari_Window (accessed March 2008).

Main, M., Kaplan, K., & Cassidy, J. (1985). Security in infancy, childhood and adulthood: a move to the level of representation. *Growing Points in Attachment, Monographs for the Society for Research in Child Development*, 50(1–2): 66–104.

Malan, D. H. (1963). *A Study of Brief Psychotherapy*. London: Tavistock.

Mander, G. (1998). Supervising short-term psychodynamic work. *Counselling*, 9(4): 301–304.

Mander, G. (2002a). Supervising short-term psychodynamic work. In: C. Driver & E. Martin (Eds.), *Supervising Psychotherapy: Psychoanalytic and Psychodynamic Perspectives* (pp. 97–105). London: Sage.

Mander, G. (2002b). Supervision for the brief therapist. *Counselling & Psychotherapy Journal*, 13(5): 22–27.

Mander, G. (2002c). Timing and ending in supervision. In: C. Driver & E. Martin (Eds.), *Supervising Psychotherapy: Psychoanalytic and Psychodynamic Perspectives* (pp. 140–152). London: Sage.

Mander, G. (2002d). Supervision of supervision: specialism or new profession? In: C. Driver & E. Martin (Eds.), *Supervising Psychotherapy: Psychoanalytic and Psychodynamic Perspectives* (pp. 132–139). London: Sage.

Manning, M. (1994). *Undercurrents: A Therapist's Reckoning with Depression.* San Francisco, CA: HarperCollins.

Martin, T. (2006). Death of a supervisee. *BAPPS e journal, 1.* www.supervision.org.uk (accessed 15 March 2008).

Marton, F., & Saljo, R. (1976). On qualitative differences in learning. *British Journal of Educational Psychology, 46:* 115–127.

McCurdy, K. G. (2006). Adlerian supervision: a new perspective with a solution focus. *Journal of Individual Psychology, 62*(2): 141–153.

Merry, T. (2002). *Learning and Being in Person-Centred Counselling* (2nd edn). Ross-on-Wye: PCCS Books.

Millar, A. (2007). The essential E's. *Therapy Today, 18*(2): 40–42.

Minikin, K. (2002). The challenge of supervision. *Counselling & Psychotherapy Journal, 13*(7): 30–35.

Mollon, P. (1989). Anxiety, supervision and a space for thinking: some narcissistic perils for clinical psychologists learning psychotherapy. *British Journal of Medical Psychology, 62:* 113–122.

Morrell, M. (2003). Forethought and afterthought—two of the keys to professional development and good practice in supervision. *Social Work Review,* Autumn/Winter (New Zealand): 29–32.

Nelson, H. (2002). Which frock shall I wear? *Counselling & Psychotherapy Journal, 13*(7): 10–13.

Nelson, M. L., & Holloway, E. L. (1990). Relation of gender to power and involvement in student supervision. *Journal of Counseling Psychology, 37:* 473–481.

Newbauer, J. F., & Shifron, R. (2004). Using early recollections on case consultation. *Journal of Individual Psychology, 60*(2): 155–162.

O'Connell, B., & Jones, C. (1997). Solution focused supervision. *Counselling, 8*(4): 289–292.

O'Neill, A. (2002). Called to account. Lecture 3 in *A Question of Trust: Reith Lectures 2002.* BBC Radio 4, 20 April.

Page, S., & Wosket, V. (2001). *Supervising the Counsellor: A Cyclical Model.* Hove: Routledge.

Palmer Barnes, F. (1998). *Complaints and Grievances in Psychotherapy: A Handbook of Ethical Practice.* London: Routledge.

Peluso, P. R. (2003). The ethical genogram: a tool for helping therapists understand their ethical decision making styles. *The Family Journal*, 14(3): 286–291.

Proctor, B. (1997). Contracting in supervision. In: C. Sills (Ed.), *Contracts in Counselling* (pp. 190–206). London: Sage.

Proctor, B. (2002). Towards an autonomous and accountable profession. *Counselling & Psychotherapy Journal*, 13(2): 36–37.

Proctor, B. (2008). *Group Supervision: A Guide to Creative Practice* (2nd edn). London: Sage.

Progoff, I. (1975). *At a Journal Workshop*. New York: Dialogue House.

Pryor, R. G. L. (1989). Conflicting responsibilities: a case study of an ethical dilemma for psychologists working in organisations. *Australian Psychologist*, 24: 293–305.

Rapp, H. (2001). Working with difference and diversity: the responsibility of the supervisor. In: S. Wheeler & D. King (Eds.), *Supervising Counsellors: Issues of Responsibility* (pp. 131–152). London: Sage.

Remen, R. N. (2000). *My Grandfather's Blessings: Stories of Strength, Refuge and Belonging*. London: HarperCollins.

Rennie Peyton, P. (2004). Bullying in supervision. *Counselling and Psychotherapy Journal*, 15(6): 36–37.

Rippere, V., & Williams, R. (1985). *Wounded Healers—Mental Health Workers' Experiences of Depression*. Chichester: Wiley.

Rizzolatti, G., Fadiga, L., Gallese, V., & Fogassi, L. (1996). Premotor cortex and the recognition of motor actions. *Cognitive Brain Research*, 3: 131–141.

Robiner, W. N., Saltzman, S. R., Hoberman, H. M., Semrud-Clikeman, M., & Schirvar, J. A. (1997). Psychology supervisors' bias in evaluations and letters of recommendation. *Clinical Supervisor*, 16(2): 49–72.

Rogers, C. (1976). *Client Centred Therapy*. London: Constable.

Rogers, C. (1977). *On Becoming a Person—A Therapist's View of Psychotherapy*. London: Constable.

Rogers, C. (1983). *Freedom to Learn for the 80s*. Columbus, OH: C. E. Merrill.

Rosenblatt, A., & Mayer, J. E. (1975). Objectionable supervisory styles: students' views. *Social Work*, May: 184–189.

Rothschild, B. (2002). The mind and body of vicarious traumatization: help for the helper. *Psychotherapy in Australia*, 8(2): 26–28.

Rowan, J. (1989). *The Reality Game: A Guide to Humanistic Counselling and Therapy*. London: Routledge.

Ryan, S. (2004). *Vital Practice Stories From the Healing Arts: The Homeopathic and Supervisory Way*. Portland: Sea Change.

Sanders, D. (2006). *Will I Still Be Me? A Journey Through a Transplant*. London: Day Books.

Sanders, D. (2008). When therapist turns patient. *Health Counselling and Psychotherapy Journal*, 8(1): 22–25.

Scaife, J. (2009). *Supervision in Clinical Practice: A Practitioner's Guide*. London: Brunner Routledge.

Schaufeli, W. B., Maslach, C., & Marek, T. (1993). *Professional Burnout: Recent Developments in Theory and Research*. London: Taylor and Francis.

Sell, M. (2000). Presentation at the British Association for Supervision Practice and Research Conference.

Sells, J. N., Goodyear, R. K., Lichtenberg, J. W., & Polkinghorne, D. E. (1997). Relationship of supervisor and trainee gender to in-session verbal behaviour and ratings of trainee skills. *Journal of Counseling Psychology*, 44: 406–412.

Seneviratne, S. (2004). Race, culture and supervision. In: K. Tudor & M. Worrall (Eds.), *Freedom to Practise: Person-Centred Approaches to Supervision* (pp. 99–114). Ross-on-Wye: PCCS Books.

Shifron, R. (2007). A dance of two lifestyles: an Adlerian model for supervision, using early recollections. *Therapy Today*, 18(1): 41–42.

Shohet, R. (2008). *Passionate Supervision*. London: Jessica Kingsley.

Schon, D. (1983). *The Reflective Practitioner*. New York: Basic Books.

Schon, D. (1987). *Educating the Reflective Practitioner*. San Francisco, CA: Jossey Bass.

Shroeder, T. (2007). Presentation at the Society for Psychotherapy Research Conference, Scarborough, UK, February.

Skovholt, T. M., & Ronnstad, M. H. (1992). *The Evolving Professional Self: Stages and Themes in Therapist and Counsellor Development*. Chichester: Wiley.

Stern, D. (2007). A felicitous meeting of attachment and relational psychotherapy. *Attachment: New Directions in Psychotherapy and Relational Psychoanalysis*, 1(March): 1–7.

Stoltenberg, C., & Delworth, U. (1987). *Supervising Counsellors and Therapists: A Developmental Approach*. San Francisco, CA: Jossey Bass.

Sugg, S. (2008). Creative writing—a tool for developing the reflective/reflexive practitioner? *Therapy Today*, 19(1): 37-39.

Szecody, I. (1990). Supervision: a didactic or mutative situation. *Psychoanalytic Psychotherapy*, 4(3): 245–264.

Talmon, M. (1990). *Single Session Therapy: Maximizing the Effect of the First (and Often Only) Therapeutic Encounter*. San Francisco, CA: Jossey-Bass.

Tholstrup, M., & Shillito-Clarke, C. (2005). Supervisory self-care. *Counselling and Psychotherapy Journal*, 16(3): 41–42.

Thomas, F. N. (1996). The coaxing of expertise. In: S. Miller, M. Hubble, & B. Duncan (Eds.), *Handbook of Solution Focused Brief Therapy* (pp. 128–151). San Francisco, CA: Jossey-Bass.

Totton, N. (1997). Learning by mistake: client–practitioner conflict in a self regulated network. In: R. House & N. Totton (Eds.), *Implausible Professions: Arguments for Pluralism and Autonomy in Psychotherapy and Counselling*. Ross-on-Wye: PCCS Books.

Traynor, W. (2007). Supervising a therapist through a complaint. In: K. Tudor and M. Worrall (Eds.), *Freedom to Practise, Volume II: Developing Person-Centred Approaches to Supervision* (pp. 154–168). Ross-on-Wye: PCCS Books.

Tudor, K. (2007). Supervision of short term therapy. In: K. Tudor and M. Worrall (Eds.), *Freedom to Practise, Volume II: Developing Person-Centred Approaches to Supervision* (pp. 195–204). Ross-on-Wye: PCCS Books.

Veniga, R. L., & Spradley, J. P. (1981). *The Work Stress Connection: How to Cope with Job Burnout*. Boston, MA: Little Brown.

Wakefield, M. (2005). Person-centred practice in primary health care: evidence that without time limits the majority of clients opt for short term therapy. *Person-Centred Quarterly*, August 1–5.

Walker, J., Ladany, N., & Pate-Carolan, L. M. (2007). Gender-related events in psychotherapy supervision: female trainee perspective. *Counselling and Psychotherapy Research*, 7(1): 12–18.

Walker, M., & Jacobs, M. (2004). *Supervision: Questions and Answers for Counsellors and Therapists*. London: Whurr.

Waskett, C. (2006). The SF journey-solution focused supervision is like being a taxi driver. *Therapy Today*, 17(2): 40–42.

Weaks, D. (2002). Unlocking the secrets of good supervision: a phenomenological exploration of experienced counsellors' perceptions of good supervision. *Counselling and Psychotherapy Research*, 2(1): 33–39.

Weaver, S. (2005). Ecopsychology and supervision. *Therapy Today*, 16(10): 45–47.

West, W., & Clark, V. (2004). Learnings from a qualitative study into counselling supervision: listening to supervisor and supervisee. *Counselling and Psychotherapy Research*, 4(2): 20–26.

Westland, G. (1997). Understanding occupational stress and burnout. In: D. Keable (Ed.), *The Management of Anxiety: A Guide for Therapists* (pp. 213–230). New York: Churchill Livingstone.

Westland, G. (2008). Training event and handouts, 12 March 2008.

Wheeler, S. (2001). *Assessing Competence*. London: Cassell.

Wheeler, S. (2003). *Scoping Review of Supervision Research*. Lutterworth: BACP.

Wheeler, S., & King, D. (Eds.) (2001). *Supervising Counsellors: Issues of Responsibility*. London: Sage.

Wheeler, S., & Richards, K. (2007). *The Impact of Clinical Supervision on Counsellors and Therapists: Their Practice and Their Clients: A Systematic Review of the Literature*. Lutterworth: BACP.

White, M., & Epston, D. (1990). *Narrative Means to Therapeutic Ends*. New York: Norton.

Wigram, P. (2002). Supervising therapists in training. *Counselling & Psychotherapy Journal*, 13(9): 28–30.

Wilkinson, S. R. (2003). *Coping and Complaining: Attachment and the Language of Dis-ease*. Hove: Brunner-Routledge.

Wilmot, J. (1987). Presentation at the British Association for Supervision Practice and Research (BASPR) Conference.

Worden, W. (1983). *Grief Counselling and Grief Therapy*. London: Tavistock.

Worthen, V. E., & Lambert, M. (2007). Outcome oriented supervision: advantages of adding systematic client tracking to supportive consultations. *Counselling & Psychotherapy Research*, 7(1): 45–53.

INDEX

abuse, 40, 46, 213
  child, 54, 124, 179, 213
  of power, 21, 30, 155
  sexual, 54, 124, 179, 213, 218
Acker, S., 132, 233
Addison, J., 29, 233
Adlerians, 21, 34, 42, 105–106, 194,
  230–231
Allen, P., 68, 90, 233
American Psychiatric Association,
  229
Anderson, S. A., 168, 233
anxiety, 11, 19, 22–23, 30, 33, 46,
  55, 66–67, 71, 81–82, 91, 93, 99,
  103, 109, 114, 116–117, 123,
  125–128, 130, 132–133, 137, 157,
  165, 167, 175–176, 200, 205, 207,
  211, 220
Artemis Trust, 165
attachment, 27, 172, 174, 177, 199
  early, 27, 200, 202
  insecure, 27, 32
  secure, 27

theory, 29, 33, 219
Auden, W. H., 212, 233
autonomy, 7, 20, 53, 60–61, 124, 127,
  136, 150

Balint, M., 195, 233
Barden, N., 180, 233
Beattie, M., 41, 234
Beaumont, H., 104, 238
Belbin, R. M., 80, 234
Bell, J., 92, 105, 234
Bennet, G., 57–58, 234
Benton, P., 143, 236
bereavement, 8, 40, 52–53, 58, 60–61,
  66, 94, 131, 171–174, 176–178,
  180, 182–183, 203–204, 226,
Bernard, J. M., 31–32, 78, 81, 84, 86,
  98, 166, 223, 234
Bloom, W., 44, 234
Bolen, J. S., 54, 234
Bollas, C., 104, 122, 234
Bolton, G., 89, 92, 234
Bond, T., 130, 196, 234